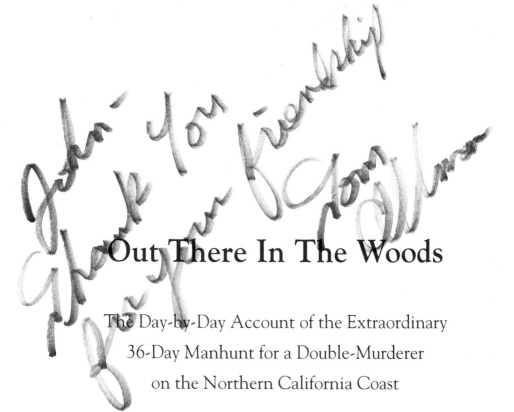

Out There In The Woods

The Day-by-Day Account of the Extraordinary
36-Day Manhunt for a Double-Murderer
on the Northern California Coast

Stephen Sparks
and
Mendocino County Sheriff Tom Allman

Contents

Maps / Diagrams

Northern California Coast
(Graphic by Loren Doppenberg)

West Mendocino County
(Graphic by Loren Doppenberg)

About the Authors

Stephen Sparks

Stephen Sparks was born and grew up in the industrial city of Birmingham, U.K. After graduating from university he traveled around the U.S. in the early '80s before settling in Austin, Texas for a couple of years and then on to San Francisco in 1985. He married Patty Liddy (from Detroit, Michigan) in 1987 and a couple of years later they opened 'The Mad Dog in the Fog' English-style pub in the Lower Haight district of the City. In 2002, after 13 years of running this very successful operation with its 30 staff, he and Patty sold up, left San Francisco, and moved to Anderson Valley in Mendocino County where they had previously bought a 10-acre parcel of land. They planned to stay for six months or so—they are still there.

In 2004, Stephen began to write a column in the local newspaper, The Anderson Valley Advertiser, and then added a weekly biography of various folks living in the Valley and some beyond—including County Sheriff Tom Allman. When not writing, Stephen coaches the high school boys' soccer team, produces and presents a weekly General Knowledge and Trivia Pub Quiz, and is Vice President of the Senior Center Board. He also organizes numerous Valley events for the benefit of various local groups—the veterans, the seniors, the animal rescue organization, and high school sports.

He and Patty have five Border collies, two cats, and thirty-eight sheep.

Tom Allman

For a detailed biography of Sheriff Tom Allman, see page 8 in 'Principal Characters.'

Introduction

October, 2011

Aaron Bassler was a 35-year-old Fort Bragg resident, reportedly suffering from undiagnosed paranoid schizophrenia, who was wanted in connection with the murder of two local people. After the murders, Bassler disappeared into the vast forests and bush country east of Fort Bragg.

Bassler had a lengthy criminal history, including a number of 5150 citations—police code for persons judged to be a danger to themselves or others because of mental illness. Bassler had first been arrested in Mendocino County in October, 1994, when he was 18, for receiving stolen property. This was charged as a misdemeanor and he was convicted in January, 1995 with no jail time served. Apart from another minor incident in November, 1995, he had no further contact with the police for the next 14 years. In 2009, he received a federal misdemeanor conviction in San Francisco when he was apprehended after a series of bizarre attacks on the Chinese Consul's offices at Geary and Laguna. Bassler had thrown parcels resembling small bombs onto the Consulate's property. Each time a bomb squad was summoned to disarm what turned out to be packages containing incoherent claims alleging Chinese military designs on the United States. This was the only time he received court-mandated psychiatric treatment as a result of his crime.

In the period from September, 2010 to March, 2011, Bassler was arrested a number of times for various offenses, including public intoxication, DUI, vandalism, and battery of a peace officer. This series of episodes culminated in his arrest following an incident at the Fort Bragg Middle School tennis courts. Bassler, driving at night under the influence of alcohol and methamphetamines, crashed his pick-up truck into the tennis courts. Local police subdued him but not before he'd proved impervious to pepper spray and the police had to deploy a taser device to stun him into submission. He was charged with reckless driving, DUI, obstruction of a public officer, and vandalism. He served a month in jail, during which time, according to jail staff, he showed no signs of mental instability.

Each of these unhinged incidents represented an escalating recklessness and a clear hazard to whatever community Bassler was living in, although each was adjudicated as a misdemeanor. Bassler, clearly in deteriorating mental health, had served a few days in county jails in San Francisco and Mendocino County before he was granted probation; as mentioned above, only in San Francisco did he undergo mandated mental health counseling.

In late September, 2011, as the search in the woods for Bassler continued, Mendocino County Sheriff Tom Allman commented, "People have said that the Mental Health Department failed Aaron Bassler. Whatever you may think, law enforcement is not in a situation of corrective action. The mental health issue has to be taken out of the equation from our perspective and any questions in that area are purely academic. Our mission at this time is twofold—we have a double-homicide situation to investigate and we have an armed subject in the woods that we are trying to apprehend to prevent another homicide from occurring.

"There has never been a 'green light' given to law enforcement to end this mission with a bullet. On the other hand I haven't told law enforcement officers that they have to arrest him. They will follow their training if they think he is going to open fire. While many people in the community are asking how this will end, my response has always been the same—Aaron Bassler's actions will always decide how this will end."

∽

September, 2012

Author's note: In late 2011, Sheriff Allman met with Aaron Bassler's father, Jim, over breakfast, and they discussed the possibility of a book describing events that occurred during Aaron's 36 days on the run. These would be told primarily from the point of view of the Sheriff and, at the Sheriff's request, I would be the writer. I am a regular contributor to the Anderson Valley Advertiser newspaper, "America's Last Newspaper," a weekly publication based in Boonville, Mendocino County, whose unique blend of local news and national commentary has resulted in a small but loyal readership in various cities and towns across the country.

Mr. Bassler was very supportive, even more so when he heard that the plan was to donate some of the proceeds, beyond the costs incurred from the publication, my salary, and that of Loren Doppenberg, the map illustrator, to the local branches of the National Alliance for the Mentally Ill (N.A.M.I.), probably the most organized group of advocates for the families of the mentally ill, many of whom continue to be very frustrated with the current system. Hopefully in some small yet perhaps significant way, the monies resulting from this publication will help provide assistance for those in most need when mental health issues arise—the patients and those nearest and dearest to them—their families and friends.

Along with a share of any profits being donated to N.A.M.I., equal amounts from book sales will also be given to the following two organizations:

A fund for Environmental Education and Conservation established by Matt Coleman's family:

Community Foundation of Mendocino County
Matt Coleman Fund
290 South State Street, Ukiah, CA 95482

And, in Jere Melo's memory:

Mendocino Coast Sports Foundation
P.O. Box 2812
Fort Bragg, CA 95437
www.timberwolfstadium.org

Further donations may be made in Matt Coleman's or Jere Melo's memory to either of these organizations.

Steve Sparks

☙

The Sheriff's Thoughts…

The story you are about to read is true. It is a story that shocked a rural county and taxed the resources of a rural sheriff's office. Several people were interviewed for this "firsthand" view of the interaction that occurred during this criminal investigation. The perspectives that have been documented are the individual perspectives of some key people who were intimately involved with this incident. What is not documented in this book is the lack of mental health services offered to citizens in rural counties. As tax dollars continue to become more scarce, rural counties have the same needs as metropolitan communities.

The mental health crisis has affected almost every person in this country in one fashion or another. A family member in need of counseling, a co-worker who feels alone, or an individual who does not know where to turn are all examples of how this crisis presents itself. It is the hope of the authors and of the people interviewed that solutions for California's mental health issues continue to be sought. This incident documents an extreme case, with an extreme outcome.

The Mendocino County Sheriff's Office spent 36 days investigating a horrific set of homicides and there are many people whose efforts should be mentioned. The assistance that we received from the community and from allied agencies allowed the investigation to be conducted methodically and thoroughly. The United States Marshal Service, in particular, U.S. Marshal Don O'Keefe, Deputy Marshal Mike McCloud, and the SOG (Special Operations Group) Division; the FBI; and the California Department of Justice all played very important roles as they worked with the many local law enforcement agencies in this investigation. The police departments of Willits, Ukiah, and Fort Bragg gave their support and professionalism, and their contributions will never be forgotten. And a special mention of gratitude goes to Julie Whipple, the secretary at the Fort Bragg Substation who kept the other parts of the Sheriff's Office functioning on the Coast. I must also mention China Comer, the wife of a sergeant on our SWAT team, for attending to many of the logistical (food) needs of all of the guys going into the woods (by providing sack lunches) and the Fort Bragg community for their support during this incident. The Fort Bragg Lions Club also held several barbecues at the Substation for the guys coming in from the woods.

The County of Mendocino will be forever indebted to the hundreds of brave peace officers who put their lives on the line each day. My appreciation for the dedication of the men and women of the Mendocino County Sheriff's Office, and the support of their spouses and loved ones, is deep and heartfelt, while special mention must go to Captain Kurt Smallcomb, who is the most dedicated and professional leader I have ever worked with.

Tom Allman, Mendocino County Sheriff—September 2012

☙

Acknowledgments

We express our gratitude and appreciation for the help received on this project from the following:

- Patty Liddy for all of her support as husband Steve Sparks was "lost" for several months due to his involvement in this project.
- Laura Allman and Susan Clarabut for their valuable comments during the early editing process.
- For their significant contributions—Jim Bassler, Robert Pinoli, and Jack Rikess.
- For their excellent coverage of the investigation, some of which appears herein—Santa Rosa Press Democrat reporters Mary Callahan, Glenda Anderson, Julie Johnson, Cathy Bussewitz, Brett Wilkison; and photographers Christopher Chung, Kent Porter, John Burgess, and Beth Schlanker.
- Ukiah Daily Journal reporter Tiffany Revelle.
- Photographer Michael Macor and the San Francisco Chronicle.
- Bruce Anderson and Mark Scaramella at The Anderson Valley Advertiser for their knowledge and fine editing skills.
- Castle Skip Newell III and Barbara Newell for their support.
- Lt. Greg Van Patten of the Mendocino County Sheriff's Office.
- Bill Harper for his editing work and ideas in the initial stages of the project, and Brian Brown for his later editing work.
- Tim Stelloh and Kym Kemp for their articles on the case.
- Loren Doppenberg (www.LorenDGraphics.com) for his many hours of work on the maps and diagrams; hours that mounted up as he, with his "perfectionist" nature, strived to get them "just right."
- Steven and Leya Booth at Genius Book Services for their excellent editing, layout, and cover art services.
- Kate Brown at ESP-Media for design of the website.
- Brian Hemphill for providing the front cover photograph.

Principal Characters

Mendocino County Sheriff Tom Allman

Tom Allman was born in 1961, the youngest of four children born to parents Dean and Norma Allman in Sylva, North Carolina, a rural mountain community in the shadows of the Great Smoky Mountains.

"My mother was a teacher and her family was in the logging industry, while my dad was an accountant for a timber company for much of my life. My dad's family was from North Carolina and my mom's from Northern California, and we moved between the Garberville area of Northern California and Sylva. I count myself lucky to have grown up in two such beautiful rural areas as the mountains of North Carolina and the redwoods of Northern California. I attended schools in both areas before my final two years were spent at South Fork High from where I graduated in 1979."

After working as a public safety officer and police officer in Fairfield, CA, Allman and his wife Laura moved to Mendocino County in 1985, where he worked for then Mendocino County Sheriff Tim Shea and where Tom and Laura raised their two sons. Tom was initially the resident deputy in Laytonville before transferring to the county's Narcotics Task Force in 1987 and moving to Willits. In 1990, he returned to patrol deputy and then became patrol sergeant in 1993 for three years before becoming a sergeant in Internal Affairs.

Allman was with Internal Affairs for two years before he became acting Lieutenant in Willits and was back to patrol again. "In the Summer of 1999, I noticed a flyer on the bulletin board that was from the U.S. Department of State asking for 400 American police officers, nationwide, to act as civilian peacekeepers in Kosovo, a war-ravaged region of southern Yugoslavia. I thought this sounded very exciting and, after many, many family discussions, I applied and was accepted. In retrospect, I look at this adventure as my 'mid-life crisis,' and I learned more than I could have imagined and truly gained a new perspective on life during my year there."

In October, 2000, Allman's tour ended and he settled back into his job in Mendocino County but was still prepared to travel if necessary. Following Hurricane Katrina he went to New Orleans as a contract employee for three weeks to protect a couple of hospitals from looting. Then, in March, 2005, he volunteered with members of his Rotary

Club and went to southern India to help clear up the mess left by the devastating tsunami a few months earlier and, helped by the $10,000 that he and others raised in Willits and Ukiah, the group built an orphanage. He was elected as the Mendocino County Sheriff in November 2006 and, in 2008, he was awarded the Governor's Medal of Valor by then-Governor Arnold Schwarzenegger for assisting a motorist trapped in a burning vehicle.

Allman says that budget problems, marijuana cultivation, and the issues that come along with small, isolated areas of the county, like Covelo, take up a surprising amount of his time. He looks forward to when the economy has bounced back and he won't have to worry about fiscal issues as much as he does now. Along with budget problems and marijuana, Tom sees methamphetamine abuse and domestic violence as his priorities. "I have learned that the absolute primary responsibility of law enforcement has to be focused where the people are the victims; all other crimes come after that. I like to wear my uniform every day; I drive a marked patrol car and I walk through the jail at least twice a week. I am very aware that not everyone in jail is a bad person. I try to stay involved at the street level, to know the trends and to keep in touch with investigations. I always worked for good sheriffs and I am grateful for all that they taught me. I love my job and I am lucky to have a core group here in the department that has been here a long time. Good employees are our most valuable asset in so many ways."

Aaron Bassler 1976-2011

Aaron Bassler was a shy but seemingly normal boy until his late teens, when he began a dark descent into mental illness, according to his family.

"He was fine. He was happy," his father, Jim Bassler, said. There were no signs in Bassler's youth that his life would turn violent. He played baseball and had a job delivering newspapers, but that changed when Aaron reached the age of 18 or 19, according to family members, who believe he suffered from schizophrenia.

Bassler had several brushes with the law after he turned 19 in 1995, when he was given two years' probation for driving under the influence.

He had been arrested and charged with crimes that included prowling, vandalism, carrying a concealed Glock pistol, and resisting arrest, according to court records. Bassler liked and collected guns, said his father.

Initially, Jim Bassler blamed drugs and alcohol use for the change in his son's behavior. But, as the behavior became increasingly strange, he became convinced his son suffered from mental illness. Aaron Bassler was unable to hold a steady job for any length of time, his father said. Over time, Aaron's behavior became more bizarre.

He built a wall around the home in which he was last living, carved into its walls, and drew strange, child-like pictures, including some of aliens. The aliens were a recurring theme. In early 2009, Aaron was arrested for throwing packages containing drawings of aliens over the fence of the Chinese consulate in San Francisco. Authorities initially thought they were bombs. He was placed on federal probation for about a year, during which time he seemed to improve mentally, his father said.

During that time, Bassler was required to attend regular counseling but privacy laws kept Jim Bassler from learning whether his son had been diagnosed or treated for mental illness. Once the probation ended, Aaron Bassler regressed. But the probationary period left Aaron Bassler's family with hope that, with treatment, he could improve. Their hopes were dashed by Aaron's unwillingness to get treatment and their inability to get forced help for him through the courts.

They pleaded with officials to evaluate Aaron and get him into treatment. They never heard back. After he was released from jail in March, 2011, Aaron Bassler began living in the forest. "He's beyond help, I think," his father said at the time.

(For a detailed history on the life of Aaron Bassler, please refer to Chapter 11, "The Thoughts and Reflections of Jim Bassler.")

Matthew Coleman 1965-2011

"Matt's heart was so big, it surrounded him."
by Betty Stechmeyer, Mendocino Land Trust (MLT)
Volunteer

Matt's heart was so big, it surrounded him. It reached you even before his extended hand, which soon turned into a hug. He nurtured his volunteers. He told us his priorities but allowed each of us to work according to our ability, energy, and interest. I think some of the more rewarding days for Matt were when he was just being here, comfortable with seasoned volunteers, each of us engaged in hacking away at the hated English ivy or weed, wrenching out the old growth broom. He would stand with his weed eater in hand, saying, "I'll just clean up some of the recent regrowth," and he'd disappear down the trail. Forty-five minutes later, there he would be, head to toe in grass clippings, looking for all the world like a camouflaged salad, but smiling... "Ran out of gas (him or the machine?)... but I guess it's about time to head back... Are you all ready?... Looks great! Thanks... Tools? Yeah, thanks again." He knew lots of families: plants, birds, insects... and people, too. His sentence structure was quite amazing: halfway through a sentence on the proper use of a weed wrench, he'd identify a bird call or sighting, including a few nifty facts, and without skipping a beat, finish the wrench explanation.

"...The Ideal Person for the Job."
by Art Morley, MLT Volunteer

Matt was the ideal person for the job. He was willing to take on tough jobs and new tasks, like the bird surveys. He learned his subject quickly and well. He was very diligent and kept all of his many projects going simultaneously. I thought his ability to organize large volunteer groups, such as schools, was quite exceptional.

"Matt Coleman Was My Friend, Mentor, and Colleague."
by Michael Miller, Big River Program Manager

Matt Coleman was my friend, mentor, and colleague. He was

14

also the Big River Stewards Volunteer Coordinator. We shared many things, but foremost was a passion for restoring streams with the goal of enhancing Coho salmon habitat to aid in their survival. We shared a vision of a vibrant and healthy Big River Watershed, finally healed from past abuses and neglect.

Matt's past work experience with the California Department of Fish and Game was invaluable in assessing potential restoration opportunities. We worked as a team. Matt provided the detail, locating stream assessment data, water quality information, and "on the ground knowledge" of the site conditions. Matt's strategic and critical analysis of potential restoration projects was the best filter I had to judge a project's worthiness. If it passed the muster with Matt, I knew we had a shot at success with our grant funders.

He was voracious in his search for new knowledge regarding watershed restoration, providing emails and updates almost on a daily basis regarding new methodologies and their potential here on the North Coast. These efforts exemplified a quality which I greatly admired, evident in all aspects of his life—his unselfish sharing and giving nature.

This quality was exemplified in his educational efforts with both youth and adults, whether it was educating others with respect to invasive plants or conducting bird surveys. Matt's approachable manner, depth of knowledge, and energetic delivery made learning from him fun and exciting.

Matt's sense of humor, wry wit, sarcasm, and sensitivity were a part of our somewhat unorthodox daily routine and will be sorely missed. His love of life was contagious. Matt was comfortable in his own skin and tried to not take himself too seriously. "The perfect is the enemy of the good," he would say, quoting Voltaire, whenever we would get too caught up in the minutia. I can still hear him saying "No worries," which was his way of reminding all of us to not take life too seriously, and to keep our eyes on the bigger picture. We will all miss his gentle and patient leadership, sense of passion, and wonder for all creation.

Matt Coleman is survived by his mother and her husband, Judy and Herb Gifford of Schnecksville, Penn.; his father and his wife, Roger and Frances Coleman of Levittown, N.Y.; his sister, Jeanne Coleman and her partner Greg Smith; and his longtime sweetheart, Susan Coulter.

Jere Melo 1941-2011

A city councilman since 1996 and Mayor of Fort Bragg from 2000 to 2004, Jere Melo (pronounced like *"Jerry Mellow"*) had lived in or near Fort Bragg, a seaside town of approximately 8,000 people, since 1966, when he began working for the Union Lumber Company as a forester. He continued to work for the company when it was purchased by Georgia-Pacific. He received the Redwood Region Logging Conference annual lifetime award in 2002. He had started in the timber industry more than 50 years before as a teenager shoveling sawdust in a Mount Shasta sawmill. He had paid his own way through U.C Berkeley, graduating in 1964 with a degree in forestry.

A community leader who worked tirelessly with numerous organizations, Melo touched the lives of countless people. He was not one to seek out praise and many will never know the good that Melo did for them. Melo fought for his country, his state, his county, and his city. He served in South Korea in the U.S. Army for two years, including a year-long stint on the 38th parallel, and achieved the rank of Captain.

When Union Lumber Company sold the local mill to Boise Cascade in 1964, Melo moved to Boise, Idaho to work in their corporate office. When the Fort Bragg mill was acquired by Georgia-Pacific two years later, Melo returned to Fort Bragg.

Melo retired from Georgia-Pacific when the Fort Bragg mill was closed in 2002. After that, he worked as a contractor for Campbell Timberland Management providing property management services on the 170,000 acres of forestland that they oversee in Mendocino County. Melo loved working in the woods. He was dedicated to keeping the woods safe for timber workers and to protecting forestland from degradation by illegal trespassing, marijuana cultivation, dumping, and encampments. It is an unspeakable tragedy that Melo lost his life trying to protect the forests that he loved.

According to many, Melo was one of the most civic-minded people the Mendocino community has ever known. Melo began his long and distinguished political career in 1992 when he was appointed to serve on the Fort Bragg Planning Commission. In 1996, Melo was elected to his first term on the Fort Bragg City Council. He served as Vice-Mayor from 1998 to 2000 and as Mayor from 2000 to 2004. At the time of his death, Melo was in his 15th year and his fourth term of office as a City Councilmember. Melo was the quintessential small town Councilmember. He was considered an old-timer and a conservative voice on the Council. As many have noted, Melo was a bridge between Fort Bragg's old mill town past and the community's future. He was well-respected by the entire spectrum of community interests in large part because he was kind, good-natured, and always willing to listen to divergent viewpoints and to respectfully present his own principled positions. He came to council and community meetings well prepared and with an open mind. He was a thoughtful listener and was willing to change his positions based on information and testimony presented by his colleagues and the public. Melo gave freely of his time and was always willing to jump in and help resolve a constituent problem or a community issue.

During his time in public office, Melo served on many local, regional, and statewide boards and commissions. More often than not, Melo found himself in a leadership role in these organizations. His diplomacy, sense of decorum, and skill as a chairperson were exceptional.

Melo came from a large Italian family. He had innumerable actual and honorary nieces and nephews. To so many people, he was Uncle Jere. He was married to Madeleine and they had two grown children, Greg and Christine, and one granddaughter, Alison.

(Much of the above came from a statement issued by the Melo Family in response to the community's support following Jere Melo's murder.)

Mendocino County

See Map, Page v

Mendocino is a rural California county consisting of 3,509 square miles situated approximately 150 miles north of San Francisco with a population of less than 90,000 citizens. The events that are depicted in this account took place there in the late summer and early fall of 2011. The west side of the County includes over 90 miles of rugged Pacific Ocean coastline with many miles of dense coastal forests, while the east side stretches into the Mendocino National Forest, a vast national treasure which spreads over six California counties.

The County is noted for its distinctive Pacific Ocean coastline, redwood forests, wine production, micro-breweries, and liberal views about most things, particularly the use of cannabis and support for its legalization. Mendocino County's economic base is dominated by the wine and marijuana industries that are supported by thousands of acres of wine grapes and a vast but unknown number of acres of illegal marijuana gardens and associated activity.

Law enforcement is provided countywide by the Mendocino County Sheriff's Office that has the same number of deputies today as were there 40 years ago. Following the double murder of Matthew Coleman and Jere Melo, the County's rugged, unforgiving coastal forest terrain became a major factor during the ensuing search for the suspect, Aaron Bassler, and in its own unique way became a "principal character" in this story.

Chapter 1
"A real whodunit"

Thursday, August 11th, 2011-Friday, August 26th, 2011

Mendocino County Sheriff Tom Allman attends many funerals. However, he very rarely goes to one for someone he does not know, and yet he did attend the funeral of timberland steward Matt Coleman of Albion, a man Allman had never heard of but whose shooting death on Thursday, August 11th, 2011 shocked residents of the Mendocino Coast.

Reports of this event first made the press in Northern California on Friday, August 12th, in a brief article written by Mary Callahan that appeared on page three of the Empire News section of the Santa Rosa Press Democrat (SRPD). Callahan wrote that the murder was first reported as a bear killing by those who found the body, but emergency medical personnel soon determined that the man's death was likely to have occurred some other way. This was the beginning of what would turn out to be a landmark investigation of historical significance and a story that would, over the ensuing eight weeks, repeatedly make not only Northern California headlines but also those throughout the State and, as the hunt for the suspect dragged on and on, the national news and beyond.

When he was killed, Coleman, 45, was believed to have been clearing brush from one of many roads on a 400 acre oceanfront ranch, located about 8 miles north of Westport, a town 17 miles north of Ft.

Bragg, which in turn is a four-hour drive north of San Francisco. He had been working at this location every Thursday for six weeks and was last seen alive on August 11th at 8:30am when he left his residence in Little River. He went to his office in Fort Bragg, then drove north to the property. It is believed that upon arriving Coleman retrieved a chainsaw, weed eater, and other yard tools from a barn at the property to begin his day's work of clearing the trails of weeds. He took photographs of these tools to show that he had been there—a common practice for the land steward to do. The final photograph was taken at around 9:30am.

He was found late that night, lying dead by his vehicle. Co-workers had become concerned about his whereabouts when his girlfriend reported he had not come home, and they had gone out to search the area he was known to have been in. Coleman had been a land steward, coordinator of volunteers, and wildlife population surveyor for the organization for about six years. He previously worked for the California Fish and Game department and, at the time of his murder, was employed by the Mendocino Land Trust, a company that has a contract to manage and maintain the property known as Cape Vizcaino, owned by the Save the Redwoods League.

℀

A press release* went out late at night on the day of the shooting:

> On August 11th, 2011, at approximately 10:35pm Mendocino County Sheriff's Deputies, along with Coastal Medical Personnel were dispatched to the 44000 Block on North Hwy 1, Westport, CA, regarding a possible bear attack, which caused the victim's death. On arrival, medical personnel along with deputies examined

*All press releases are shown as they were originally published

the victim (who was located next to his vehicle) and found that the decedent's injuries were not consistent with a bear attack. Mendocino County Sheriff's Detectives were summoned to the location and are conducting a further investigation into the victim's death. A forensic necropsy will be conducted on August 15th, 2011 and the decedent's name is expected to be officially released at that time.

☙

Another marijuana-related crime—or not?

Initially, Coleman's murder was widely assumed to have occurred when, while working on this remote Mendocino Coast ranch, he encountered a person or persons involved in the thriving and ubiquitous North Coast drug trade.

Reporters for the Santa Rosa Press Democrat investigated the marijuana culture of the area and soon discovered that making the marijuana connection was an easy one for the public to hold on to, despite the Sheriff's comments to the contrary. The drug trade is hardly new to Mendocino County. In the 1960s and 1970s, urban refugees homesteaded the hills as part of the "back-to-the-land" movement, a call to reject consumer society and create new, self-sufficient lives.

They planted tomatoes, lettuce, bell peppers, sprouts—and pot. "It was a private garden culture," said Beth Bosk of Albion, who as publisher of the New Settler magazine has written about what she terms the "cannabis culture" for three decades and supports the legalization of marijuana. Bruce Anderson, editor and publisher of the Anderson Valley Advertiser, believes it "began with the hippies and spread throughout the rest of local society."

Either way, it became a trade among neighbors and then, over time, grew into one with a broader reach. By the 1980s, Mendocino County pot was sold nationwide and the rise of marijuana as a staple of the local economy sped up as the county's fishing and logging industries withered. In 2002, Georgia-Pacific Corp., which once employed 2,200 workers, closed its Fort Bragg lumber mill. In 2003, Mendocino Forest Products Co. shut its Fort Bragg mill, the Coast's last, leaving 4 mills in a county that once had 200. More and more, local people began to grow marijuana to make ends meet.

"There's people depending on it because they need to make a living," said John Ross of Little River, a lumberman for 60 years whose family entered the timber trade in 1869.

"Social workers and teachers and nurses, it's been a portion of people's livelihoods for over two decades here," said Bosk. "When we lost the last jobs, the loggers who stayed became growers; their kids became growers."

The county's marijuana crop turned into a true commercial industry after 1996 when California voters approved Proposition 215, the statewide ballot measure that legalized medical marijuana use. "Then it became a cash crop," Bosk said. "Since then there's just been this goldrush mentality."

It is a rare resident who does not know someone who grows pot. "I think I know a lot of people who are actively growing and selling," said Michael Anderson, the third of four generations of Andersons to run Anderson Logging, one of a handful of remaining local lumber companies. "You can't live in the community and not know people who are in the drug business," said Anderson, who believes that only legalizing marijuana will staunch the growing violence.

But today, drug enforcement officials say, the bulk of marijuana grown in Mendocino County is being managed by Mexican drug-trafficking outfits operating gardens many hundreds of acres in size. It's armed guards with night-vision goggles and AK-47s. It's becoming a major problem and people didn't think of it that way before—when it was just pot.

(For further background and insights to the pervasive marijuana culture of Mendocino County, and an interview with Sheriff Tom Allman on this topic, refer to Addendum C).

℘

No motive, no witnesses, no suspect

Nevertheless, despite the widely-held belief of the general public, law enforcement was far from sure that this case had the usual marijuana connection. Sheriff Tom Allman remembers, "On the night of the murder, a detective had sent me a text saying there had been a shooting on the Coast and there was one person dead. Informing me promptly was the routine thing to do in the event of a major crime—a homicide, a rape, a major traffic accident. I need to know so that if I am asked by the press then I am aware and can tell them we are working on the case at all levels. My first thought, as it always is, was that this murder must be marijuana-related. It was a forester and pot is often grown in the woods. 'Could it be a marijuana ripoff?' was my first thought. However, the Sheriff's Office detective at the scene, Detective Sergeant Greg Van Patten, did not bring this issue up. To solve any crime you have to look at motive—greed, drugs, love, sex, etc. It is normally apparent very quickly. In this case, I remember thinking the next day, 24 hours later, it was unusual that we still had no idea of what the motive might be, had no witnesses, and no suspect."

It appeared that Coleman had been at the scene for a short time, at least, with his weedeater, a gas can, and a pair of work gloves already removed from his car. It was estimated that he had been shot twice from about 30 feet away. In total, the killer had fired four shots from a high-powered rifle and two had hit the car. One of the other shots had hit Coleman in the right waist area, the other in the right arm and then into his chest, separating Coleman's aorta. The driver's side door was open and Coleman had fallen on the ground alongside the car with his head and shoulders on the driver's seat. His weedeater was a few feet away. It was not clear which shot had been fired first—the shot to the hip was not deadly but would have certainly slowed Coleman down. No casings were found at the scene and, very bizarrely, the suspect had defecated on Coleman's body, which made things even more confusing for the police.

Allman recalled, "This fact would perhaps signify a motive based on great anger but I had never heard of that kind of act being done.** There was nothing at the crime scene to connect this with marijuana but I was still thinking this might be the case. Meanwhile, the usual crime scene photos were taken and they made for pretty disturbing viewing. These would not be seen by anyone other than law enforcement unless the case went to a jury at some point. I believe the car was cleaned up shortly afterwards and sent off to one of those charitable organizations that people send their old vehicles to."

❧

**According to the District Attorney's Report on the case, DNA testing on the feces was not conducted due to the poor quality of the sample. It was however concluded that the diarrheic feces had been deposited on the deceased's remains post-mortem. It was believed by the prosecutor's office that such conduct by the perpetrator is indicative of some combination of an after-death demonstration of territorial or physical dominance, contempt of authority, and lack of remorse.

Mendocino County District Attorney C. David Eyster released his report on the case on August 13th, 2012. The report, reproduced in its entirety as Addendum A, will be used throughout this book to explain and/or elaborate on various events.

On Monday, August 15th, Mendocino County Sheriff's Office Captain Kurt Smallcomb issued this press release:

> On August 15th, Mendocino County Sheriff's Detectives learned that victim Matthew Coleman's cause of death was due to a fatal gunshot wound. He was found deceased on August 11th, adjacent to his vehicle. It is believed he was conducting property management at a rural piece of property north of Westport, CA, when the incident took place. Detectives are trying to establish leads into the murder of Matthew Coleman. They are continuing to work with evidence obtained from the scene and are attempting to establish a suspect/ suspects who are responsible for victim Coleman's unfortunate death.

Matt Coleman Crime Scene August 11, 2011

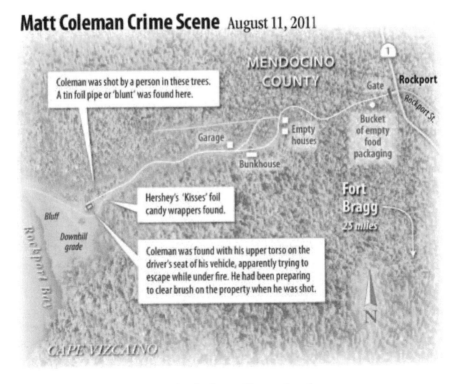

(Graphic by Loren Doppenberg)

"A real champion of the natural environment"

On Tuesday, August 16th, writing in the Press Democrat, reporter Glenda Anderson confirmed that law enforcement officials were calling Coleman's death a murder. More information was now coming out about what Coleman was doing at the rural property known as Cape Vizcaino or The Old Thomson Ranch. He was conducting regular property checks in his position as a land manager for the Mendocino Land Trust. Coleman's duties included management of this parcel recently acquired by the Save the Redwoods League. Coleman was killed while carrying out these duties, although law enforcement was still not saying publicly whether or not marijuana was being grown in the area, and whether Coleman might have stumbled into a "garden." The Sheriff's Office was asking the public for information for which callers could remain anonymous if they so wished. In the meantime, as reported in the Press Democrat, Captain Smallcomb did comment, "Where don't they grow in Mendocino County?"

Coleman often worked in remote areas alone, clearing brush and the invasive plants he despised. Friends and co-workers described Coleman as dedicated, hardworking, and likable. He was passionate about restoring land to its natural state and resuscitating endangered fish populations, said Winston Bowen, president of the Mendocino Land Trust. Bowen described his employee as "a real champion of the natural environment." He could not imagine anyone wanting to harm Coleman. "He was wonderful. He was a great big friendly bear of a guy. Optimistic, cheerful, a delightful man to work with."

At the regular Tuesday morning meeting of all Lieutenants and ranks above, the discussion was focused on this case. Sheriff Allman recalls, "I found myself being drawn in and decided I would go to the funeral on the upcoming Friday. I believed that Matt Coleman had been the absolute victim of a crime—he had been viciously murdered for no apparent reason. I should say that another reason for going was that I thought the killer might be there. However, I also wanted to find out who Matt Coleman was and the funeral turned out to be unlike any other I had ever been to."

Following the murder, there was a community outpouring of shock and concern—"clearly many people in the area loved Matt Coleman," thought Sheriff Allman. He was sent several emails expressing this and asking him not to bookshelf this case. "They could not believe how this could happen. I answered all of the emails and said, 'We do not bookshelf homicides in Mendocino County.' I found myself getting involved more than I normally would on an emotional level because of the reaction of the community and their collective outpouring of affection for this man. I had never heard of him in my world, but he was clearly beloved on the Coast."

"Nothing really made sense, except that we were never really going to make sense of it," said Scott Zeramby, a close friend of Coleman who owns Dirt Cheap, a garden shop in Fort Bragg. "He [was] always face down in the creek counting fish," Zeramby said. "He knew more about the local flora and fauna than anyone I knew. When he wasn't there working and studying the fish, he was playing, studying the fish." In his work, Coleman maintained trails, monitored stream conditions, and pulled invasive species from beaches. And outside of work, he was just as likely to be doing the same while camping, kayaking, studying birds, or backpacking with his girlfriend Sue Coulter. "They were inseparable," Zeramby said.

"Like everybody else, I'm flabbergasted," said Betty Stechmeyer, a volunteer with the Land Trust who spoke with Press Democrat reporter

30

Glenda Anderson. She added that the potential for stumbling upon one of Mendocino County's countless illegal marijuana gardens is always a concern. She knew Coleman to be kind, thoughtful, and optimistic, tackling the toughest of brush clearing himself. "He was a big puppy dog. Every inch of him had love and respect. To fill his shoes will be hard. I think that is something the Trust is going to have to look at once they get over the shock of the situation at hand."

℘

Significant evidence?

Over the next few days, Mendocino County Deputies and search and rescue team members continued to comb the crime scene and the surrounding area for any clues. On August 18th, there was what would become a significant find—a wrapper from Hershey's Chocolate Kisses and a blunt, or tin foil pipe, made for smoking marijuana, located in the area from where the bullets were determined to have been fired, based on their trajectory. These items were sent for DNA testing. Initially these items led law enforcement to follow the "marijuana connection" but, ultimately, when this connection was discounted, they were to have a far greater significance in the case. *** The searchers failed to locate any shell casings that could be later used to track back to the casings by ballistics to a particular firearm, and so by the day of Matt Coleman's memorial they were no closer to having a suspect, nevermind about making an arrest.

*** *These evidentiary items, along with further DNA testing and witness statements, would eventually positively identify the individual who murdered Matt Coleman.*

The memorial for Matt Coleman took place on Friday, August 19th. Allman recalls, "It was very emotional for many of those there. Boats of flowers floated down Big River and so many positive things were said about the deceased. It struck me as very odd that nobody was angry. I felt a little awkward in that I believe I was the only person there in a suit and tie—Coleman's family, friends, and acquaintances were not a suit-wearing crowd. There were many funny and warm stories shared about him, from his high school days right up until recent times. His girlfriend spoke of their special relationship and it was all very 'flowery,' for want of a better term.

"I decided I wanted to say something too. Now, I can speak very comfortably to large groups or just one-on-one, but when I stood up on this occasion I suddenly became very emotional and my eyes started welling up. I simply said, 'As Sheriff of this county, I owe you justice. And I will get you justice.' I couldn't say any more. A few days later, Matt Coleman's mother sent me a card thanking me for 'those wonderful words.' I was so struck by the community's love for Matt Coleman. He had no enemies. As I left, somebody asked me if I thought the killer was at the funeral. 'I doubt it,' was my reply."

At that stage in the case the detectives were trying to piece together Coleman's life and were questioning some of his acquaintances and checking on any criminal activities they may have been involved in. A few days later, Sheriff Allman appeared on KZYX & Z, Mendocino County local public radio station with host Norman de Vall. "It was a live show and I was asked, 'Was the murder marijuana related?' The public wants a 'Yes'/'No' answer to that, not a 'Maybe.' I took a pregnant pause as thoughts were racing through my head. I said what I truly believed—'No, I don't believe that marijuana is involved.' There were two reasons I did that—firstly, it was what I believed to be the truth, and secondly, it would stop the rumors that were circulating about this being 'just another North Coast marijuana shooting.' This was not so. This was a real 'whodunit?', which is rare in Mendocino County, and one for which we had no credible leads."

Over the next week, as the case faded from the news bulletins and headlines, the investigation continued. The connection to marijuana was probably still in the minds of the majority of the public, but this was not thought to be so by those investigating the case. This situation was not helping in their inquiries, as "just another marijuana crime" meant that they had no leads coming in whatsoever and the case remained as much a mystery as it had been on the day of Matt Coleman's death.

This would all change following a shocking development on Saturday, August 27th, when a set of criminal circumstances, that were not necessarily connected to marijuana, suddenly confronted everyone on the Northern California coast already very aware of the murder of Matt Coleman.

&

Chapter 2
"It's not Jere Melo, is it?"

"Okay, listen to me right now. I'm being shot at…"

Saturday, August 27th, 2011

This was going to be a very busy day for Sheriff Allman. It turned out to be far busier than he could have imagined. He was going to help a friend cook a barbecue for about 200 people in the evening but had also arranged to attend a library fundraiser and wanted to do both. "At about 11:30am I received a text from dispatch reporting a 'possible shooting in Fort Bragg; forester involved.' Interesting, I thought. Ten minutes later, Sheriff Office's Captain Kurt Smallcomb sent a text saying 'Deputies near to the shooting report one down.' I called him and said, 'It's not Jere Melo is it?' 'We think so' was the Captain's reply. That was certainly an 'Oh, shit' moment. Jere Melo was a former Fort Bragg Mayor and a current City Councilman. I called my wife and said I had to cancel on both of the events I was planning to attend and go out to the Coast. I did not stop to put on my uniform and got into a patrol car and headed out."

Sheriff Allman commented, "Jere Melo was very determined to make sure marijuana was not grown on the land he was responsible for in his job at Campbell Timber Management, owner of much of what was once Georgia-Pacific timberland running east and north of Fort

Bragg. A couple of years earlier, Jere and other advocates of solving the marijuana problems faced by timberland owners had been frequently disappointed at the response they would get from law enforcement when they would report marijuana issues affecting their property. At that time, the system was changed and all emails would be forwarded to myself and Bruce Smith, the head of our marijuana team, and one or both of us would always follow-up in one way or another.

"I had received emails on this topic weekly from Melo and, during the growing season, they could even be daily. In the week of August 22nd to 26th, I had assigned a Fort Bragg Sheriff Deputy, Jon Martin, a friend of Melo's, to spend time with Jere to plan the fall raids on the grows in the timberland areas. They would not be eradicating the plants at this time, just getting GPS readings for later use by the Sheriff's Office as part of our eradication program. On the morning of Tuesday, August 23rd, I was cc'd on an email that was sent to Deputy Martin from Melo stating that he intended to go into the woods the next day. Melo had received a report from a neighboring property owner that there was a water line that went from his property onto Campbell Hawthorne Timber Company's land and had now decided to ask the neighbor's son-in-law, 31-year-old Ian Chaney, who initially found the site, to assist him in locating it. The message also mentioned that Chaney said he suspected that the culprit was a man whose first name was Aaron and it was the same person who had crashed his vehicle into the school tennis courts a few months earlier. Chaney had also informed Melo that this man was 'a bit unstable.' Melo also told us that Chaney had seen red poppies growing on the land. This was unusual. Poppy grows would normally mean Asian involvement and such a community was very small in this area. I did not give much more thought about it at the time."

This is the email sent by Jere Melo to Sheriff Deputy Jon Martin and cc'd to Sheriff Tom Allman and the management at Campbell Timber: (It should be noted that Jere Melo spelled his companion's name as Ian "Cheney" in his emails. The correct spelling is "Chaney.")

Date: August 23rd, 2011. 11:42

Subject: Marijuana and Poppies Grower Report

This morning I took a report from Ian Cheney, a local who is married to a Balassi, and who is concerned about a bunker-type camp he observed on Hawthorne Timber Company property in the lower Noyo River area. I am asking for some guidance or information about the person who is the apparent grower.

Mr. Cheney identified the person as a young man whose first name is Aaron, last name unknown. He is apparently an eccentric person. His mother lives on Sherwood Road, just about on top of the Skunk Railroad tunnel. Aaron apparently lives across Sherwood Road in a tile red (color only, no tiles) house, when he is around. Aaron is the person who ran his dark Toyota pickup into the tennis court fence at the Middle School a few months ago. Hopefully, that gives enough information for a positive identification.

Mr. Cheney has seen Aaron on the Balassi property several times this year. He describes Aaron as a tall, young man who sports a skin head and dresses in dark clothing. Mr. Cheney has seen Aaron carrying potting soil and fertilizer bags across the Balassi property on Sherwood Road. He has recently followed his tracks across on to Hawthorne Timber Company property where he claims to have observed a "bunker" dug into the ground and surrounded by barbed wire. The Balassi family hear[s] chain saws working at night. Mr. Cheney observed lots of cleared areas around the bunker. He told me that a fire had started in the area. He saw red poppies growing in the area. He did not stay around long enough to look for more, as Aaron is known to be a bit unstable.

I reviewed the Hawthorne map this morning with Mr. Cheney, and my best estimate is that the site is near N 39 degrees 25.9 minutes and W123 Degrees 44.1 minutes. For a legal description, it is located in the E1/2 of the SE 1/4 of Section 10 T18N R17W, above a mid-slope road.

It is my plan to walk the area from South Fork on the Skunk Railroad tomorrow morning to get a better location. I will appreciate any information you might provide.

Thank you,

Jere

❧

On the next day, Wednesday, August 24th, Melo spent six hours walking the company logging roads but found nothing. Meanwhile, Deputy Martin had responded by email to Melo that the Aaron in question was Aaron Bassler and that Bassler had been arrested for being under the influence of controlled substances and that Bassler was "against law enforcement."

Melo sent another email to Deputy Martin on Thursday, August 25th that read,

*Jon: Thank you. Is he in custody now? I walked for six hours yesterday on the Hawthorne logging roads, overgrown for sure, and found nothing. I have an appointment at 8:00am, Saturday, to meet with Ian Cheney to get a better location. (It also occurs to me that this may be our guy in the Scout Camp incidents.) * Jere.*

Deputy Martin responded by informing Melo that Bassler was not currently in custody. Unfortunately, neither Deputy Martin nor any other member of the Sheriff's Office was aware that Bassler had been in the Cape Vizcaino area when Coleman was murdered. Thus, no additional crime-specific warning of caution was provided to Melo.

℘

On Saturday the 27th of August, as planned, an unarmed Jere Melo went into the woods with Ian Chaney, who did have a gun. They drove out to the vicinity of a trespass grow deep in the woods about four miles

---

According to the DA's Report: Melo's "Scout Camp incidents" comment refers to burglaries that had been reported as having happened at the Boy Scout camp on the Noyo River between June 23, 2011 and June 28, 2011. The camp is surrounded by Hawthorne Timber property. A person or persons unknown had broken into buildings and stolen bedding items, small hand tools, food, alcohol, and other items commonly used when camping. One of the breached padlocks had been shot off one building by a high-powered rifle. Deputy Martin told Melo about this incident and Melo, with the help of camp staff, later located the majority of the stolen items hidden under some brush on a trail near the camp. A brown sleeping bag, folding chair, and some small items, however, were not recovered. The same day that Melo helped recover some of the stolen property from the brush, a man, identified only as a skinhead wearing camouflaged clothing and carrying an AK-47 rifle, was seen by railroad personnel walking on the railroad tracks within a quarter mile of the Boy Scout camp. In turn, Melo advised Deputy Martin that he believed there may be a survivalist camp in the area so Deputy Martin, acting on that tip, conducted an unsuccessful fixed-wing overflight looking for such a camp the following day.

east of Fort Bragg with the apparent plan of marking the garden for the Mendocino County Sheriff's Office (MCSO) to eradicate. Melo felt so comfortable in that environment that he rarely carried a gun with him. Once in the area, from approximately mile marker six, they traversed old logging trails up the brushy slope alongside the rail tracks of the Skunk Train, a very popular tourist attraction providing scenic rides through the redwoods for 40 miles from Fort Bragg to Willits.

Ian Chaney described to investigators that, as they reached the general area, the men found a water line that was now camouflaged (it had not been camouflaged when Chaney was last at the site), and the men followed that line to the open-topped bunker, a location that Chaney would later describe as a "great ambush spot." (Note: The garden turned out to contain opium poppies; no marijuana was found.)

With Melo cutting the water line on their way up the hill, neither man observed anybody around the bunker during their approach, nor did they hear or see anybody in the surrounding area. The land near the bunker had been terraced and there were plants growing on the terraces that Chaney believed to be opium poppies. At the bunker, Melo put down the wooden-handled axe he always carried and began taking photographs and GPS readings near the bunker entrance. Chaney also took a picture of the bunker. As the men were looking around, Chaney heard crackling leaves behind and above the men. He whispered to Melo, "I think he's right behind us." The two men turned around to the north and saw Bassler partially hidden in brush about 15 feet above and behind the men.

Looking directly at Bassler, Melo announced, "Hey, what the fuck are you doing over there?" Bassler immediately responded that he was an FBI agent and opened fire with what Chaney believed at the time to be a fully-automatic AK-47 assault rifle. Chaney heard three quick shots in rapid succession and, after the third shot, Chaney saw Melo "spin like a top," falling hard and sliding a short distance down the hill. Close enough to see the whites of his attacker's eyes, Chaney recognized the gunman as Aaron Bassler. Dropping to the ground, Chaney took cover against the bunker and returned fire with his 9mm semi-automatic handgun. Bassler then stood up and began "unloading" his rifle on the spot where Chaney was seeking cover. Outgunned, Chaney decided to run for it. He ran into the brush and then began to slide down the hill. He later reported that he could hear bullets whizzing by his head in rapid succession as they hit the trees around him. As he slid down the hill, Chaney was also calling for Melo. At one point, Chaney, while looking back, observed Bassler standing on Melo's back and looking downhill towards Chaney while continuing to fire on him. Seeing Bassler now trying to advance on him through the brush, Chaney got to his feet, used trees as cover, and ran hard from the area, continuing to return fire to keep the attacker back. As he was able to achieve separation, Chaney tried to connect to 911 with his cell phone.

☙

This is a transcript of the 911 call received from Ian Chaney while under fire from Aaron Bassler after their encounter in the woods and the shooting of Jere Melo:

CHP Dispatch: 911 emergency reporting

Chaney: Hi, listen to me right now. My name is Ian Chaney. I'm here with Jere Melo out in the woods. We're being fired upon by some growers. I think Jere Melo might have been hit.

CHP Dispatch: Where are you located?

Chaney: I have no idea. We are right on the tracks, ummm...

CHP Dispatch: What town are you in?

Chaney: Fort Bragg, California

CHP Dispatch: Let me put you through to the Sheriff's Office, just a moment...

(Beeping sounds, then a dialing tone; caller can be heard breathing heavily)

CHP Dispatch: You are being transferred.

MCSO Dispatch: 911, what is your emergency?

Chaney: Okay, listen to me right now. I'm being shot at...

MCSO Dispatch: Where are you at?

Chaney: I'm out in the woods and I think Jere Melo has been hit. I got... (several shots are heard in the background) Shit!...

MCSO Dispatch: Where are you at?

Chaney: God damn it! (tones heard as if buttons are being pushed on Chaney's cell phone keypad) I'm out in the fucking woods. (loud shuffling noise)

MCSO Dispatch: Sir?

Chaney: Are you still there?

MCSO Dispatch: Yeah, where are... (recording ends)

⁊

According to Skunk Train passengers riding through that same area of the woods that morning, at around 10:00am several shots rang out from the surrounding forests. Shortly afterwards, a man flagged down the "speeder car," an all-purpose service vehicle that follows a few minutes behind the Skunk Train to make sure no fire has been started by someone discarding cigarette butts or in some other way. It was Ian Chaney. As detailed above, he had already called the police from his cell phone from the woods informing them that he was under fire and shots could be heard in the background during that 911 call.

The Skunk Train had continued on to the Northspur station and the speeder car returned Melo's shocked companion Ian Chaney to the Skunk Train Depot in Fort Bragg where, over the next few hours, he was interviewed by law enforcement. After the initial difficulties for both Cheney and the dispatcher to work out exactly where these events were taking place, this issue had been resolved and deputies were dispatched to the area. The investigation was underway—one that nobody would have predicted was to take 36 days to resolve.

Ꮽ

Over the next few hours the Sheriff's Office dispatched a large number of heavily-armed deputies to the area where Melo had fallen. The suspect was armed and assumed to be possibly still in the heavily-forested area near the site where he'd shot Melo. As a result, the responding officers were forced to move into the vicinity with the greatest caution. With these law enforcement officers and SWAT** team members slowly searching the surrounding area, the passengers on

---

**SWAT is a law enforcement acronym for Special Weapons and Tactics. This concept originated in the late 1960s as a result of several sniping incidents against civilians and police officers that had occurred around the country.

Jere Melo Crime Scene August 27, 2011

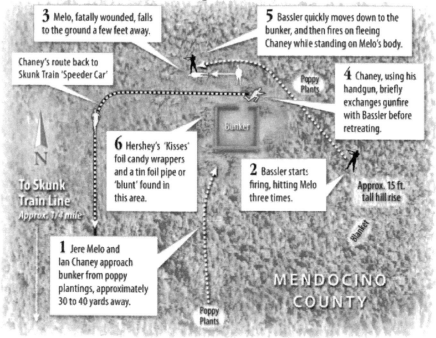

3 Melo, fatally wounded, falls to the ground a few feet away.

5 Bassler quickly moves down to the bunker, and then fires on fleeing Chaney while standing on Melo's body.

Chaney's route back to Skunk Train 'Speeder Car'

Poppy Plants

4 Chaney, using his handgun, briefly exchanges gunfire with Bassler before retreating.

Bunker

6 Hershey's 'Kisses' foil candy wrappers and a tin foil pipe or 'blunt' found in this area.

2 Bassler starts firing, hitting Melo three times.

N

To Skunk Train Line
Approx. 1/4 mile

Approx. 15 ft. tall hill rise

Blanket

1 Jere Melo and Ian Chaney approach bunker from poppy plantings, approximately 30 to 40 yards away.

Poppy Plants

MENDOCINO COUNTY

(Graphic by Loren Doppenberg)

the halted Skunk Train were kept on lockdown for several hours before being taken by bus to Fort Bragg.

In interviews with detectives back in Fort Bragg, Ian Chaney described the man at the bunker ambush as a white male with a completely bald head. The man was wearing a thick black bulletproof vest and black pants. Known to Chaney for at least 10 years as Aaron, the man had no shirt on underneath the vest. Chaney believed it was bulletproof because it had no pockets, there were Velcro straps holding the vest on the man's shoulders, and Chaney believed he struck Aaron with several of his 9mm rounds with the hits having no effect on the

43

rifleman. Chaney had not told Melo that he was carrying a loaded firearm, though Chaney had previously told Melo he would not return to the location alone or without being armed.

☙

"The name Aaron Bassler was mentioned to me"

Sheriff Allman arrived at the scene around 1:00pm. "Melo's body was in a spot we just could not get to without risk of life. The suspect had a bunker built there and it was at this time that the name Aaron Bassler was mentioned to me for the first time. I remember I kept referring to him as Bassner—the name of a friend of mine. As I mentioned, Melo had made it known to law enforcement that he knew a troubled man, named Aaron Bassler, was growing either marijuana or opium poppies or both on the timberland Melo supervised for the Boston-based Hawthorn-Campbell Timber Company. It was believed that Bassler had used heroin but that is a very different thing than cultivating it.

"I was informed that Melo and Chaney had walked into a poppy grow of 452 plants, just below a bunker that had been dug into the side of the hill. The redwood trees had been cut away to create the clearing and vantage point from the open-topped bunker, which was fortified with cut timber bound together with mud and wire. It was approximately eight feet by eight feet and had walls five feet tall, thus providing an optimal fighting position overlooking the hillside. The poppy plants were about a foot high and planted haphazardly, almost indistinguishable in the brush. Melo was in the process of checking his GPS and recording his position when he spotted some empty rifle casings on the ground and immediately said, 'Let's get out of here!' At that moment the suspect had suddenly stood up from a spot about 25 feet further up the hill from the bunker, shouted 'FBI! FBI!', and started firing. Melo was hit three times and fell to the ground where he stood. Chaney took out his handgun and fired towards the suspect several times but the suspect just disappeared into the woods, so he scrambled down to the Skunk tracks, about 200 to 400 yards away, where a train had just passed by. He managed to stop the speeder car and return to town. He was very scared. He and Bassler knew each other vaguely—he had chased Bassler off the land before, and he now feared for his safety. In fact he was scared to death. Throughout the duration of the case he chose to live away from his home and we did not reveal his name to the public. Meanwhile, we were obviously very concerned that the suspect was still in the vicinity. Melo had fallen to the ground right there and we had to work out a way to get him out without getting someone else shot."

SWAT teams from the Sheriff's Offices in Willits and Fort Bragg were soon on the scene, assisted by K-9 handlers Sgt. Mike Davis and Deputy Joseph Demarco, as well as Fish and Game Officers. Allman had every confidence in them. "They had good equipment, good training, and were good men. The SWAT team sergeant informed them that they could not get to Melo's body. We assumed he was dead but we did not know for sure, which really pained me. The SWAT teams, totaling about 10 men, knew they were going to be there for the rest of the day and night, and a deputy went and fetched about twenty sandwiches. We had also requested Ukiah SWAT and they brought in the armored C.R.V. (Citizen Rescue Vehicle).

"I began checking on our resources and by 3:00pm it was obvious we needed to get some supplies for the guys searching in the woods. There is a deli in Fort Bragg called the G and C Deli that makes dynamite sandwiches. They had heard about the law enforcement officers in the woods and they contacted Fort Bragg Police Chief Scott Mayberry who picked the sandwiches up and took them to the edge of the woods. 'Really?' I thought, 'Those guys were thinking of us!' It was very nice. Chief Mayberry also assured me that if the Sheriff's Office received additional emergency calls while we were in the woods, then the Fort Bragg Police Department would take care of them."

At that point, realizing that this situation was not going to be resolved quickly, Sheriff Allman's concern was with the preparation of the logistics for the teams of men and detectives. "Normally, the process would be to recover the victim's body, secure the crime scene, and then look for the suspect. We could not do this. I remember that the weather was good and one less thing I had to worry about. I had discussions with the SWAT sergeant figuring out both how we might rescue Melo and also arrest the suspect. Ian Chaney knew Aaron Bassler previously and had told us this was the man who had shot Melo. I saw Deputy Martin, Melo's friend, whom I had assigned to work with Melo that week, and said I was very sorry. He was not emotional, and was doing everything he was expected to do.

"Melo had been shot not far down the Coast from Rockport, where Matt Coleman had been shot just over two weeks earlier, but at this time the name of Matt Coleman was not mentioned at all. We were only concerned with the fact that we believed that Jere Melo had been shot by someone by the name of Aaron Bassler."

᳕

"Tom, do you believe that Jere is dead?"

Later in the afternoon, Sheriff Allman met with Fort Bragg Mayor Dave Turner and Fort Bragg Police Chief Scott Mayberry at Turner's house. "Turner kept saying, 'Tom, we need to get him out of there. Madeleine [Melo's wife] is very upset that he is lying out there.' I agreed. Perhaps there was a one percent chance that he was alive, but I told them we could not get to him any time soon. I remember drinking a soothing glass of cold water. I had been talking and listening so much over the previous few hours that it tasted so good... I then decided to do something a little unorthodox. I told them 'I have to talk to Madeleine.' Turner and his wife were in the same church as the Melos and he had a church address and phone book. I called and got the answering machine. I did not leave a message. I called her sister and left a voicemail there, asking her to tell her sister to call me. At about 4:00pm Madeleine called and I arranged to go over to her house.

"I told her everything I knew and that a certain Aaron Bassler was the suspect. I told her we had lots of resources at our disposal from within the County but she kept asking why we couldn't get him out. The SWAT teams had reported that there had been no sign of life from Melo's body. It was very heavy brush and dense woods. Even through their binoculars they could not see well. He was lying face down, he had fallen that way and had not moved. The only factors that would lead me to think he might be alive were emotional. No actual facts allowed me to think that he might be alive or that I could rescue the body without risking the lives of more people. Finally, she took my hand and said, 'Tom, do you believe that Jere is dead?'...

"You cannot prepare for such a question and for a brief second or two I hesitated. It was a very lonely moment before I answered, 'Yes, I do'... There was about five seconds of silence. There were just a few family members, the Mayor, and myself in the room. It was a deafening silence. Madeleine, like most people, believes that what law enforcement and fire departments do is save people. I'm sure that to hear that from me was very upsetting and frustrating, but it would not have been right to give her false hope. Before she posed it, I hadn't yet asked myself that question and come up with a definitive answer. It was a defining moment for me at the time and I wanted to think that there was a one percent chance he was alive but had no real reason for thinking that way. My whole thought process changed—Jere Melo is dead. Let's find the suspect."

❧

Sheriff Allman left the Melo home and headed to the Fort Bragg Fire Department. "I did not want to interfere with the SWAT teams who knew what they were doing but I wanted to make sure that they had every resource available. I arranged for generators and lights from the fire department, lots of them. We had never had a situation like this. It was not uncommon to leave a body at the scene but to not even be able to get to the scene was not common at all. I believe a C.H.P. [California Highway Patrol] officer had taken a photograph of the scene from a plane and had given it to the SWAT team but I did not see it."

The Sheriff next met with representatives of the Boston-based Hawthorne Campbell Timber Company. "The big boss was there because the previous day, Friday, had been a company picnic. Jere Melo had been at that picnic but had left early as Saturday was the opening day of the new deer-hunting season and he had to open up a number of locked gates on the timber company property so that employees could go in and hunt. I met the company representatives but had no time to chitchat, telling them we needed to have a closed-door meeting. Several of us sat down around a long table in a dark conference room. I told them everything I had told Madeleine earlier and we exchanged cell phone numbers. I said I would be in touch if anything changed. They were offering logistics—food, coffee, etc. I shook hands and left.

"By this time the press was starting to get wind of all of this and the shocking news of the popular councilman's murder began to reverberate up and down the Mendocino Coast. A reporter from the Press Democrat had even driven her car close to the crime scene—directly to an area that, because we were still undermanned at that point, was not secured by any law enforcement officers. It was a very unsafe thing to do—the shooter could have been there. I was livid. I was also frustrated by not having enough staffing, but, mostly, I was angry with her. We would be doing press releases regularly and neither I, nor Captain Smallcomb, wanted them calling us all day. Sure, she wanted her story but my priority was not her story, it was getting the logistics together for people to be in the woods all night long. I was upset but moved forward and left her to her own devices. I kept the SWAT teams in the woods and worked on getting new people for the next day. Detectives interviewed Bassler's parents that evening and it was an all-nighter for everyone involved."

જી

Around this time a press release was prepared by Lieutenant Greg Stefani of the Sheriff's Office:

On August 27th, 2011, at approximately 10:20am, this office was contacted regarding a shooting incident which took place approximately four miles east of Fort Bragg in an area on private timber company land, adjacent to the Noyo River. The property is in remote and rugged terrain. The property is also adjacent to the Skunk Rail lines.

Mendocino County Sheriff's Deputies along with Fort Bragg Police personnel, California Highway Patrol, and Fish and Game Officers proceeded to the area and contacted a witness to the shooting who advised law enforcement personnel that he and Jere Melo had been conducting property management in the area and the suspected gunman started shooting at them. The witness was able to flee the area and contacted law enforcement by cellular phone.

The County's SWAT team has at this time been deployed to this rural and rugged area, in an attempt to locate any victim or the suspect regarding this shooting. The suspect has been positively identified as Aaron Bassler, a transient from Fort Bragg, CA.

A Reverse 911*** was sent out to residents in the general area of the incident. Once the suspect is in custody, a second Reverse 911 call will be sent to notify residents that the area is secured. No further press releases will be done until August 29th, 2011. All inquiries should be directed to Captain Kurt Smallcomb at 707-463-6536.

⌘

***A "Reverse 911" call is a method that law enforcement uses to get the word out to the public at times when public safety is impaired. A police dispatcher can send out a message to every listed phone number in any given vicinity. This technique was used on several occasions in the Noyo Basin during the investigation as a way of informing the public of various developments.

"This might be big"

Captain Smallcomb, who was at the crime scene, decided that the lights and generators from the fire department were not necessary so they were cancelled. He reasoned that the lights would expose the law enforcement officers and, despite lots of planning going into implementing this idea, they decided to cancel the use of the lights. Sheriff Allman, who had arranged for this equipment to be made available, agreed. "That was a very smart strategic decision to make. Nevertheless, the Fire Department emphasized that they would help in any way they could with anything else. At this point Jere Melo was assumed dead—a shocking development for the Fort Bragg community to face. He was a city council member and had many, many friends in the area. I was concerned about vigilantes taking things into their own hands. I was also worried about the next day being opening day of the deer-hunting season and people being in the woods with guns. At that point we did not know that Aaron Bassler was a very skillful survivalist. The vigilantes and hunters were a concern but, apart from the fact that his crop was not marijuana but poppies instead, everything else seemed to be the same as a regular raid on any marijuana grow in the woods following a shooting. How wrong I was."

✥

Captain Smallcomb and Sheriff Allman sat in the Sheriff's Substation in Fort Bragg. "We were both looking at each other, hoping the other had an answer. The enormity of the situation started to sink in and the conference room there became the Command Post, whereas normally it would be in the field or a small office. I called my wife Laura

Captain Kurt Smallcomb
(Beth Schlanker/ The Press Democrat)

and told her I would be at home at midnight. I continued planning, yet in doing that I really did not want this whole thing to snowball into something it wasn't. However, I could see that this might be big and I had never been involved in anything like it before. I worked on getting the next day's operation organized and at about 11:00pm or so I went home."

☙

Chapter 3
The "Manhunt" begins

"We had our mission—find Aaron Bassler"

Sunday, August 28th, 2011

The day after Melo's murder, SWAT teams began to arrive from other parts of the county and officers were pulled off regular patrols to deal with the developing situation in the woods. The Detectives Unit, the Mendocino County Major Crimes Task Force, Mendocino County District Attorney's Office Investigator Andy Alvarado, and California Department of Justice Crime Scene Technician Matt Kirsten also hiked into the woods towards the crime scene to process evidence.

Sheriff Allman was in touch with the crime scene team early that morning. "I got up and checked in with those at the scene. Melo's body was still there where he fell. I was scheduled to attend a Rotary Club fundraiser further down the coast from Fort Bragg in Little River and so I drove over, explained the situation, and immediately left for the crime scene. I met with Smallcomb who was becoming worth his weight in gold at this point. He had previously been a Lieutenant in charge of detectives and, as such a big part of this investigation involved detective work, he reverted to his previous job and this worked very well as he focused on that aspect. This allowed me my first sign of some relief on this and I knew he and I could work through this together. Technically, everyone involved was answerable to me but I do not micro-manage. The specialists in various fields brought things to my attention and I listened to what they had to say. My job, at that point, was with logistics, dealing with the press, and to be assured that the direction of our investigation was correct. We had little to go on other than we knew we were searching for Aaron Bassler and that he was armed and very dangerous, out there in the woods."

That morning the Press Democrat made its first report of the Jere Melo shooting. Law enforcement was not commenting to the press other than the fact that there had been a shooting and they were attempting reach the victim's body deep in the woods with a SWAT team. Meanwhile a search for the suspected shooter, a transient from Fort Bragg by the name of Aaron Bassler, was being carried out in the woods by additional SWAT team members.

❦

At 9:00am, the SWAT team, who were about 100 yards away from the body of Jere Melo, decided it was time to move in, estimating that it would take them about two hours to cover that distance. Sheriff Allman was informed of this decision. "They had no idea of where Bassler was. They would be slowly crawling uphill through dense brush. It was horrendous. That morning was very, very foggy and this had prevented a helicopter from flying over the scene and seeing if they could spot anyone. After about an hour they were about 30 feet from Melo's body and they said there was no question that he was dead. Ultimately, it did take the full two hours to cover those 100 yards, and at about 11:00am they confirmed that Melo was dead, shot several times with a 7.62 x 39mm round. The rifle was later determined to be a Norinco

Mak 90 Assault Rifle. He was shot in the back as he spun around in reaction to the initial shot to his head. He had died almost instantly. The Department of Justice had by this time sent their C.S.I. (Crime Scene Investigation) team down from Eureka and they processed the crime scene. Various items of evidence were found and there was also a blanket in the brush where we assumed the suspect had been hiding or sleeping, several yards from the bunker area and close to the spot from where gunshots had been fired at Melo and Chaney.

"After getting confirmation from Smallcomb, I called Madeleine Melo with the confirmation of her husband's death. Her brother-in-law answered and I asked for Madeleine. He stayed on the line when she came on and I said I was very, very sorry to say that Jere was dead. Now, I have been a coroner for 30 years and I know what the next question always is. Rather I know what the next thought always is, whether they ask the question or not—'Did they suffer?' In this case nobody had seen Melo for 24 hours so any suffering was difficult to confirm without an autopsy, but it certainly did appear that his death was somewhat instantaneous. Madeleine did not ask the question but there was very little blood on the scene and I did offer the information that it appeared he had not suffered. We tell people the truth. They need to know the truth, whatever it may be. There was a silence for a few seconds before I said I would call her with any further details I might get. The autopsy later confirmed that Melo had died within seconds of being hit—his aorta had been separated, his death was instant, his heart stopped and therefore very little blood flowed.

"After the call to Madeleine I began to focus again on what lay ahead. We had our mission—find Aaron Bassler. This was going to require lots of logistics; not just finding personnel, but also making sure we could support these people and at the same time making sure that the Sheriff's Office was still functioning effectively around the rest of the County. Smallcomb and I had several meetings on these topics. These were one-on-one meetings. We did not want subordinates seeing that their leadership was not sure about the answers to some of the questions confronting us. The secretary at the Substation, Julie Whipple, was doing a great job of coordinating things in the field in terms of food, etc., and the Fort Bragg Police Chief, Scott Mayberry, was doing a fantastic job too. Meanwhile, I was in contact with the District Attorney, C. David Eyster, who sent several of his investigators to assist with the interviewing of people who might know Bassler. For me, all day Sunday was spent working on logistics for the local agencies apart from our own, such as the C.H.P., CalFire (the California Department of Forestry and Fire Protection) and Fish and Game, and also dealing with the press.

"Kurt Smallcomb and I already had the gut feeling that this was going to be a big investigation. The former mayor had been killed, there would be a large press presence, detectives could well be in the woods for a long time. There were going to be some big logistical problems to overcome. We had made the decision to use the Substation as the incident command center with its large briefing room, 20 feet by 20 feet, being a great choice as it turned out—we would eventually need space for twenty to thirty people. We set up phone lines and installed a dispatcher service operating 24/7—when there is a name for the suspect the tips are more frequent. We would need coffee 24 hours a day, flashlights, batteries, and of course radio chargers. There are no wall chargers out there, as there are here, where we have a wall of them that deputies just plug their radios into at the end of their shifts each day so they are ready for their next shift. I was also concerned about the possibility of rain and the extra clothing and equipment required for that scenario. Meanwhile, I was also staying on top of the developments in the woods—the crime scene was still under investigation, we were removing the body, and discussions were underway on how to move forward in the search for Aaron Bassler."

እን

Later on Sunday, the Bay Area television stations picked up the story of the city councilman who had been murdered by what police described as "numerous gunshots from a high-powered rifle." The story was gathering steam and Sheriff Allman, as head of the overall operation, was soon going to be making many important decisions for which he personally would be ultimately responsible. "I was a support person for the SWAT teams and the detectives from both our Sheriff's Office and the Department of Justice, plus the two who had been sent over by the DA's office who would be reporting any developments to District Attorney Eyster. I would also be the main person dealing with the press, although Kurt Smallcomb would take over many of those responsibilities in the ensuing weeks. Having said that, the press knew that they could go to Smallcomb and then on to me if necessary."

እን

SWAT teams on Skunk Trains

Monday, August 29th, 2011

The following morning, the Press Democrat had the front-page headline, "Fort Bragg official slain."* This was printed above a large

---

*It should be noted that the Santa Rosa Press Democrat (SRPD) does not use capital letters for all the words in its headlines. Many newspapers do. Throughout this publication, the headlines are represented exactly as they appeared in the original newspaper editions.

photograph of the local Skunk Train, a Fort Bragg tourist attraction, with two SWAT team officers riding on the front, and also smaller photographs of both Melo and Bassler, the latter appearing to have some sort of black eye. (It turned out to be a booking photograph following a pepper spraying and his detainment earlier in the year when Bassler crashed a vehicle into the high school tennis courts and after some resistance had then been arrested.) They also reported that sources close to the investigation were saying that law enforcement agents who had searched the area of the shooting had found opium poppies and not marijuana but that County Sheriff Allman declined to discuss any further details at that time.

℘

The Skunk Train has been in continuous operation since 1885, when it was established to bring redwood timber from the coastal hills to a mill in Fort Bragg. It officially started to carry tourists in 1904 along a line that snakes 40 miles through Noyo Canyon, crossing 30 bridges and passing through two tunnels. It carries about 50,000 passengers a year, with most trips from either Willits inland or Fort Bragg on the coast, going to and from the station at Northspur, midway between the two towns. In the days following the Melo shooting, the tourist attraction was closed to the public and the trains were instead used to transport law enforcement officers and SWAT team members in and out of the woods as the search for Bassler continued.

With news of the popular Melo's death reverberating around the region, Sheriff Allman met with County C.E.O. Carmel Angelo and briefed her with all the information he had, informing her of the costs that were being incurred. "I assured her that this was going to be costly but that I would keep it as low as I possibly could. I had many meetings scheduled that day, one being a seminar dealing with tribal police issues in Redwood Valley with the Community Oriented Police Service (C.O.P.S.), whose director was in town from Washington D.C. Captain Smallcomb took over the running of operations at 'ground zero' as it were and I knew things were in good hands, although I did check in with him on a number of occasions throughout the day."

഍

Early in the afternoon the second press release on the Melo shooting was issued from the Mendocino County Sheriff Office (MCSO):

> On August 29th, 2011, a forensic medical exam was conducted on victim Jere Melo and the cause of death was determined to be multiple gunshot injuries. The MCSO and other city and state law enforcement agencies continue to conduct searches in their attempt to locate suspect Aaron Bassler. Residents are reminded that the suspect was last seen armed and he is considered dangerous. Anyone with any information is encouraged to contact (707) 463-4086 or (707) 961-2479.

഍

Sheriff Allman felt by this time that the case was not going to be over in a short time. "About 24 hours into the investigation we started to feel with some conviction that there was not going to be a quick solution to this. Ninety-nine percent of homicides where you know the suspect, as in this case, are solved very quickly. I knew this investigation might well be very different. I felt it would present us with a number of

Armed Skunk Train
Heavily armed SWAT team members on the front of the Skunk Train
as it heads out into the search area east of Fort Bragg.
(Christopher Chung/ The Press Democrat)

unusual things to consider. Captain Kurt Smallcomb and his detectives were concerned that perhaps we might not be committed to this for a lengthy period of time. They were also wondering if we could assume that the suspect was still in the area. Other factors in deciding how to move forward were the economic issues—two of which were the cost to the County and the Skunk Train ride through the woods, a major tourist attraction to the town that would not be operating over the upcoming Labor Day holiday weekend. A further financial consideration was the fact that several logging operations had been shut down by order of the timber companies, thus causing many timber-fallers and foresters, whose jobs were in the woods, to be out of work until the situation was resolved. I made a commitment to Smallcomb that we were in this for the long haul; in for a penny, in for a pound; 24/7. However, despite having expressed that, all along I kept thinking that this might actually end very simply, perhaps as basic as Bassler being picked up hitchhiking on Highway 20!"

There had never been an extensive operation like this in modern-day Mendocino County, and Sheriff Allman had little or no experience he could call on. "Such manhunts were only in the history books—Sheriff Doc Standley had hunted down cattle rustlers from Little River to the Sacramento Valley back in the 1880s. There were so many things we did not know, one of the most basic of which was how to maintain a 24/7 investigation and to keep control of the desired outcome. I knew we didn't want to fill the woods with guys with guns, walking around searching under every bush. All we knew in that first day or so was that a suspect by the name of Aaron Bassler had a rifle and that he was in a thickly forested area of 400 square miles that we believed he knew better than we did."

℘

The local community was in shock. Jere Melo was very well known in the area and admired by many as a prominent community member. He was serving his fifteenth year on the City Council, having devoted much of his life to helping Fort Bragg, raising funds and political will to fight for many civic-minded causes. As the tributes for him came in from many local residents, co-workers, and city officials, the hunt for Bassler continued with teams of searchers working in shifts, each returning exhausted after several hours in the rugged terrain.

There had been no sign of the suspect but the generally held view was that this was another drug-related crime. Mendocino County at marijuana harvest time is always tense but, according to many locals, this season the tension seemed greater than ever. Growers were armed against the numerous pot thieves, also armed, who preyed on the valuable ripening cannabis, and many areas of the County had become no-go zones to ordinary citizens as trespass grows became harvest-time armed camps.

Mike Delbar, a former County Supervisor and friend of Melo's, speaking to the Press Democrat and on a Facebook post, expressed a view commonly held among the North Coast communities—that the forests were being overrun by people exploiting the area's rural terrain to make money in the drug trade. He commented, "When law-abiding, taxpaying citizens can't use their own property without fear, and now real consequences, of this runaway illegal drug problem, then we as a society will never succeed with healthy and secure communities."

✂

"He will decide how this ends"

Tuesday, August 30th, 2011

Sheriff Allman normally had his regular schedule planned two weeks in advance. Following the Melo murder, he asked his secretary, Liz Evangelatos, to put off whichever of his appointments she could, although the necessary regular work had to continue, of course. Two more days of meetings for Sheriff Allman followed, during which time he continued to talk often with Captain Smallcomb, who was on the scene in Fort Bragg, and who continued to keep the public informed with press releases.

The public learned of the increasing number of law enforcement agencies becoming involved when Smallcomb put out this release on the 30th:

> Mendocino County Sheriff's Office, assisted by Fort Bragg Police, Cal Fire, Willits Police, California Highway Patrol, Fish and Game, Ukiah Police, Federal Bureau of Investigation, and the National Guard, are continuing their search in an attempt to comprehend suspect Bassler for the murder of Jere Melo. Officers are being supported by the Department of Justice as well as the Mendocino County District Attorney's Office.
>
> Law enforcement officers are conducting ground and aerial searches in an attempt to locate Bassler and to obtain evidence to assist in the successful prosecution of Bassler. The ground search efforts are focused from the northern coast to the east towards Willits, CA. They also include any type of possible sightings by the public. Efforts will continue until the suspect is apprehended by law enforcement.
>
> All residents in the area should remain vigilant and conscientious of their surroundings. Anyone with information as to the whereabouts of suspect Aaron Bassler are encouraged to contact the Mendocino County Sheriff's Office at 707-463-4086 or 707-961-2479.
>
> The Mendocino County Sheriff's Office would like to thank those residents and private companies, including the Skunk Train personnel and local media, who are supporting law enforcement by assisting in public address efforts in regards to law enforcement search efforts in our attempt to safely apprehend suspect Bassler for the murder of Jere Melo.

WANTED
ARMED AND DANGEROUS

Photo Date: 9-14-2010

LAST NAME:	BASSLER	RACE:	WHITE
FIRST NAME:	AARON	HEIGHT:	6'00"
MIDDLE NAME:	JAMES	WEIGHT:	160 LBS
DOB:	5-1-1976	HAIR COLOR:	BROWN
CURRENT AGE:	35	EYE COLOR:	BLUE

"Armed and Dangerous" poster

The Sheriff's Office posters described Bassler as six feet tall and about 160 pounds with blue eyes and brown hair. He was last seen wearing dark clothing. Bassler's father, Jim, informed the press that his son had in recent years kept his head shaved clean and any hair would be turning grey.

The public also learned more details from the front pages of the Press Democrat that day. These revealed that Bassler had been living in the woods for four months before the fatal encounter and it was believed that he was the sole tender of more than 100 poppy plants, an uncommon endeavor, according to Captain Smallcomb. Bassler's father called his son a "practiced hider," explaining that there were times when Bassler was a child when he would disappear in the woods to play and his father couldn't find him for hours.

On the same front page, Jim Bassler stated that he had tried to get help for his son for years as the young man grew increasingly threatening and anti-social. He added that law enforcement and court authorities had not acted on the family's requests for help. Jim Bassler, a commercial fisherman out of Fort Bragg, was quoted as saying, "It's anybody's guess what is going through his head. I don't think he is going to throw down his gun when they find him."

Jim Bassler went on to talk about how this was a nightmare come true. He said he had long feared that without mental health intervention his son would end up hurting someone. His son had several brushes with the law since turning 19 in 1995, when he was given two year's probation for driving under the influence. According to court records he had since been arrested and charged with crimes that include prowling, vandalism, carrying a concealed weapon, and resisting arrest earlier that year following an incident where he had smashed his truck into the school tennis courts and then fought with the police who had in turn used pepper spray and finally a taser before he could be restrained.

Jim Bassler further discussed with the press his concern about the difficulty of getting help for mentally ill people and the repercussions of the failure to do so. Laws protect patient privacy and prohibit forced treatment, and he believed this to put his son and hence the community at large at risk. He believed his son to be schizophrenic but did not know if this had been formally diagnosed due to the privacy laws. Jim Bassler and the family say that following the brief imprisonment of his son after the tennis court incident they wrote to the police asking them and the courts to insist that Aaron received treatment. "I said, basically, 'I'm worried about his safety, the family's safety, and the community's safety.' I never heard a word in reply. I even had a hunch that he might have been involved in the Coleman murder, particularly when I learned that he had a rifle with him when he was dropped off in the Westport area. I feel guilty about not running down to the police station. No one had listened to me before though."

☙

Later on this day, three days after the shooting of Jere Melo, Jim Bassler explained to police that when he was at a recent family barbecue, his ex-wife, Laura Marie Brickey, the biological mother of Aaron Bassler, told him she'd driven their son to Westport around the time that Coleman was shot and killed on August 11th. He recommended that she call the Sheriff's Office and report what she knew. Brickey later confirmed that Jim Bassler had indeed asked her at the barbecue to report what she knew to the police. She explained that she did not contact law enforcement because she did not know at that time where to find her son and she didn't know for sure that her son had done anything wrong.

❧

According to the DA Report, in those first few days following Jere Melo's murder it had been determined by investigators that Laura Brickey had driven her son north on Highway 1 on August 10, 2011 and eventually dropped him off before noon at the driveway designated as 44000 North Highway 1. This is the same roadway leading out to the scene where Mr. Coleman was found murdered. It was a planned trip; Bassler had gone shopping at the Safeway and Purity markets in Fort Bragg for food and other provisions. Investigators found out that his mother had also taken him to Safeway to shop on August 8, 2011. In addition to items purchased at the two stores, the mother also belatedly disclosed that her son was armed with a rifle when she transported him to the Point Vizcaino area. She also said that this was not the first time that she had dropped Bassler off in this area.* Approximately one month prior, his mother had dropped Bassler off across the highway from this same location. Bassler had told his mother that he had two camps in the Westport area.**

---

*According to the DA Report: There is no record that the mother had attempted to disclose important information to obviously interested law enforcement. The mother admitted, however, that she was aware of the timely media reports of the death of Coleman and the general location where it was reported Coleman had died.

**In searching the entrance area at 44000 North Highway 1, investigators found a bucket hidden in the bushes near the unlocked gate that blocked that access road—see diagram of Matt Coleman Crime Scene on page 28. While animals had apparently scattered the contents of the bucket, several Top Ramen noodle wrappers were found spread on the ground. A store receipt provided by the Safeway store in Fort Bragg documented that Bassler had purchased Top Ramen noodles on August 8th, three days before Coleman's murder.

When asked to provide background on her son, Aaron Bassler's mother, Laura Brickey, explained to investigators that she believed something was wrong with her son because he had anger fits and he was paranoid around people. His mother placed blame for these personality manifestations on a claim that Bassler had used "acid" and had experienced a bad trip. When asked about her son's Federal court-ordered counseling flowing from a 2009 incident where he lobbed notes about aliens and stars into the Chinese Consulate in San Francisco, his mother told law enforcement that no diagnosis of mental illness resulted from her son's nine-month long interaction with mental health professionals in that matter. Laura noted that her son had recently taken up chewing tobacco. When her son smoked marijuana, his mother said he would use the aluminum foil off of the top of plastic bottles, though she further added that she didn't think her son would ever smoke marijuana in the form of a joint. When asked about her son and opium poppies, his mother said he had tried to grow poppies wherever she had lived. She believed he was trying to get opium out of the plants. Finally, when her son had access to a television, Laura reported that he only watched English language stations broadcasting the daily news of China or weather channels.

Meanwhile, his father reported to law enforcement his opinion that his son was a "paranoid schizophrenic" who thought that everybody was following him. A friend of Bassler reported that Aaron, starting in early 2011, was becoming more radical about being able to survive any type of armed encounter with the federal government. Aaron Bassler talked with this friend about making bunkers and how he considered himself a survivalist.

Furthermore, also according to the DA Report, after the death of Jere Melo, Bassler's mother provided some information as to her son's whereabouts before and after Coleman's death. It was disclosed that his mother received a telephone call from her son on or about August 18, 2011 at about 2:00 in the morning. She told investigators that her son did not sound "screwed up" during the short call. Bassler told his mother not to call the Sheriff. He also wanted his father to be told that he had checked in so nobody would come looking for him. (Bassler and his mother had an agreement that she would report him missing to the Sheriff's Office if he ever failed to check in with her within a week of his being gone from the immediate Fort Bragg area.) This call was traced back to a cell phone of young woman who, when eventually located, confirmed that she had loaned her cell phone to a man she later was able to identify as Bassler from a photograph. The man approached the woman who was sitting in her vehicle at the Ettersberg Road junction of Briceland Road. He told the woman that he had walked to the junction from Usal and was looking for the nearest telephone. The woman offered the man the use of her cell phone. After he finished his call, the man asked the woman where she was heading and if he could have a ride. She replied she was heading towards Whitethorn. She agreed to give the man a ride and eventually dropped him off at the Shelter Cove/Whitethorn junction. When specifically asked, the woman could not remember the man carrying anything with him. After being dropped off by the woman, the man was last seen walking briskly into the night in the direction of Shelter Cove.

Sheriff Allman realized that every lead had to be followed up. "I immediately contacted Humboldt County Sheriff Mike Downey and advised him of the situation. Bassler's mother had said that he knew the backwoods so well that he could hike from their house to Westport in four hours—a distance of about 15 miles. It is possible to then go through the Usal forest to Humboldt County and the town of Whitethorn, where the witness had seen him. We believed he had not done this but the information got out and we now had terrified citizens in that area too. This was very bad news so we decided to put about 10 cameras on the route he might have taken. I do not know how this information reached the public but it was very irresponsible for that to have happened. I remained in contact with the Sheriff Mike Downey, who I'd known for 20 years and, in fact, he was the first person to send us a SWAT team and I wanted him to know everything that was going on."

It was around this time, in those early days of the investigation, that Sheriff Allman really started to think with some conviction about how this might end. "Jim Bassler had told Captain Smallcomb that he 'didn't believe that his son would give up without a fight,' and I thought from that moment on that [Aaron Bassler] will decide how this ends."

❧

"Are 2 killings connected?"

Wednesday, August 31st, 2011

On this day, the Press Democrat, underneath a sub-heading of "Fort Bragg manhunt grows," carried the main headline "Are 2 killings connected?" The general public was now being confronted by and talking about the possible connection between the two recent slayings in the area.

As a result, for the first time it was being suggested that there might be a link between the Melo killing and the murder two weeks earlier of Matt Coleman. Captain Smallcomb declined to say whether Bassler was a suspect in the Coleman case, although he did comment, "Anything's possible. It's all under investigation."

Sheriff Allman recalls that someone, and he could not recall who, had informed the press that Aaron Bassler had been in the Westport area at the time of the Matt Coleman shooting. "We knew we would have to confirm or deny this. The DNA tests on the blunts found at both scenes were still a few days from being completed so Smallcomb's comment that 'Anything's possible' was perfect. We could not confirm any link, but neither did we wish to deny that there might be one.

"Law enforcement hates to say something that is later disproved. We must be seen by the public to only give credible information. I was only going to say Aaron Bassler was responsible for both murders when I knew for certain that he was, although my gut feeling at this point was that he was. This was two random shootings with no motives. This is very, very rare; in fact, we could not remember any other similar situation happening in the County. There were no financial issues in play, no love interest, no family intrigue, nothing. However, Bassler's connection to the Coleman murder could not be confirmed yet and so we had to wait for information from the Department of Justice before we could confirm it. Meanwhile, rumors continued to spread. Matt's parents had flown out here from the East Coast and I was in regular contact with them, assuring them of the facts and informing them when rumors were false. Officers Smallcomb and Van Patten also helped with this and they did a great job."

Allman recalls being surprised at the newspaper headlines and calling Captain Smallcomb. "He had commented the previous day to the press that 'anything was possible' as a way of expressing that nothing could be ruled out at that point, but we had no evidence that could actually support the headline. Nevertheless, given the lack of motives for either killing, I think we were both beginning to believe that it was entirely possible, though we were not sure how, although the public was still generally of the belief that drugs were the reason behind the murders. However, one of our deputies, Detective Sergeant Greg Van Patten, who had been at both crime scenes, pointed out that Hershey Kisses wrappers and tin foil blunts had been found at both. This was kept under wraps initially as we did not wish to start fears that a possible serial killer was on the loose. Bassler was never thought of as that—he killed when people encroached on 'his land.' The links were becoming more apparent. We had also talked to Bassler's mother in those first few days and she remembered dropping off her son, with a rifle, close to Westport and near the spot where Matt Coleman was killed. DNA was taken from both scenes but this takes a few days to analyze. We would have to wait a little longer."

The similarities of the killings appeared to contradict any thoughts that illegal drug production was involved. While the Melo crime scene was at a location known previously as a spot for a marijuana garden, no evidence of marijuana, poppies, or any other drug cultivation was found where Coleman was killed. Neither victim had any connection to the drug industry, both were "ethical and moral, doing their legal and lawful jobs," Smallcomb was quoted as saying. Meanwhile Allman surmised, "So perhaps any link, if there was one, was something else entirely. Very soon evidence began to show up that pointed to no clear and direct link, but the fact that the murders were random was actually the link between them. As a result of such randomness, the suspect would be even more difficult to track than had previously been assumed."

As for the weapon used to shoot Jere Melo, in The Ukiah Daily Journal, reporter Tiffany Revelle, who would follow and write about the case throughout its development, wrote that Captain Smallcomb had said that ballistics tests were being carried out by the state laboratory and that the gun used in the Coleman shooting had been a "large-caliber rifle." He had previously stated that the weapon allegedly used by Bassler to kill Melo was also a high-powered, high-caliber long rifle. He continued to refuse to speculate further on any connection between the two killings and stated that ballistics testing results were not yet available.

❦

Around this time, those leading the search discussed at great length the "Skunk Train issue" and the effect it being open or not would have on the local community. The popular tourist attraction had resumed business the previous day, Tuesday, August 30th, despite the continuing search. Until a few weeks earlier, Fort Bragg was perhaps best known as one terminus of the scenic Skunk Train's excursions through the California redwoods, a working-class town of about 8,000, most of them fishing and logging families supplemented by a healthy dose of sightseers. The very popular tourist train ride through the woods ran right through the crime scene. At the Fort Bragg end of the Skunk line the tracks double as a path to town for the homeless whose camps have been long entrenched between the Fort Bragg Cemetery and the train tunnel. The investigators assumed that the tracks served as Aaron Bassler's resupply route between his apparent opium poppy garden and Fort Bragg. It was at this garden, close to the Skunk Train's first tunnel, four miles from the train depot in central Fort Bragg, where Jere Melo had been killed.

Meanwhile, as reported in the Press Democrat, the Department of Justice had issued a statement that if the poppies found growing at that garden, the scene of Melo's shooting, proved to be the opium variety, then it would be a rare find. In fact this would be just the second time such a quantity of poppies had been found in almost three decades. Captain Smallcomb, who had been on the force for 28 years, said he was unaware of any rise in opium poppy production, "If it's a trend, it's something very new," he said. Authorities also added that neither marijuana nor opium poppies had been found at the Westport scene of Matt Coleman's death, thus adding more weight to the increasingly held view among law enforcement that the murders were quite possibly linked in a random way, not by any sort of connection with the illegal drug industry.

Nevertheless, a drug connection was still suspected by many members of the public—"What else could it be?" remained the generally held view. A Fort Bragg resident posted this assessment of the weekend's events on Facebook: "You're on vacation on the Coast, going for a nice ride on the Historic Skunk Train, and just before you go through the tunnel into the warm country, you hear seven or eight shots, then some guy comes running toward the train to flag it down saying someone has been shot. The train can't go back to Fort Bragg through the woods because the shooter is still around somewhere. So several hours later, halfway between Fort Bragg and Willits, Mendocino Transit Authority buses pick up the passengers and take them back to the Coast over Highway 20. End of pleasant rejuvenating vacation. What's this going to do for the reputation of this area? There's no more fishing or logging, and tourism is the supposed cure-all, except that the real industry up here is pot, with this kind of tragic fallout."

In the town

Following the murder of Jere Melo, Fort Bragg residents study the "Armed and Dangerous" poster issued by law enforcement as the search for suspect Aaron Bassler continues. The reward being offered for information on the Matt Coleman murder, that had taken place a couple of weeks earlier, was also posted at this time.

(Kent Porter / The Press Democrat)

Chapter 4
Double-murder suspect?

Tin foil pipes and Hershey's Kisses

Thursday, September 1st, 2011

With the Labor Day weekend fast approaching, Congressman Mike Thompson visited Fort Bragg. Sheriff Allman recalls, "We met at City Hall and then had a full meeting with City Manager Linda Ruffing, Mayor Dave Turner, City Council member Doug Hammerstrom, and Heidi Cusick Dickerson, Thompson's representative in Mendocino County, who co-coordinated the meeting. I gave this group a full and up-to-date briefing. I informed them that this was becoming a very big concern but assured them that we were committed to its resolution. The tourist economy was being affected and there were over 100 timber workers and truck drivers unable to go to work due to their work areas being cordoned off. Several of these were calling me and asking why. I told them it was not our decision—their employers had made that call."

That morning, Melo's employer, Campbell Timberland Management, issued the following statement regarding his death: "We are deeply saddened by the tragic incident that occurred this past weekend. Staff members continue to mourn the loss of Jere Melo, a dear friend and colleague. Since 2003, Jere provided contract security services for properties managed by Campbell Timberland Management in Mendocino County. Jere Melo had a passion for forestry that was unmatched, setting a standard that we aspire to achieve. He cared deeply for the forests of Mendocino, and worked tirelessly at the local, County, and State level to help maintain living wage jobs in rural communities along the North Coast. We have tremendous respect for Jere's civic contributions and his efforts to secure a future for the timber industry in California. Our thoughts and prayers are with Jere and his family during this difficult time."

‹›

As the sixth day began in the search for his son in the rugged forest by a heavily armed force of law enforcement officers, Aaron Bassler's father, Jim, appeared on the front page of the Press Democrat. He reflected on the mental illness that could have made his son capable of possibly two murders and reiterated that he wished people had listened to the concerns of his family. "I told the sheriff's deputies he's likely responsible for both murders," said Jim Bassler. He added that his son was anti-social and delusional, and preferred to retreat to the wilderness rather than hang around town. "He does very, very bizarre things. They are not really tied to any rational thought."

Quite apart from Bassler father's comments, Sheriff Allman recalls that the investigation was now piecing together actual evidence that showed similarities between the Coleman and Melo murders. "Detectives had found out that Bassler's mother had dropped him off at the gate to the Vizcaino property in Westport a day prior to Coleman's shooting, not far from where that murder took place. She was aware that he had food supplies and a scoped rifle. Furthermore, Hershey's

Kisses candy wrappers and blunts, or foil pipes, had been found at both the Coleman murder scene and the bunker near to where Melo was killed. These had been sent off for DNA testing and whereas this would normally take perhaps six weeks to do, we were assured by the Department of Justice that it would be given a one-week priority.

"We were beginning to make the connections and this meant that perhaps we were not looking for two suspects, there might be just one. We needed more information to confirm this and this was now being accumulated. Both were killed with a high-powered assault rifle, both were just 'doing their job,' there was no marijuana involved in either case—this was important. We had found a place close to where Coleman was shot where we thought the killer might have been bedded down, watching Coleman arrive. Similarly, he was believed to be initially hiding a little further up the hill from where Melo was shot—some bedding was found there. In each case he had been watching the men approach."

☙

While this evidence gathering continued, the hunt in the woods moved to a higher gear. Allman remembers, "By this time we had started to place about 40 unmanned heat-activated surveillance cameras on the trails we believed Bassler might use and also ground sensors to detect any foot traffic. These cameras took still photographs at intervals when a heat source came close. It was one thing to put the cameras out, another thing entirely to get back out there and download the footage in the field onto a laptop. We were trying to predict his movements and any patterns he may have developed. However, he was so elusive. Although I do not think he ever fully realized just how many men we had out there, more than 50 at one point, there was no pattern that could be found and we never knew where he might be. He always seemed to be about 20 to 30 hours ahead of us and we were not completely sure if he was still within the 400 square miles that all of our resources were focused on." (See Map, page v.)

✎

Later that afternoon, Captain Smallcomb was quoted as saying he would prefer it if the news outlets refrained from using the term "manhunt." "I don't like that term because it's hunting season. I prefer 'suspect apprehension.'" A press release was issued with regards to the use of the term in the reporting of the case:

> I request that all media outlets refrain from using the term "Manhunt" in connection with the search for suspect Aaron Bassler. Law enforcement is attempting to safely apprehend suspect Aaron Bassler and believes that sensationalizing the situation may panic the public. Your continued efforts to keep the public updated on this investigation is appreciated by law enforcement personnel, the community, and the Melo family. Thank you.

(Despite this request, most media outlets, and certainly the Press Democrat, continued to use the term "manhunt" throughout the search for Bassler. It would appear that the Press Democrat's editorial staff regarded what was going on in the woods east of Fort Bragg as being precisely that.)

With the two murders being slowly connected, it is worth noting that other crimes that might be linked to the killings of Melo and Coleman in some way were also studied by law enforcement at this time. One of these certainly seemed as if it too might have a possible link to the Matt Coleman murder. This involved another local conservationist, one who had mysteriously disappeared in 2010 while working in the coastal forests. The case had never been resolved.

Sheriff Allman commented, "The case of the missing forester, Eric Grant of the Mendocino Redwood Company, was reviewed for a time. His vehicle was found last year at a turnout on Highway One where Grant was known to enjoy his lunch breaks. He had been working on MRC (Mendocino Redwood Company) property on Navarro Ridge Road just before he disappeared. His remains have not been found. I started to wonder if we had a serial killer or a person who killed people for coming on to his 'territory.' These discussions were taking place in our meetings as the search for Bassler continued but nothing was ever really developed to make the link between Bassler and any other incidents. To this day, Grant's body still has not been found – I imagine he fell into the river and drowned, nothing more sinister than that, but we continue to receive a lead on this every week or so."

Another discussion topic at this time among the investigators was that over the previous two years there had been a series of burglaries at vacation cabins in the Noyo Basin, all with a similar pattern of doors broken in, some but not all the food taken, and a few guns going missing. There were no leads on this but it was suspected that it might be the homeless transients who moved up and down the Skunk Line railroad tracks between the town of Fort Bragg and the vacation cabin area who were responsible.

As far as Sheriff Allman was aware, the name Aaron Bassler was not mentioned as a possible suspect in any of these crimes. "Earlier in the year, the Department of Fish and Game had spoken to Jim Bassler, Aaron's father, about their belief that his son had poached an elk in Westport. Bassler Sr. said he would be very surprised, believing his son would not know what to do with an elk once he'd shot it. Even after the Coleman shooting, we never got to hear any of this. Perhaps Fish and Game might have contacted us, given that Coleman was shot nearby to the elk shooting. As it turned out, apart from the Jere Melo email mentioning Bassler just a few days before Melo was killed, that incident with the elk would have been as close as we would have come to Aaron Bassler's name before Jere's murder."

℘

"We just need the instruction manual on how to solve this"

Friday, September 2nd, 2011

The search for Bassler continued in the vast forests that continued to remain off limits to the public. Normally these woods are used by hunters, loggers, and hikers, but it was search team members, totaling somewhere between 30 and 50 in number, who were the sole inhabitants as the hunt dragged on with little to encourage them. Progress was virtually nonexistent and the working conditions couldn't have been much tougher.

Bob Nishiyama, commander of the Mendocino Major Crimes Task

Force, was quoted in the Press Democrat as saying, "It's frustrating, it's tedious. The terrain we're searching is absolutely miserable." Nishiyama's men returned from the woods each day with poison oak rashes and blackberry bramble scratches and little to show for their efforts. Sheriff Allman insisted that "We're making progress" but did not share with the public what that progress was, adding that "We're looking for a safe resolution for everyone involved, and we hope the suspect will surrender and have the judicial system run its course," vowing that the teams would continue to search the forest until Bassler was found.

At the heart of the 20 by 20 square mile area where Bassler was still thought to be is the 50,000-acre Jackson Demonstration State Forest, with its towering redwoods, Douglas firs, madrones, and very thick and inaccessible undergrowth. CalFire had ordered this closed to tourists and timber companies on August 30th because of law enforcement action inside its perimeters. As a result of the difficult terrain, everything at the disposal of law enforcement was being used in the search. While keeping their tactics a secret, Nishiyama did inform the press that aircrews, off-road vehicles, and all means available were being deployed to assist the search teams. "You name it; we've been using it," he said.

Meanwhile, law enforcement remained ambiguous about the role of private citizens in patrolling remote areas for illicit drug operations. Melo was acting in his capacity as a security contractor for Campbell Timberland Management. The company refused to comment on whether Melo made regular searches on the company's property in the woods. Melo was unarmed but his companion, still unnamed for reason of safety as this person was known to Bassler, fired back at the gunman before escaping and calling 911. Speaking to The Ukiah Daily Journal's reporter Tiffany Revelle, Nishiyama went on, "My dilemma is this—in this economy every law enforcement agency is taking a hit, consequently there are less law enforcement resources to go out there and do the job, which, quite frankly, should be a job done by law enforcement. However, it has been falling to private citizens to do this and they are putting themselves at risk. I understand that the community is sick and tired of dealing with this issue, and of law enforcement not having the resources to respond."

Sheriff Allman remembers, "Jere Melo had been helping law enforcement for years, providing GPS coordinates for marijuana grows and staying in weekly contact with us. The vast majority of information we gather on marijuana, other than from aerial overflight, is given to us by citizens and those working for private timber companies. Sometimes they go out there first to see if a pot garden is there before they report to us. Is it a safe duty for them to perform? Apparently not always, but it is a job that has to be done. The timber companies traditionally help us find about 20 large gardens annually." Allman stated that budget and staffing woes were having a significant effect on what he could do. "I really wish I could have 10 more deputies [he had 38 patrol deputies for all of unincorporated Mendocino] so I could assist in these problem areas but right now we're strapped."

☙

During the first week there were several brainstorming meetings to discuss how the investigation should proceed. Sheriff Allman recalls, "We were relying on the newly-arriving SWAT teams from the nearby counties of Humboldt, Sonoma, Lake, and Marin. Traditionally, law enforcement goes after the suspect; the police do not sit back and wait for them to come to us. In this situation, there was clearly a need for us to change our mindset on this and we would have to adapt to new tactics to make this happen."

In the first week or so the California Air National Guard agreed to fly over the area at night and use the heat-seeking devices known as FLIRs (Forward Looking Infra-Red devices) to detect Bassler. "According to his father, he was a coffee addict," says Allman. "We thought we'd track him if he started a campfire to boil some water and make coffee. The flights took place every night based on the map grid, back and forth over the Noyo Basin, from the Sinkyone Wilderness Area, 100 miles south to the village of Mendocino and then 10 to 20 miles inland. The FBI out of the Bay Area also had a fixed-wing aircraft flying over the area as part of the search effort."

Not long after the flyovers began, Sheriff Allman found out that the press had been told about these. "I heard it on the radio, on the news being read out by Joe Rigelski on K.O.Z.T. The Coast, Fort Bragg's local FM station, and was initially very frustrated about that. Let me explain. Traditionally, law enforcement likes to keep any intelligence operations secret. If Bassler was still inside the immediate 400 square miles where we thought he was, then we did not want to scare him away. We knew he did not have a cell phone but maybe somebody else was getting information to him, and if the public was aware that these heat-seeking missions were taking place then he would hear about this from his source and would try to slip away, out of our search area. However, with hindsight, I believe that Captain Smallcomb made the right decision to let the press know. The entire psyche of the Coast community was being affected. People were scared, business was being affected—both regular and tourist—and rumors were running wild, creating a lot of paranoia. In some circumstances, the flyovers included, it was good for the public to know about some of our efforts.

"Kurt Smallcomb made the decision to tell the press for reasons that were correct, despite my initial reaction to the contrary. He and I had never worked together in a situation like this. There was an immediate mutual respect that prevented either one of us from second-guessing the other. So after my initial frustration at the news on the FLIRs being public knowledge, he explained to me why this was done, and I could see it made sense and could see the benefits. We were in unknown territory; every day was a new learning experience in many ways. In fact, on one occasion, when somebody remarked at one of our many command post meetings that 'We just need the instruction manual on how to solve this,' everyone in the room laughed.

"Letting the public know about the flights meant that they would be comforted to know that we were not doing the same old 'stuff' every day. It was important to them and [to] us that they knew that each day we were coming up with new methods and making progress. It was a constant balancing act between keeping intelligence close to your chest and maintaining public confidence and morale by keeping them informed of progress."

❧

Meanwhile, Jim Bassler had continued to express his feelings to the press about what he saw as a failure of the system to take care of people such as his son suffering with mental illness. He and the family saw the opportunity to finally get treatment when their son was sentenced to a month in jail earlier in the year. His paranoia and delusions that he had been plagued with since his late teens were getting worse. After repeated arrests, all for misdemeanors, Aaron Bassler's father hoped that the court system would finally intervene. The Press Democrat reported that Jim Bassler claimed to have written letters with the help of Coast mental health advocate Sonya Nesch, author of "Advocating for Someone with a Mental Illness" and a member of the National Alliance on Mental Illness (N.A.M.I.). However, the letters went unanswered. Jim

Bassler claimed that he faxed a letter to the Mendocino Jail psychiatrist and two were hand delivered to the public defender, Tom Croak, to be passed on. Croak said he could not comment on this, or whether any letters were handed on to the judge on the case or the District Attorney's Office. Sheriff Allman said he was unaware of any letters and Captain Smallcomb declined to comment on any communications the Sheriff's Office may have had from anyone in Bassler's family prior to Melo's slaying.

Jim Bassler believes that what he considers the County's failure to take seriously his warnings and his son's mental illness are at least partly to blame for the deaths. Quoted in the Press Democrat, he said, "If he had a little more attention and guidance and control, this would never have happened."

Laws that put civil liberties and privacy laws above families' desires to help their mentally ill relatives also are at fault, said Nesch. She hopes Bassler's history will convince the county to implement provisions of the state's so-called "Laura's Law"* that would make it easier for the

---

*Laura's Law—see Addendum B. Laura's Law is a California state law that allows for court-ordered assisted outpatient treatment or forced antipsychotics in most cases. To qualify for the program, the person must have a serious mental illness plus a recent history of psychiatric hospitalizations, jailings or acts, threats or attempts of serious violent behavior towards self or others.

The law was named after Laura Wilcox, a mental health worker who was killed by an American citizen who had refused psychiatric treatment. Laura was a 19-year-old sophomore from Haverford College working at Nevada County's public mental health clinic during her winter break from college. On January 10, 2001, she and two other people were shot to death by Scott Harlan Thorpe, a 41-year-old American citizen who resisted his family's attempt to force psychiatric treatment. Thorpe was found incompetent to stand trial and was sent to Atascadero State Hospital and was later transferred to California's Napa State Hospital. After the incident, Laura's parents chose to advocate for forced treatment of individuals considered to have mental illness.

Modeled on Kendra's Law, a similar statute enacted in New York, the bill was introduced as Assembly Bill 1421 by Assemblywoman Helen Thomson, a Democrat from Davis. The measure passed the California Legislature in 2002 and was signed into law by Governor Gray Davis. The statute can only be utilized in counties that choose to enact outpatient commitment programs based on the measure.

courts to mandate mental health treatment. County cost-cutting measures have contributed to a dearth of public treatment services in and outside of the jail, Nesch added.

☙

It was a strange Labor Day weekend both for everyone involved in the case and the North Coast community. It is a weekend that is usually a time of fun with many tourists in town enjoying the festivities, including the Skunk Train. Sheriff Allman remembers, "Some Skunk Train employees had actually run into Bassler a few weeks previously. One of them said, 'We were working on the tracks when suddenly he appeared—just appeared from nowhere. We talked for about 10 or 15 minutes and then turned away to carry on working. We glanced back to where he had stood and he was gone.' They were alluding to something that was slowly becoming apparent to many of us—Bassler's natural ability to be in the woods without making any noise. He had seemingly perfected this skill and, after spending so much time in the woods over most of his life, he was now in his absolute element. I believe he liked being in the woods as much as Elvis enjoyed being on stage."

By Friday lunchtime, the results from the DNA testing had returned from the lab. The evidence located at the Melo crime scene and the Coleman crime scene tied the murders to a single perpetrator. The tin foil marijuana pipe/blunt, scientifically tied to Bassler by DNA, was found at or near the location where it is likely Bassler was firing upon Coleman on August 11, 2011. Hershey's chocolate Kisses wrappers were also found at the Cape Vizcaino location, wrappers that were not associated with Coleman. Later, at least one marijuana blunt fashioned from tin foil was located at the bunker, the scene of Melo's murder, along with more Hershey's chocolate foils. As one Sheriff's investigator noted in his report, finding the "marijuana pipe fashioned like a cigarette out of tin foil" at the bunker was only the second time in his law enforcement career that he had seen a smoking pipe fashioned from tin foil in this fashion. The first time, he noted, was at the Coleman murder scene.

Sheriff Allman felt there was more than enough evidence to obtain an arrest warrant for Bassler on two counts of murder. "The DNA analysis of the foil pipe showed a match with Bassler's blood taken from his previous DUI arrest and this, together with the other evidence we had accumulated, led to our decision to proceed with the arrest warrant at that time. District Attorney Eyster wrote the warrant that then needed to be presented to a judge. There were none available on the Coast at the time and it's not a duty I usually perform, the deputies do it, but I personally drove, very fast I should add, from Fort Bragg to Ukiah and met with Cindy Mayfield, the presiding judge. She read the warrant very thoroughly and after 45 minutes signed it. In my hand I had the warrant for the arrest of Aaron Bassler for both murders. Clearly the community wanted and needed to know that we were looking for one suspect for both murders. I faxed the warrant to Fort Bragg for a press release."

A criminal complaint was filed against Aaron James Bassler in Mendocino County Court charging him with two counts of first-degree murder, the attempted murder of Chaney, and the special circumstance of lying in wait, making him eligible for the death penalty or life imprisonment without possibility of parole if found guilty of the crimes. Judge Mayfield also signed a no bail warrant for the arrest of Aaron James Bassler that same day. District Attorney Eyster said through a spokesman that it was too early to determine whether prosecutors would seek the death penalty.

SUPERIOR COURT OF CALIFORNIA – COUNTY OF MENDOCINO
700 S. FRANKLIN ST.
FORT BRAGG, CA 95437

WARRANT OF ARREST

AARON JAMES BASSLER
Alias (if any):
SHERWOOD ROAD
FORT BRAGG CA 95437

WARRANT NO: **AW 8627**
REPORT NO: 11-1856
CITATION NO:
CASE NO: MC-TM-CR-CR-11-0018683-002

1	PC	187(A)/189	F	MURDER	08/27/2011
1	PC	190.2(A)(15)	F	SA-MURLYING WAIT	08/27/2011
1	PC	12022.53(D)	F	SA-USE OF FIREARM	08/27/2011
2	PC	664/187/189	F	ATMPT MRDR 1ST DEGRE	08/27/2011
2	PC	12022.53(D)	F	SA-USE OF FIREARM	08/27/2011
3	PC	187(A)/189	F	MURDER	08/11/2011
3	PC	190.2(A)(3)	F	SA-MULTIPLE MURDER	08/11/2011
3	PC	12022.53(C)	F	SA-USE OF FIREARM	08/11/2011

Driver's License & State	Birthdate	Sex	Race	Hair	Eyes	Height	Weight
B3593886 CA	05/01/76	M	W	BRO	BLU	6ft01in	170

THE PEOPLE OF THE STATE OF CALIFORNIA TO ANY PEACE OFFICER OF THIS STATE:

The above named and described defendant was convicted in the court of the offense set forth above or an order was issued; or an accusation was filed charging the defendant with the offense set forth above and the above named defendant subsequently failed to obey the order of the court or other requirements of law, or

NEW COMPLAINT

You are ordered to arrest the defendant and bring him/her before me or in the case of my absence or inability to act, before the nearest or most accessible magistrate in this county.

Y	Defendant to be admitted to bail in the amount of $ NO BAIL
	Bail Forfeitable
Y	May be served at night (840PC)
Y	Mandatory Appearance Required
Y	No O.R.
Y	Do not cite out

CINDEE MAYFIELD   RICHARD HENDERSON
DAVID NELSON   CLAY BRENNAN
ANN MOORMAN   JOHN BEHNKE

_____
JUDGES OF THE SUPERIOR COURT

ISSUE DATE: September 2, 2011

If the offense charge is a misdemeanor or infraction, this warrant may be served between 6:00am and 10:00pm unless endorsed for night service, or any time if served in a public place.

BWARRANT-FAW (rev 0111)

Aaron Bassler Arrest Warrant

The following press release was issued by Captain Smallcomb:

On August 11ᵗʰ, 2011, Matthew Coleman was shot and killed in a remote area located near the 44000 block of Hwy 1 near Westport, CA.

On August 27ᵗʰ, 2011, Jere Melo was shot and killed in an area approximately six miles east of Fort Bragg, CA.

Both victims were shot and killed while conducting duties related to their forestry management profession.

Mendocino County Sheriff's detectives are continuing to collect evidence, speaking with witnesses, and conferring with both the California Department of Justice Forensic Laboratory analysts and the Mendocino County District Attorney's Office.

Based on evidence collected at both murder scenes during this ongoing investigation, the Mendocino County Sheriff's detectives have obtained an arrest warrant for suspect Aaron Bassler in connection with the shooting death of victims Matthew Coleman and Jere Melo.

Mendocino County Sheriff's Office personnel, with the assistance of officers and agents from the Fort Bragg Police Department, Willits Police Department, Ukiah Police Department, Cal Fire, California Department of Justice, California Highway Patrol, California Fish and Game, Federal Bureau of investigation, United States Marshals Office, United States National Guard, and the local timber industry, are continuing their search efforts in an attempt to apprehend suspect Aaron Bassler.

That afternoon, U.S. Congressman Mike Thompson issued a statement through the Fort Bragg Mayor's office: "Words cannot begin to express the magnitude of the tragic loss of Jere Melo to our community. Jere was part of the fabric of the Fort Bragg community and the glue that kept all sides working together. He was a dedicated public servant and a dear friend."

The influx of visitors for the Labor Day holiday weekend was already well under way at the kickoff ceremony for Fort Bragg's 72nd annual Paul Bunyan Days festival, celebrating the town's more than a century of logging, an event that extends through Monday. At that ceremony, Fort Bragg Mayor Dave Turner asked the handful of residents attending for a moment of silence to remember Melo, his friend. Behind the stage where Turner spoke, a massive flag was draped over City Hall in Melo's honor. "He would want us to have fun," Turner said. "He helped us many times to keep the Paul Bunyan days going. I just want to welcome everyone and ask to keep Jere in your mind this weekend." Turner said that attendees of Monday's parade were encouraged to carry the U.S. flag in honor of Melo, a veteran of the U.S. Army who had served in Korea. "Jere always wore a flag pin on his lapel. He would like that."

As Friday came to a close, no contact with Bassler had been made in almost a week, since the Melo shooting, but the searchers remained optimistic and, in the words of Captain Smallcomb, they were determined to "stay the course and keep at it until we get him."

☙

"No one listened to me…"

Saturday, September 3rd, 2011

The Press Democrat reported that news of the arrest warrant confirmed the worst fears of Jim Bassler, who had said earlier in the week that he believed his son was responsible for Coleman's death in addition to Melo's slaying. Bassler said his ex-wife told him she had dropped off their son near Westport around the time that Coleman, 45, was found slain on an oceanfront ranch. Jim Bassler said he later learned his son had a rifle with him at the time he was dropped off nearby.

Captain Smallcomb declined to comment on any communication the sheriff's office may have had from anyone in Bassler's family prior to Melo's slaying. He said both of Bassler's parents had been cooperative with authorities during the investigation.

Jim Bassler had said a few days earlier that he first had a "hunch" that his son could be involved in the Coleman homicide before Melo was killed, but he never acted on his feeling or alerted authorities. "I feel guilty for not running down to the police station." He added, "No one listened to me before though." In letters to jail medical staff, the county psychiatrist, and his son's public defender from a previous case, Jim Bassler had pleaded for help for his son, whom he said suffered delusions and paranoia. He said he received no response from authorities.

Bassler's father said his son had become increasingly unstable and isolated, and had made the heavily forested coastal hills his home for the past several months. He said his son had some contact with his mother from time to time, and she dropped him off north of Westport on or around August 11ᵗʰ, the day of the Coleman shooting. She declined repeated requests for interviews.

❦

On Saturday morning, the citizens on California's North Coast were digesting and reacting to that morning's front page headline in the Press Democrat—"Fort Bragg suspect linked to two slayings." This headline was accompanied by three photographs—of Aaron Bassler, Jere Melo, and Matt Coleman, presented over a map of the North Coast from Rockport down to Fort Bragg and inland to Willits, depicting the locations of where the two men had been murdered. There was also a photograph of Fort Bragg mayor, Dave Turner, shown asking a crowd for a moment of silence in memory of Melo at the previous evening's kickoff party for the town's annual "Paul Bunyan Days" festivities. The article stated that law enforcement officials would not discuss evidence but had nevertheless obtained an arrest warrant for Bassler in both cases.

Meanwhile, the article went on to report that at the close-knit town's big holiday weekend celebration of their logging industry roots, the mood was certainly quieter than usual, understandably, given the fact that Jere Melo was such a popular figure around town and a significant link to its proud history. For the second consecutive year, "Paul Bunyan" was portrayed by Mike Stephens, a wildlife biologist who has his own wildlife consulting company and often worked in the woods himself. Stephens commented, "It's more and more dangerous in the woods— an unfortunate reality." He wondered how he could better protect his employees out there. They already carried radios and checked in at the end of their shifts to confirm they made it out of the woods. "I can't think of anything else we can do. We're all trying to figure out what we're going to do next year because we're pretty vulnerable."

The Press Democrat reported that the loss of Melo was particularly poignant on that weekend, emphasizing Melo's link to the town's logging history. Many townsfolk expressed opinions that there was a cloud over that year's event but they agreed that the celebration had to go on. "Jere would have kicked our butts if we didn't bring the community together," said Johanna Jensen, who organized the Ugly Dog Contest. "He liked to party as much as anyone."

Before the annual firemen's water fight between firefighters from Fort Bragg, Comptche, Willits, the Coast Guard, and Cal Fire, Fort Bragg Fire captain, Glen Beck, paused to remember Melo. "Jere Melo was a hard-working gentleman, a friend, and we're going to miss him dearly." He asked for a moment of silence and a hush fell over the large crowd. The festivities continued with saw demonstrations, the vintage costume dress show, the Ugly Dog Contest, tricycle races, and a parade. Meanwhile, in the woods a few miles in land to the east, the 24-hour a day search for Aaron Bassler continued.

⁊

Sheriff Allman was not in Fort Bragg that day. Accompanied by wife Laura, he drove his son Josh to Sacramento Airport from where the young man, just 18, was going to fly to Alaska where he would be taking on a job for two months as a hunting guide for moose and bears. "I was in touch with the investigation for that whole journey, thinking about it and calling in; on the phone every five minutes when I had cell service, calling other sheriffs for information, thanking those who had helped already. I also called Mike Thompson, our Congressman, who was a friend of Melo's and who was paying very close attention to the developments. I rarely talk about work when I am at home but it was a topic of conversation on this occasion. My son, a very big hunter and outdoorsman, was intrigued by all that had happened so far and the continuing investigation and search. He actually knows more about bullets and such than me. Also, coincidentally, he had just spent the summer in Fort Bragg working with the commercial fishermen there, a group that Bassler's father, Jim, is a part of, although they had not met. Throughout that journey my mind was elsewhere, as it was for most of the following month."

℘

Dutch almost gets his man

Sunday, September 4th, 2011

The following morning, Sheriff Allman was back out in Fort Bragg. "I was planning to once again spend the day working on the logistics for the men in the woods. By this time SWAT teams from out of the County were arriving and one came in that day from Marin. Each of these was joined by one member of our own SWAT team to make them aware of the communications we had set up, to inform them of the local geography and terrain, and to give them any information we had on Aaron Bassler. Coincidentally, our own deputies and SWAT teams had undergone a week-long training course in rural patrol tactics earlier that year, in the spring of 2011. This was in preparation for the "Full Court Press" program to deal with the marijuana in the fall, an expensive but necessary project. Thankfully, we were therefore incredibly prepared for the conditions we were now facing in the Noyo River Basin and the situation that confronted us.

"The new SWAT teams were very proficient at what they did. I felt a little more relaxed as some aspects were taken out of the hands of the County Sheriff. Support was coming from many places; other county sheriffs were calling me and offering support, and this was all very comforting. On top of that, I have a good friend in the British military who had spent a day working with our SWAT team a year or so earlier. Our wives are good friends and I am the godfather to his son. He was just back from serving in Afghanistan and is very tactically oriented so I called him on that Sunday for a chat and we talked for half an hour or so. It was a very good call in terms of boosting morale. He told me, 'Tom, your SWAT team is very capable. Do not worry about that at all.' I already knew that but it was very comforting to hear it from him too."

☙

At 8:15am, Sunday, September 4th, a sheriff's deputy was driving by Bassler's mother's house when he spotted somebody behind the building. Sheriff Allman remembers, "The deputy stopped and investigated. Bassler's stepfather came out and when asked if somebody else was there, he replied, 'I don't know what you're talking about.' Meanwhile, a new SWAT team had recently arrived from Humboldt County and they were in the vicinity. They had also seen somebody there and believed the person, who they had seen from the chest up, fitted Bassler's description. He had quickly disappeared into the woods. They did not see any gun or a backpack on the man and a search dog and his handler were immediately called in to search the nearby woods. This was one

Working Dog
Mendocino County Sheriff's Office search dog, ever vigilant, relaxes
on the Skunk Train after a hard day's work.
(Beth Schlanker/ The Press Democrat)

of our best dogs—Dutch—and a short time later he returned from the woods with a fanny pack. The pack was taken from the dog and he was sent back into the woods again, with his handler some way behind. The handler caught up with Dutch who was standing in a creek, unable to detect any scents to follow. This incident was very unusual. The dog is trained to grab on to the suspect's left arm and hold on for two or three minutes. It is very painful and lots of screaming and shouting is usually heard. Not this time—nothing at all was heard. I have no doubt that Dutch got hold of him but somehow Bassler was able to get the dog off. He was so self-controlled he did not utter any noise at all. Bassler's father had called his son a 'practiced hider,' explaining that there were times, when Bassler was a child, that he would disappear in the woods to play, and his father couldn't find him for hours. I was now beginning to form the opinion that we were dealing with the most accomplished outdoor survivalist and woodsman I'd ever heard of."

◌◌

Immediately following the sighting, local, state, and federal law enforcement agencies flooded the neighborhood and nearby woods, growing in strength from around 30 to somewhere between 50 to 70 officers, many with their guns drawn, according to witnesses. Despite added assistance from aircrews, no further sighting of Bassler was made. Between 10:30am and 11:00am that morning, the Sheriff's Office's "Reverse 911" call system was activated in the area to warn local residents within a five-mile radius of this Bassler sighting, informing them that a homicide suspect had been seen in the area and that they should lock doors and windows and stay inside. A call went out to the Skunk Train office asking them to cancel their operations for the day. Mayor Dave Turner said that word of the sighting had spread quickly around town but had not caused undue alarm, commenting that "People were optimistic and that a sighting is good."

Sheriff Allman recalls the events that followed this eventful morning. "As far as the press was concerned, Captain Smallcomb informed them that it was the first confirmed sighting and that the deputies were close enough to engage with him, had verbal contact, and then sent a police dog after him. We added that the dog made some type of contact, not mentioning the fanny pack. We said it was unknown if Bassler was injured—which was the truth.

"The fanny pack recovered by Dutch contained a bag of ground coffee—his father had told us he was a coffee addict; 18 playing cards—

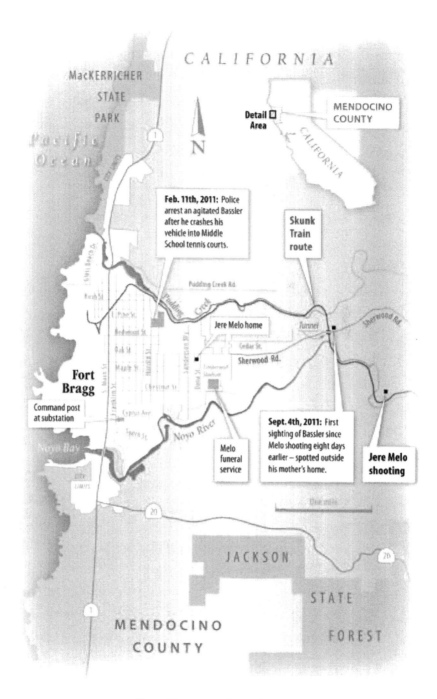

Fort Bragg and environs
(Graphic by Loren Doppenberg)

all the eight of spades, our first encounter with this odd phenomenon; 7.62x63 mm cartridges; a book of the local ocean tide timetables; fishing hooks; razors and shaving cream; Band-Aids; aspirin; two bags of suspected poppy seeds; a tin foil blunt; a can opener; and, inside a sock, an Electronic Benefit Transfer (E.B.T.) card—a food stamp card.

"It turned out that the card had been used at the Purity Market in Fort Bragg on August 10th, the day before Matt Coleman had been killed. It was next used on August 26th, the day before Jere Melo was shot. On that occasion it was used twice in the Fort Bragg area. It had not been used after that.

"The sighting of Bassler and securing of the fanny pack was a big boost to the search teams—confirmation that he was a hundred percent definitely still in the area. We had been trying every avenue we could think of as the search for Bassler continued. We knew he had a food stamp card that would be swiped, and the transaction recorded electronically, every time he bought something, such as eggs, bread, soup, etc. We also knew there were two things he really liked—coffee and candy. People had confirmed this. He had used the card at a store in Cleone, just north of Fort Bragg, to buy these items and we paid obvious close attention to that store and the store workers who knew him. We were working closely with Welfare Fraud investigators at that time and there were people watching computer screens 24/7 to see if that card was used, but then Dutch recovered his backpack—and inside was the food stamp card! That was very disappointing—we wanted Bassler to have it and hopefully use it, and perhaps lead us closer to him. Captain Smallcomb suggested that we put the card and a sock on the trail Dutch had come along with the backpack as if it had fallen out, hoping Bassler would find it and use the card again. The Welfare Fraud team had installed a program that would alert us within five minutes if and where Bassler used the card so if he did we would then move quickly to that location. We placed the card on the trail, inside the sock, but Bassler never returned to look for it. There was also a can opener and we were initially pleased that we had that, thinking he would have to come out of the woods to get food from somewhere but he no doubt broke into one of the vacation cabins and stole another one—he was to survive on stolen canned food for most of his time in the woods."

Also inside the backpack, as mentioned above, was a stack of 18 playing cards—each one the eight of spades, from a variety of different decks. "We initially went back to all of the cabins that had been broken into to see if any sets were missing the eight of spades. None of the ones we checked were. I believe that some may have been from there though—some sort of trophy from the burglaries Bassler had committed. We researched this very thoroughly. There is not much symbolism attached to the eight of spades in comparison with the ace of spades or the queen or the jokers."

❧

During the day, Jim Bassler offered to talk to his son if any sort of a standoff developed, stating to reporters that he "wanted there to be a peaceful ending." However, there was no further sighting, and by late afternoon several groups of officers in camouflage and bulletproof vests began to walk out of the woods after a day of searching. They were returning to the command post near Bassler's mother's house. This was less than 10 minutes' drive east from downtown and two miles west of the spot where Jere Melo had been shot. At 9:00pm, Captain Smallcomb confirmed that Bassler had not been found. He added that the search would continue through the night.

Allman remembers, "That night, I did not sleep. I spent the night on the computer trying to crack the 'code' of the playing cards, as it were. There is a gothic band in the United Kingdom that goes by the name

Searching with dogs
Following the contact with Bassler by Dutch, law enforcement officers
from a half dozen jurisdictions, along with more dogs, searched for the
suspect on Sherwood Road near his mother's home.
(Kent Porter/ The Press Democrat)

'Eight of Spades'; some people believe it is connected to immortality;
others believe it has some sort of power. After three days of 'off and on'
thought put into this I stopped. In 31 years as a cop, I've seen many
different symbols left at crime scenes. Perhaps in the end this was just
Bassler's business card, a trophy that at some point would be used to
tell police where he had been. I came to realize that Aaron Bassler was
mentally ill and I stopped believing that his explanation for the cards
would be understood by anyone other than himself. However, I do have
a Top Ten list of questions for Bassler and his explanation of the cards
is certainly on there."

⁓

Chapter 5
A frustrating week, then...

"The biggest day of the year..."

Monday, September 5th, 2011

The following day was Labor Day and in Fort Bragg that means the "Paul Bunyan Days Parade." Sheriff Allman remembers, "It's the biggest day of the year for the town and we're there in the middle of the biggest manhunt in the County's history. How do we have a great time and say everything is okay when everyone knows that there is a killer within a few miles of the biggest crowd of the year?"

℘

Allman spent the day with District Attorney C. David Eyster, and the two rode together in the parade. "I drove us in a Sheriff's Office truck and we did lots of waving but my mind was not on the celebration at all, knowing I'd be glad when it was over and nothing had gone wrong. I wanted to get back to the Command Post. Every day, about 100 times a day, I was asked 'Did you get him yet?' It was constant. I always replied, 'When we do, you'll hear about it.' Kurt Smallcomb and I discussed this a lot. What did people think we were going to say? 'Oh, yes—we did. I just forgot to tell people'! I know it was human nature to ask that question, I'd probably ask it myself. But sometimes it just was overwhelming. I often added, 'I think we're closer today than yesterday,' thinking this had to come to an end sometime soon."

As the various law enforcement teams continued with their efforts to get more intelligence and insights into Bassler's movements, a further complication arose as another homicide took place in Fort Bragg when 40-year-old James Kester strangled a man by the name of Jason Blackshear. In the early hours of this investigation, Kester was described in a press release as "a white male adult with a shaved head; with tattoos on his throat and neck, and believed to be living a transient lifestyle on the Mendocino Coast," thus somewhat matching the description of Bassler.

Sheriff Allman recalls, "When I mentioned this moment to Captain Smallcomb recently he rolled his eyes. It was a sidetrack he could have done without at the time and as a result further adding to the workload of the investigation. It was around 8:30pm and detectives were sent to the scene of the crime, along with a couple from the DA's office too. I'm sure that any homicide report in the area at that time would have led police officers to make Aaron Bassler their first thought. In this case, as soon as the officers arrived it was obvious that the suspect was still there." Kester was arrested and charged with the murder of Jason Blackshear but not before, for a few hours at least, the task facing Sheriff Allman and the many others involved in the Bassler investigation appeared to have become even more complex and difficult.

Obviously the newspapers were all over the events of the previous day when Bassler had been seen near his mother's home off Sherwood Road about two miles east of town and contact had been made with him via the police dog "Dutch." The Press Democrat continued to run the sub-headline of "Fort Bragg Manhunt," despite Captain Smallcomb's request to not use that term. Their main headline that morning was "Suspect slips away." This was accompanied by photographs of heavily armed law enforcement officers from several different agencies, one picture of a County Sheriff officer with his dog, and also one of the home of Bassler's mother, Laura Brickey. In the Ukiah Daily Journal, Sheriff Allman was quoted as saying, "It's the closest we've ever been. It's obvious he hasn't gone far."

∽

Bassler's mother's home
Bassler, by this time a suspect in two North Coast murders, was spotted close to the home of his mother, Laura Brickey, about two miles east of Fort Bragg, before vanishing into the woods nearby.
(John Burgess/ The Press Democrat)

"This was not 'Andy Griffith'..."

Tuesday, September 6th, 2011

The Empire News section of the Press Democrat featured on its front page a photograph of the lead car in the Labor Day Parade the previous day, showing a large photograph of Jere Melo with grieving Fort Bragg city council members riding alongside while the story inside the paper concentrated on the continuing sadness and grieving of the townsfolk over Melo's death. A number of people commented on the

Labor Day Parade
At the Labor Day Parade in Fort Bragg, Jere Melo was honored as Grand Marshal. Vice Mayor Meg Courtney, left, holds back tears. Council Member Doug Hammerstrom, is left rear and Mayor Dave Turner is on the right.
(Kent Porter/ The Press Democrat)

smaller crowds for this year's event, and while some explained that the drizzly, cold weather was a factor, others mentioned that there was a general concern about the fugitive at large.

☙

Speaking to the Press Democrat, Lt. Dennis McKiver, a game warden who ran the State Department of Fish and Game's North Coast District, just one of the many law enforcement agencies aiding in the search for Bassler, stated, "the forest provides incredible shelter for animals—and people. A person could pass 10 yards away from you unnoticed, and the dense tree and brush cover blocks much of the heat-seeking equipment. Mendocino County has the highest number of bears in our woods in the state, but how many do you see when you're out in the woods? A person can easily hide and survive for quite a while at this time of year when the forest offers lots of food.

"Huckleberries, blackberries, and bugs are plentiful, as are deer, rabbits, and other game. The apple, pear, and other fruit trees from orchards established when logging communities settled deep in the canyons a century earlier are still producing fruit," McKiver added.

Meanwhile, Captain Kurt Smallcomb insisted that the tactics of the search must balance the drive to apprehend Bassler with the safety of the deputies and officers entering a forest better known to the suspect than to them. He declined to describe what kind of contact Dutch, the police dog, had had with Bassler on September 4th, or say if evidence had been recovered. He also refused to explain what evidence had led the authorities to connect Bassler with the earlier death of Matt Coleman.

A noticeable change in the community at this point was the suspension of the Skunk Train rail tours through the woods. They had been stopped on the previous Sunday morning following the contact with Bassler. Owner/operator Robert Pinoli said he received a call from a Sheriff's official that morning just before the 10:00am train was to depart and was "instructed not to operate." He gave refunds to the customers who had bought tickets and then he received a similar call on Monday and had placed a notice on the door announcing "There are no trains today." Pinoli explained to the public that his trains had become a key method of transporting equipment and people involved in the search into areas of the forest not accessible by road. Sheriff Allman remembers, "Robert Pinoli Jr., the Skunk Train owner, was stellar during this whole thing. He ended up closing his business for quite a number of days over the Labor Day weekend and at other times, costing him about $130,000 in total."

☙

Sheriff Allman has clear memories of speaking to some members of the press on September 6th. "It was time to give a full explanation of the situation to date. We had been sending out many press releases, believing the more we did this the less likely it would be that people would call us with questions. This preempting of possible questions was very important and saved us much time. Prior to each of the press meetings various talking points that we felt were needed to be focused on were discussed. The ongoing safety of the public was often one of these talking points and we constantly emphasized that we were not willy-nilly on this. This was not 'Andy Griffith' and we needed to show that we knew what we were doing.

"At an informal conference at the end of the week following the Melo murder, I had officially said in public for the first time that the suspect was the same for both the Melo and Coleman murders. Many people had been asking whether we had two killers or one that we were looking for. Jim Bassler said we had known that for some time but we actually didn't know for sure. However, the mounting body of evidence—the blunts, the Hershey Kisses wrappers, the whole M.O., Bassler's mother dropping him off in Westport the day before the Coleman killing, were all now pointing to that scenario and the warrant for Bassler's arrest for both murders had been issued on Friday, September 2nd. The DNA on the wrappers had been returned to us in just a few days and we were very comfortable in saying that Aaron Bassler was at the crime scene of the Coleman murder. We had no reason to believe that it was not the same suspect as in the Melo murder.

℘

The Press Democrat has the scoop

Wednesday, September 7th, 2011

Sheriff Allman was at home in Willits, sipping his morning coffee, watching the news on San Francisco's Channel 2. "Suddenly, on the scroller at the bottom of the screen, came the words, 'Aaron Bassler, the suspect in the Fort Bragg murder, may be responsible for the Jenner

---

* Jenner Beach murders—The Jenner, California double murder of 2004 came to the public's attention on August 18, 2004, when the bodies of Lindsay Cutshall, 22, and her fiancé Jason S. Allen, 26, were found on Fish Head Beach between Russian Gulch and the mouth of the Russian River, in the small coastal hamlet of Jenner, California. Both Cutshall and Allen were killed with a .45-caliber Marlin rifle as they slept in their sleeping bags on the beach. The Sonoma County Coroner's Office estimated that the couple was slain on either the night of August 14, 2004 or in the early morning hours of August 15, 2004. In the days following the murders, the case received considerable attention from the national media. The case remains unsolved.

Beach murders seven years ago.'* Reporter Rita Williams appeared on the screen and repeated the words. There was no reason to believe that at all, but it was possible, I suppose. I immediately called Channel 2 and angrily demanded to know why they were saying this and not only scaring the public even more but also putting the families of the Jenner victims on an emotional roller coaster. It was incredibly irresponsible of them and fortunately it disappeared from the bottom of the screen in a couple of minutes, following my call."

☙

Earlier that morning, Kym Kemp, a local news reporter writing in "Redheaded Blackbelt," an online publication focusing on Humboldt County and its marijuana culture, commented:

"Today, the Noyo News finally addressed a question that has been bugging me. Why has the Mendocino Sheriff's office given great information to the Santa Rosa newspaper, the Press Democrat, and given little information to sources closer to home? Frequently, a piece of information from the department is in the Press Democrat before it is in the official press release. That might be understandable if the local papers were getting the scoop but instead it is a paper a good two hours away from the site of the crime.

"Furthermore, the Noyo says somewhat skeptically:

In a highly unusual series of events, the MCSO [Mendocino County Sheriff's Office] has not conducted an open press conference on the situation since the witnessed murder of the town's former mayor and current city councilman, Jere Melo. The sheriff's office has instead relied on highly contrived releases of information through a spokesman, Kurt Smallcomb, to the Santa Rosa Press Democrat Newspaper, and occasional updates by head sheriff Tom Allman by telephone interviews with selected local radio stations.

'Despite the fears and concerns for the safety of the people in the nearby town of Fort Bragg, Sheriff Allman has claimed that release of information regarding the details of the search might aid the suspect, whom Allman claims might possess a radio.'

"Don't get me wrong. The coverage of the Press Democrat has been outstanding. The photographs are beautiful. The other papers could have done more. But, as an outsider looking in, I can't help feel it bodes badly that the local papers and the Mendocino Sheriff's Dept. appear to be on such bad terms that basic information goes to the Press Democrat hours or even, it appears, days before it goes out to the Mendocino papers."

[The Noyo News concluded:]

'Meanwhile, the operation has sapped the tight resources of a sheriff's department recently involved in threatening to sue an already broke County of Mendocino, over attempts to cut back the sheriff department's budget. So far, neither county officials nor members of the media have demanded that Allman conduct a routine press conference, either after the murders, or after the reported contact with the suspected killer.'

Sheriff Allman responds, "The Press Democrat had two full-time reporters in Fort Bragg, Initially Glenda Anderson was one of these but not later in the case, when it was two of Mary Callahan, Julie Johnson, and Cathy Bussewitz, I believe. They wanted full headline coverage but we could not tell them everything we had. We had several press releases, a number of phone calls with reporters were taken by

Smallcomb and myself, and many impromptu conversations were held as myself or Captain Smallcomb were arriving or departing the crime scenes or the police stations, usually jump-started by a reporter asking, 'Anything new, Sheriff?' We wanted information to get out and the press were generally our 'friends' in this. If I had to do it over again, I would have a full official press conference at the end of the first week, instead of waiting for as long as we did, albeit for what we thought were good reasons at the time. I was also getting three calls a day from the timber companies asking when it would be safe for them to go back into the woods to work. We were not going to rush this. We wanted to be methodical, both with our dealings with the press and the public."

⁊⁊

Speaking of the Press Democrat, that morning the newspaper featured the investigation on its front page with the headline, "Fort Bragg dragnet tightens" in a story by reporter Julie Johnson outlining the details about the wide perimeter over a swathe of forests that law enforcement was convinced Bassler was inside. The official comments from the County Sheriff's Office did not reveal the exact parameters of this area but they did inform the press that there were about 20 or more officers from other agencies such as the F.B.I. and U.S. Marshals Service, as well as another 20 from their own department, working on the search.

Several local people who were interviewed expressed thoughts that the case would not last much longer and were buoyed by the fact that there were so many law enforcement people involved. They believed that Bassler would "make a mistake" sometime soon. Bassler was believed to have lived for the past four months east of the town in the untamed timberlands and state forest but Fort Bragg Mayor Dave Turner commented, "They're going to get him. Sure he knows the woods, but he'll trip up."

According to Johnson's report, the wait for the search to reach a conclusion had been excruciating to Bassler's father, who said he had made several offers to help the search crews call for his son's surrender. "I could use a bullhorn from the train tracks or a forest road," said Jim Bassler He said he was in too much anguish to go to work at his commercial fishing business and felt it was his responsibility to help bring in his son. He had previously stated that his son was mentally unstable and that his son's behavior had become increasingly threatening in recent months.

℘

"Bassler's territory"

Thursday, September 8th, 2011

Following the sighting of Bassler on the morning of Sunday, September 4th, the Skunk Train had been closed for three days but had re-opened on Wednesday, September 7th. However, keeping it running and being able to assure people that it was safe was something that was the subject of many hours of serious discussion. Sheriff Allman decided this was a good thing. "Everybody knew what was going on and I'm sure some people were riding the train to visit the 'crime scene.' Initially we had placed fully equipped SWAT team members on the front of the train although we really felt that Bassler was not looking for us. As the investigation continued, there were uniformed officers inside the carriages at times and also plainclothed law enforcement personnel. He was the hunted, not us, although that was to change a few weeks later, but by keeping a high profile on the train we helped the public psyche. It was felt that it was in our interests to keep that train running as it ran through Bassler's 'territory' and he knew the train schedule as well as anyone, I'm sure. When it stopped, he obviously knew and it disrupted his schedule. We believed it was to our advantage to get normalcy back into Bassler's life and for him to go back to his patterns of behavior. We were operating in his territory but I do not believe he knew that we had so many cops in the woods."

Tips about Bassler's whereabouts continued to come in to the Sheriff's Office with Detective Sergeant Greg Van Patten estimating that this amounted to about 10 to 15 a day before this number dropped after the Bassler sighting the previous weekend near his mother's house. "I call it 'America's Most Wanted Syndrome,'" said Van Patten, adding that after the sighting it had become easier to rule out many of the leads. There had been calls reporting Bassler as far away as San Francisco, 150 miles away, and Paso Robles way down south on the Central California Coast. "We believe he is still in these forests. He's very resourceful and he's not out there eating berries. People have called in because food has gone missing from the vacation cabins and things were out of place, and I would discourage anybody from going into a heavily-wooded area to check on their homes."

❧

The investigation once again featured on the front page of the Press Democrat's "Empire News" section, although the focus on this occasion was the recollections of a veteran prosecutor in the area who knew both Melo and Bassler. Mendocino County Deputy DA Timothy Stoen had seen both of them in court, one as a defendant and the other as a witness in a marijuana cultivation case involving private timberland. He reflected on the search and flipped through the files from the occasions when Bassler had appeared in court in Fort Bragg. He had tested positive for oxycodone following a September, 2010 arrest for being intoxicated in public, and again in February, 2011 for vandalism and resisting arrest—the incident at the high school tennis courts. The story went on to mention the latest update on the previous day's reports out of the Bay Area media that linked Bassler with the Jenner Beach murders of 2004 (see September 7th). Both Captain Smallcomb and Sonoma County Sheriff Lt. Dennis O'Leary, who oversees violent crimes investigations in that county, strongly disputed this. "We have nothing to tie him to the Jenner case whatsoever," said O'Leary.

❧

The whole week between September 4th and 12th the U.S. Marshals were arriving with equipment, setting up a cell phone service and better communications. Sometimes the command post officers were having problems with their radio connections with the searchers in the woods, so the U.S. Marshals Service put up a 100-foot radio tower and things were greatly improved, although occasionally there were still some radio problems due to the terrain and very thick brush and ground cover. It was a week of organizing, logistics, and long-term planning for Sheriff Allman. "Our portable radios were just not working well out in the woods but the Marshal's new communications setup improved things tenfold. I had met with Don O'Keefe, the U.S. Marshal for the Northern District of California, and he had presented me with what was described as a "memorandum of understanding" between the U.S.

Marshals Office and the County Sheriff's Office. It was bureaucracy at work, with pages of details on the rules and protocols of the Marshal's involvement in this case. I knew this was necessary but it was a very wordy document to deal with at the time. Marshal Mike McCloud was the main guy we had with us from that organization and he really and truly showed his unwavering commitment to this, often working 24-hour days. He is the epitome of what you want and expect when you ask for assistance—he was very knowledgeable, kept calm, had many useful connections, and had a good sense of humor.

"One morning I walked into the Command Post and there were just two people in the room—Kurt Smallcomb and Mike McCloud. I had no idea what they were talking about, and Kurt turned to me and said, 'Can we talk to you for a minute?' 'Sure,' I said, and Kurt asked me, 'We are in this for the long haul, right?' I figured that they had been wondering whether I was getting to the point where I might have to consider pulling resources back. I was not. I assured them of this, but McCloud asked again, 'You're still committed to this, right?' I told them it had not crossed my mind to pull back. I could certainly have justified reducing our resources but there were too many 'knows'—we knew who the suspect was; we knew he was armed; we knew he was inside a 400 square mile area as there was no indication he was elsewhere or anything to make us believe he had gone.

"Furthermore, at least a quarter of the deputies were born and raised in this County and that was an important factor as we proceeded with the investigation. They love this County and wanted to end this situation. They had no problem doing whatever was required. Placing men as guards on the front of the Skunk Train, for example. That was a dangerous assignment but there was no hesitation when we asked for men to do that job. We had six cops on each train and when the picture came out of the heavily armed SWAT team members riding on the front of the train it certainly had a positive effect on the morale of the community.

"Having said that, our applications for 'Concealed Weapon' permits tripled in one month following the death of Jere Melo. We have about 2,500 permits and a few hundred were applied for at this time, over 100 by women. The quality of life and personal safety of the residents was deeply affected for many weeks. I fully supported people's desire to protect themselves, but not if they wanted to go after Bassler in the woods. The 2nd Amendment gives people the right to arm themselves, unless there's some reason, such as criminal history, to deny them, and it is a very respected policy in this County."

಄

Bassler's Mother—under surveillance

Friday, September 9th, 2011

From early in the manhunt, a three-person team was stationed in an empty house next to Bassler's mother's house. "We had maintained surveillance on Laura Brickey's house from very early on in the investigation. They were there 24/7 with cameras feeding us real-time video of her home," recalls Sheriff Allman. "There was a computer at the Command Post giving us the information on every single phone call that Laura was making, incoming and outgoing, on her landline and cell phone. This was done after we secured a warrant at the federal level. We did not listen to the phone calls themselves; we just wanted to know who was making and receiving them. We wanted to know if she was telling us everything. We soon decided that she was. However, as Bassler's mother, who knows what she might want to do to help him. She did drop him off with his rifle in Rockport the day before Matthew Coleman was murdered close to that location. We tested her a number of times and encouraged her to write messages to Bassler and leave them in the woods. She told us what she wanted to write and she did as she said. She wrote all of the notes; we did not write any. At the very beginning she told us that her 'goal' in this was to persuade Aaron to come and see her; she wanted to give him a meal, and then she would call us.

"We soon got to know the habits of Bassler's mother, Laura, and his stepfather, Greg Brickey—everything from their nightly visits to a local bar for a few drinks to the fact that they were up feeding their chickens every morning. As time went on we had no reason to doubt her 'goal.' We wanted the same as she did and she realized this and never bad-mouthed us. During those weeks I had a number of her neighbors asking me if I thought they were safe. I assured them we had men in place around the vicinity and told them that if they saw anything suspicious to call the Command Post immediately. We also placed about 20 ground sensors around the house. These came from the U.S. Marshal and looked like eight-inch nails with a large head and were pounded into the ground. When footsteps were nearby a radio signal would be sent to the communication center with the location where a team would be listening for it. Throughout the whole 36-day search we had a Rapid Response Team consisting of about a dozen law enforcement officers ready and waiting for a call that would require them to go out and encounter Bassler. Ultimately the only information all this equipment gave us was that Bassler was not going to his mother's house.

"That evening at home, and thinking about Melo's funeral that was set for the next day, I really wished there was some good news to share with the family, but at that time there was nothing new."

℘

Jere Melo's Funeral

Saturday, September 10th, 2011

The Coast was enjoying an afternoon of very pleasant weather as Jere Melo's funeral began at 2:00pm the next day. This event took place at the Fort Bragg High School's Timberwolf Stadium and was planned by the City of Fort Bragg and the fire department.

Sheriff Allman recalls, "We had no idea how many people might show up and there were some estimates that perhaps as many as 5,000 people might be there. In the end, it was about 1,000. The psyche of the family and citizens was on my mind and we had a full security operation in force, and had requested a helicopter flying overhead. The day before the event we were told by C.H.P. that this would not be provided. It was very frustrating that we could not get a commitment to do that. As I said the psyche of the attendees at this event was important and the presence of a helicopter would have greatly helped with that. The area to the north and east of the stadium is all forests and woods. Fortunately I believed that Bassler was not looking for people, but was rather trying to stay away from them so, while the helicopter issue was disappointing on some levels, the threat from Bassler was not there in my opinion.

"Along with uniformed law enforcement officers positioned all around the venue, we also had SWAT vehicles present. If something happened we would be able to respond in an organized way, and we had worked on the plans for this for many hours during the previous week. On the day we had the communications trailer from Ukiah set up and operating on the scene at the stadium. There were probably over 40 officers in and around the venue—sheriff deputies, Fort Bragg police, C.H.P., probation officers, parole officers. We were also going to make sure that the visit of our U.S. Congressman, Mike Thompson, was going to go smoothly and without any incident—we wanted to get him in and out quickly.

"Not long after I arrived, I asked where the Melo family members were. To my dismay I was told they and about 100 friends were walking to the stadium from the Melo home, about eight blocks away. 'They're what!!?' was my response. This was not a parade! I immediately sent some cops and a medical vehicle over there, and when the family arrived it was the biggest relief of the day."

Madeleine Melo had expressed several times that her greatest wish was to have the whole search for Bassler resolved as soon as possible, and Sheriff Allman was certainly hoping it would be before the funeral. "That morning I talked to Madeleine and she once again expressed this wish. She told me she was seriously counting on us to have it resolved. I told her we hoped so too but that we had to stick to our plans and not push too much too quickly. I assured her that the moment Bassler was caught she would be notified immediately. It seemed that she was waiting and hoping for that to happen that very morning before the funeral.

"I talked to Congressman Mike Thompson on our cell phones as he was on his way and knew his time of arrival accurately. I was dressed in a suit and met him outside the stadium as he arrived, immediately introducing him to the family, handing him off to them and the city officials—I knew he was in good hands and, while I was glad he had come, it was an extra concern to have. The funeral went off without a hitch and there was no sign of the suspect. A number of people thought that Bassler might hide out in the woods behind the stadium so I assured them we would have added security there. In my opinion, Bassler would not be there—he was trying to stay away from being captured and I felt there was little danger from him at the funeral."

The service took place in bright sunshine at the football field that Melo had helped build. Many people referred to Melo's love of forestry, his passion for his community, and his ever-present laugh. Mike Thompson said, "Jere's dedication to getting this stadium built was the stuff of legends. He was a friend and colleague whose legacy and contributions are long-lasting, not only throughout Fort Bragg, but throughout Northern California and the timber country."

*

A message from Madeleine Melo was read out by niece Erin Timinsky at the service: "My heart is broken, your heart is broken. At the very beginning of this horror, I was swept up by friends who delivered the most awful messages of their lives. They held me together, quickly followed by my loving family, and a town of such incredible character... In my horror you held me, loved me, and held together my broken heart, even as your own hearts were forever broken."

Allman recalls, "The service was very uplifting, a fitting tribute to Jere Melo and the huge amount of dignity given to him. The community of Fort Bragg really came together for him. They donated so much food and I had never seen so many volunteers helping out. As the Sheriff, I felt very good about how it had all gone but it was a big relief when it was over."

*

121

Melo Family at the Funeral
The family of Jere Melo, including, from right, his cousin Tony Melo,
wife Madeleine, daughter Christine Melo, and son Greg, receive
the American flag from the Army honor guard during the memorial
service on Saturday at the Fort Bragg High School.
(Beth Schlanker/ The Press Democrat)

Burglaries, eights of spades, and the crosshairs

Sunday, September 11th, 2011

This was the tenth anniversary of the terrorist attacks of 9/11 and
people all over the country observed it in ceremonies of remembrance.
The Press Democrat had this event on its front page but the Empire
News section featured the previous day's Jere Melo funeral as its lead
story with a large front-page photograph of Madeleine Melo and
members of the immediate Melo family attending that memorial.

Searchers go into the woods
Camouflaged searchers and their dogs disembark from the Skunk Train
and head into the woods for another long day.
(Michael Macor/ The San Francisco Chronicle)

☙

Once again, the woods east of Fort Bragg, stretching all the way
to Willits, saw at least 40 officers searching for Bassler, many of them
transported there by the Skunk Train. Captain Smallcomb, admitting
he was tired, had little new information to add. "We are just continuing
to follow up leads today and trying to safely apprehend Mr. Bassler."

It turned out that there had been a possible sighting of the suspect,
but Smallcomb refused to comment either way. According to the Press
Democrat, the previous day, September 10th, an informant reported
to law enforcement his having had face-to-face contact with a man

he identified as Bassler at approximately 5:00 that morning along the railroad tracks. While camping in the woods, the man accidentally stumbled into a camp and surprised Bassler. He reported that Bassler was armed at that time with a rifle, as well as a smaller pistol. The man characterized Bassler as paranoid that his camp had been discovered but eventually calmed down and the two men ultimately shared the informant's marijuana joint. Bassler was informed during this interaction that he was a wanted man, and they discussed whether Bassler should either surrender or flee the area. Following directions provided by this informant, a law enforcement apprehension team went to this location where they only found signs of a recent camp. Detective Sergeant Greg Van Patten recalls, "I think the possible sighting by the transient was an important event as it was considered to be a valid contact by many, but some people were skeptical because of the circumstances being reported." In other words, concrete evidence that Bassler was still within the search area remained beyond the searchers' grasp.

The Skunk Train had reopened on the previous Wednesday after being closed for three days, and Sheriff Allman recalls that, on that Sunday, Jim Bassler was allowed to ride on the Skunk Train with a bullhorn along with several deputies. "We focused on the area three miles either side of the Melo shooting. We hoped Bassler would trust his father and agree to his pleas for his son to surrender. He said stuff a father would say—how he loved him, how he wanted no harm to come to him, and [for him] to come out and give himself up. Actually, Bassler's mother, Laura, also went into the woods, without a bullhorn, and yelled out asking Bassler to come and see her."

Sheriff Allman further recalls, "We had a list of the phone numbers for every cabin in the woods but there was nothing on camera to confirm he was still in the vicinity. A number of burglaries had been reported by this time also—on September 3rd, on Irmulco Road with forced entry and foodstuffs taken; on September 5th, on Ramsey Ridge Road with canned food items and blankets taken; and on September 11th, at four houses or cabins in the area of Northspur Road, one of which was missing a 12-gauge shotgun, a .22 rifle, 40-50 cans of food, and a bottle of vodka. We were pretty sure this was all Bassler but there had still not been any sightings.

"We continued to find the eight of spades playing card at a number of the burglarized homes during the first three weeks of the search but we also found a symbol—carved in wood in one case—of an eight-inch circle with a plus sign inside. We found this made out of some sticks on the Skunk Train tracks near Noyo and also at Bassler's bunker near where he shot Jere Melo. Some people said it was 'crosshairs' as in a rifle sighting. Other people said it was an Indian medicine wheel and that he was injured. Jim Bassler told us it meant nothing and was just part of his son's illness. He may well have been correct. However, it did cause us some concern and we told the SWAT team guys to be on the lookout for it. If it was crosshairs, what was he telling us? I'm sure that he knew that we were going to see that. Was he telling us 'I see you'? Along with a number of other things, that's one of the things I'd love to have asked Aaron Bassler."

ↀ

Food donations and decomposing sea urchins

Monday, September 12th, 2011

As reported in the Press Democrat, Fort Bragg residents were rallying their cooking forces in support of the worn and hungry law enforcement officers who for three weeks had been searching the dense forests for the murderer of two men. On Monday morning, about a dozen apron-clad locals were in a church kitchen preparing enough spicy beef and fixings to make Sloppy Joe sandwiches for about 60 people. Swithenbank Construction had donated the beef; Subway donated vegetables, cookies, and other desserts; and Kemgas Propane Gas Services supplied the buns. These were just a few of the many organizations and individuals who had been taking turns to buy and prepare food for the search teams. One family donated 25 pizzas; someone else made 30 burritos; a restaurant provided roasted chickens to which the Chamber of Commerce added a side of potato salad. Tri-tip and garlic mashed potatoes were on the menu courtesy of Harvest Market, with a barbecue from Campbell Timberland Management, for whom Jere Melo worked, planned for the upcoming Sunday. While the Chamber of Commerce's Chief Executive, Debra de Graw, saw the town's efforts as "great therapy"; others, such as Harvest Market's Jennifer Bosman, admitted that the "whole town was uneasy" and would love Sunday's meal to be a "celebratory dinner instead."

Around this time, Sheriff Allman recalls that the searchers thought they had made a major breakthrough. "After three nights of using the FLIRs we had realized we were not making much progress, but we persevered, just in case. The terrain on the ground was so dense they could not detect anyone or anything. We even tested these on our guys in the woods, as we obviously knew where they were situated, but they could not be detected either. We kept trying and searched all over the area, even up to Humboldt County, but we found nothing in almost two weeks of flyovers. Fortunately, given the financial issues of maintaining the investigation, a subject that was never far from my thoughts: the National Guard were paying for these, not the County Sheriff's Office.

"Finally the FLIRs did detect a heat source and a SWAT team was sent in very covertly, heading for the location based on the GPS reading. We were hopeful that this might lead us to Bassler. It didn't. What the source of that heat was turned out to be a large pile of decomposing sea urchins' guts and clamshells, left in the woods by fishermen. It was about 10 feet wide. That was a very disappointing moment. Who knew? Heat from decomposing sea urchin guts was not something you learned at school, or in regular police work. I believe this was the last time the FLIRs were used. I should point out that we later did find a number of fires that Bassler had started during the five-week search but he was very smart—they were never any wider than about eight inches in diameter, too small to be detected by the FLIRs."

ᔓ

The Reward

Tuesday, September 13th, 2011

After much discussion, a reward was announced in the form of a press release on the morning of September 13th:

> The Mendocino County Sheriff's Office has been contacted by private citizens as well as the U.S. Marshals Service and the Mendocino Land Trust, each providing reward funds for information leading to the capture and arrest of Aaron Bassler. The reward amount is at $30,000 at the time of this press release.
>
> Aaron Bassler is the lead suspect in the homicides of Matthew Coleman and Jere Melo. Residents of the Fort Bragg and surrounding

area should remain vigilant and conscientious of their surroundings as suspect Bassler is considered armed and dangerous and thought to have remained in the area. Suspect Bassler should not be approached. Law enforcement is looking for information, not active participation in the search. Please notify authorities at 707-463-4086 or by e-mailing report@mendocinosheriff.com with any information you may think would be helpful. Anonymous information can be sent via email to the same address.

The Mendocino County Sheriff's Office wishes to thank the many individuals and local, state, and federal agencies assisting in the search for suspect Bassler in our attempt to safely apprehend the suspect. See attached Reward Poster.

☙

The Mendocino Land Trust had previously offered a reward for $17,000 for information on the homicide of their employee, Matt Coleman. Sheriff Allman explains, "We had waited and waited, we did not want vigilantes out looking for Bassler in the woods, but by this time we hoped that emotions were calming down a little. The Land Trust now increased this by $5,000 to $22,000, and an attorney from the Bay Area, who said he was a friend of Jere Melo's but did not wish to be identified, offered a further $5,000. With $3,000 being donated by the U.S. Marshals Service, it stood at $30,000 for information on either murder. I don't believe the Sheriff's Office had ever done this before.

"There were many hours of conversation on this and our legal team was also heavily involved in the preparation of the 'Wanted' poster. It was designed with the posters of over 100 years ago in mind. It is illegal in California to say on a wanted poster 'Dead or Alive.' As a result it was agreed that the main headline on the poster would be 'Wanted for Murder' and the reward would be paid for information leading to the 'arrest and capture of the suspect.' This left a grey area that had to be sorted out.

"By this time, many of us involved in the case had the idea that the outcome might be a conviction, but just as likely it might end in a shootout. I called the Land Trust and asked them if the money would still be paid if someone gave us information telling us where Bassler was and this led to a shootout and his subsequent death. The guy at the Trust said that the wording as it stood meant that the money would not be paid in such a situation. I said that this was not satisfactory and he agreed, saying he would talk to 'his people' about it. Just 20 minutes later he called back and said they understood and a wording change would have to be made in their agreement with us. We dealt with our counsel for hours on this and eventually their attorney agreed to a change and a binding agreement was signed. It was decided that the term 'legal deadly engagement' would be added to the letter of obligation from those putting up the money as a possible alternative scenario to 'arrest and capture.' This new wording confirmed that if someone's information leads to a shootout or, in other words, if Bassler would not go easily and he was shot and killed, the informant would still be paid. It was a strange sequence of events. The Land Trust had completely changed their stance. I did not expect that from them, from the NRA perhaps, but not from this group. I signed off on it which meant that the Sheriff's Office was liable for the payment if the donors backed out."

Speaking to the Press Democrat, Mendocino Land Trust President Winston Bowen said, "It's a substantial reward and we're hoping it results in the capture of Aaron Bassler." Their largest donors to the Land Trust were The Conservation Fund and the Save the Redwoods League, on whose ranch north of Westport Matt Coleman was working when he was killed.

'Wanted for Murder' poster

The photograph of Bassler on the left is the booking photograph following his apprehension earlier in the year after the incident at the high school tennis courts. He had resisted arrest and had been pepper sprayed. On the right is a photograph of Bassler in his early 20s. It led to some members of the public to suggest that the suspect might be a transvestite or perhaps transgender.

The Photograph

Wednesday, September 14th, 2011

Sheriff Allman recalls this morning vividly. "We had gotten nothing from the cameras to that point but then a detective had returned to a cabin in the Northspur area where we had placed a camera looking down on to the cabin entrance. He found that the door was off its hinges. The detective set up his laptop right there and began to download the footage from the camera to his computer. Suddenly on the screen the detective was watching he saw a man with a rifle standing in the exact same spot on the porch where he was now standing. The photograph could have been taken just minutes earlier! Perhaps Bassler was watching him there and then. A heart-stopping moment for the detective, I'm sure." (It transpired that the photograph had been taken in the early evening on Monday, September 12th, about 40 hours earlier).

en

After a long frustrating week of little progress, these photographs were a huge breakthrough for those involved in the search. Sheriff Allman was obviously delighted. "We were pretty certain Bassler was still in the vicinity but, having received no definite proof for over a week that this was still the case, those photographs were very good news indeed. The cabin owners were contacted and, after further investigation, it was discovered that some, but not all, of the food had been taken. Also, a sewing kit was missing so our assumption was that

Cabin break-in photo
To Sheriff Tom Allman and many involved in the investigation, this
is the most important photograph of the whole 36-day search—Aaron
Bassler, high-powered rifle at his side, breaking into a cabin in the
woods. The discovery of this picture confirmed to law enforcement
that Bassler was still within the search area and that they were on the
right track.

perhaps he needed to do some first aid on himself after the dog had attacked him. We studied that footage for hours and hours. He looked to be in good health; his left arm—the one the dog would have bitten—seemed to be fine so perhaps our sewing theory was incorrect. His hair was well groomed and he was in the same jacket he had been seen in a week earlier when spotted by his mother's house. He was also in an offensive firing position—his finger was alongside the gun's trigger—the usual tactical maneuver. You do not have your finger actually on the trigger. Cops are trained to not have their finger on the trigger in case they trip and fall, perhaps shooting themselves in the process."

With no sighting of Bassler for 10 days, since Sunday, September 4th, Sheriff Allman and the other officers at the command post leading the manhunt did not know whether or not someone was feeding Bassler information. "Perhaps word had got out that we had many unmanned cameras hidden in the woods, watching various thoroughfares and roads. We had made the conscious decision to adopt the tactic of not releasing certain confidential information and the hidden camera operation became one of those. As it turned out, the information did not get out, even though this tactic was known to be in use on this case at every briefing room in the county.

"After we had the breakthrough of the photographs showing Bassler breaking into a cabin, I was convinced that if he had not taken all of the food at the various cabins then he was planning to return later. Furthermore, each time he left a cabin with the hinge pins removed—once again, an indication that he would return. I wanted to covertly put people inside the cabins and wait for that eventuality. I was adamant about this but was told that we couldn't do it because there was nowhere inside the cabins that could not be seen from at least one window. [Also,] we would need at least three men inside, with one sleeping at any one time, and this wouldn't work. I remember a letter to a newspaper suggesting we do what I had wanted to do. I wish it had been that easy.

"As a result of the cabin photo we greatly improved our search patterns, concentrating on structures and cabins and being very cautious every time we were within 100 yards of such a building. Jim Bassler had told us his son was not a hunter and this was confirmed by all the canned foods that were being taken from cabins. We certainly felt we were on the right track after seeing that photograph."

Captain Smallcomb was convinced that Bassler should not know we had cameras set up in the woods. Sheriff Allman agreed. So despite the breakthrough, it was agreed that this information would not be shared with the public at this time and Captain Smallcomb briefly commented to the press that day, "Efforts continue. We continue to follow up leads."

Some law enforcement officers had told members of the media that they had found signs of Bassler's presence, including temporary shelters made from sticks and brush, but again Smallcomb would not comment on such reports. He did confirm that a specially trained bloodhound had been used in the search but nothing significant had transpired from this to date.

Meanwhile, Fort Bragg residents remained on edge and later that day, just after 3:00pm, Fort Bragg Middle School locked down its after-school program after rifle-carrying law enforcement officers were spotted in the area. There was no Bassler sighting but the principal was not prepared to take any risks and he decided to lock down the kids inside the premises.

The photograph had been a massive boost to every law enforcement officer involved in the search and the decision to keep this under wraps was a unanimous one, but as time passed and the public became increasingly restless, it was an option that was to be constantly reviewed and discussed by Sheriff Allman and others leading the search.

∽

Chapter 6
"Why is this taking so long?"

Keeping the cameras a secret

Thursday, September 15th, 2011

Throughout the two weeks that followed the publication of the reward, the investigation continued in much the same way. The searchers were in the woods every day and, although boosted by news of the photograph of Bassler breaking into the cabin, their frustrations grew as further progress was slow. Meanwhile, the public remained unaware of the photographs placing Bassler in the woods on September 12th. It was decided to keep the public in the dark about that sighting. Sheriff Allman and the senior investigators on the case were adamant about this. "We had many long discussions about this and there were several points to address. The overriding reason to keep this information from the public was to keep anyone in contact with Bassler from knowing about the cameras. We thought for some time that he was in contact with friends on the 'outside' and did not wish him to work out just how much we knew and how we were getting information, or not, from our cameras and other search techniques."

☙

"It's a drain emotionally and economically"

Friday, September 16th, 2011

Authorities announced that signs of Bassler's activities were showing up as the search continued. Makeshift campsites and break-ins at a handful of remote cabins scattered miles apart all appeared to be the work of the suspect, sometimes just a day or two old. Detective Sergeant Greg Van Patten of the Mendocino County Sheriff's Office, acting as spokesperson in Captain Smallcomb's absence, explained to reporters from The Press Democrat, "There are certain things that we think are unique to him. These include the secluded places he chooses to camp, the way he is known to craft a fire, and the items that are going missing from the cabins."

Authorities believed that Bassler remained in a 19-mile corridor between Fort Bragg and Northspur, roughly parallel to the Skunk Train rail tracks. The overall area covered by the search stretched from Fort Bragg east as far as Willits, and from Westport in the north to Highway 20 in the south, and although the area had been reduced it remained a vast forested expanse of over 300 square miles. However, this was decreasing steadily as law enforcement's knowledge of the terrain and Bassler's tendencies improved.

Van Patten continued to explain that tips and sightings were still being received and investigated, but would not confirm if the perimeters of the search area were being tightened given that Bassler, based on the distances between some of the cabins, seemed to be frequently on the move, covering long areas of difficult terrain in relatively short periods of time. Van Patten did add that with a search team comprising 30 to 60 officers, while there was no plan to cut this back at this point, this might happen in the future "if things [weren't] working."

Later that day, speaking to the Ukiah Daily Journal, Captain Smallcomb, who was continuing to coordinate logistics, communication, and strategy for the ongoing hunt for Bassler from his base in Fort Bragg, said, "It gets emotional at times, with the pressure of making sure nobody else gets hurt before he is apprehended. It's a drain emotionally and economically." Although fewer hunters and transients were being seen in the woods than in previous years, the downside was that the timber companies were unable to get their goods out of the forest and into the marketplace.

Make-up
A SWAT team member preparing for his day in the woods.
(Christopher Chung/ The Press Democrat)

Smallcomb also confirmed that the Skunk Train would continue to operate for the public but under heightened security, as least through the upcoming weekend. According to Van Patten, at least two armed peace officers rode in the engine of each train and, although the idea was for these officers to be mostly Sheriff's deputies, law enforcement officers from other agencies had taken some of these shifts on the trains, which ran from 10:00am to 2:30pm daily. Apart from the first few days of the search when the tracks were shut down as a precaution, the hunt for Bassler didn't seem to have affected the numbers of people taking the scenic ride through the woods. "Every day we hope is the last day," Van Patten said.

⁂

Three weeks into the search

Saturday, September 17th, 2011

Three weeks into the search, a $30,000 reward had been posted for the capture of Aaron Bassler; the Skunk Train was running but manned with armed guards; "Armed and Dangerous" flyers papered the streets; several experienced SWAT teams were in the forests every day, along with U.S. Marshals whose specialty was hunting for fugitives from justice; Behavioral Health Department employees who had profiled the suspect had apparently been ordered not to talk about the case; and local citizens were living on the edge as they dealt with various rumors persistently sweeping the town like a California wildfire, everyday being all too aware that the killer remained at large in their "backyard."

Prep for the woods
Various law enforcement teams congregate and plans are made before
a day of searching begins.
(Michael Macor/ The San Francisco Chronicle)

☙

Sheriff Allman remembers, "We continued to be very aware that the public was thinking 'Why is this taking so long?' and we constantly discussed how much information we could give out. We wanted to tell them progress was being made, no matter how slow it was at times, but we could not tell them too much and risk the possibility of tipping Bassler off on some of our tactics. We continued to emphasize their safety and that there were significant numbers of ground personnel in the woods, where the deep thick wilderness provided a nasty terrain for our searchers. I always made sure to mention to the media and anyone who asked that there was no reason to believe Bassler was anywhere else except in the areas we were searching."

e/o

Beer for the informants

Sunday, September 18th, 2011

Despite all of their efforts, tactical skills, and equipment, Sheriff Allman and the many other law enforcement officers involved were making slow progress towards apprehending the suspect. With the exception of the pictures, one snapshot in particular, and the fact that some of his survivalist activities had been discovered, there were no other significant leads at this point, although the search area was gradually being decreased. Allman commented, "We did hear from three transients, who were at the east end of the Skunk Train line, that they had met Bassler in the middle of the night, on Saturday, September 17th. They said he had a handgun on his belt [and] carried a rifle, and [they] accurately described the clothes he was wearing based on what we had seen on film. They did not feel threatened by Bassler, smoked some marijuana with him, and then he just disappeared into the woods. This was one of the very few tips on a Bassler sighting that we believed. They identified Bassler from a photograph and did not know about the reward. Captain Smallcomb believed they were credible witnesses and he gave $20 to a detective who bought the transients a case of beer for their help."

∽

Bizarre sightings

Sheriff Allman recalls that in the week following the reward's announcement the number of tips dramatically increased. "We had all kinds of reports of Bassler sightings, many of them bizarre and none useful. However, we had to follow up on them as it only takes one to lead to a solution. We had a clairvoyant who called virtually every evening to tell us that Bassler was to be found 'around tall trees near to a large body of water.' Well, considering we knew he was in a redwood forest on the edge of the Pacific Ocean, I'd say that was pretty accurate! Someone else told us we would have success if we went into the woods with a loudspeaker system and announce[d] that we were Mother Earth at which point Bassler should turn himself in. Then, as a result of the second of the two photographs on the poster we had maybe 30 people call in and say he was transgender and that we should be looking around Fort Bragg for a woman. Another tip told us that Bassler had been seen in Fort Bragg riding a bicycle and wearing orange overalls, as worn by convicts—needless to say we didn't spend much time on that one! Another tip said he was in Safeway buying ice cream at 11:00pm one night—we checked the surveillance camera at the store and he wasn't, but as I said we had to check everything and we did continue to encourage the public to contact us with anything they might think suspicious or any possible sightings of the suspect. Many cases are solved as a result of one person seeing one strange thing and reporting it. We were learning as we went along; nobody working on the case had ever been involved in something like this before. Even the U.S. Marshals Service, which specializes in tracking fugitives, found this case full of situations they had not faced before, particularly the unforgiving terrain."

Apart from the reports of sightings, the public was showing their continuing support for law enforcement in the form of greeting cards. Allman comments, "Every other day we would receive a card from someone, thanking us for our efforts and for being there for the public. We received one card with encouraging words from many members of Jere Melo's family. Madeleine Melo wrote, 'I pray for each of you—God knows who you are. I pray to him to protect you and guide you. I know you are working sooooo hard. I have such huge respect for you and the work you do. I wish I could speak to each of you and tell you what is in my heart. Some of you know. Be safe, Madeleine.' Other family members understandably expressed their wishes more pointedly for us to go get Bassler and end this thing."

&

Two bloodhounds

Tuesday, September 20th, 2011

The search stepped up a further notch when it was announced that two new dogs were to be added to the search for Bassler in the rugged, poison oak-infested timberland. This would bring the number of dogs involved in the search to six, although these two additions, Mandy and Maddy (from the Riverside County Sheriff's Department and the Murrieta Police Department respectively), were bloodhounds, a breed known for its keen sense of smell. They are therefore more effective than the shepherd-like breeds used by the local Sheriff's Department, particularly when it comes to "cold tracking"—following older scents over longer distances.

The Press Democrat reported that on the previous occasion a bloodhound was used in the hunt for Bassler, it was a couple of weeks earlier, shortly after he was spotted by his mother's home, east of Fort Bragg. On that occasion, it was actually Dutch, the Mendocino County Sheriff Office's German Shepherd, who returned from the chase with what Captain Smallcomb said at the time was a small piece of clothing, although other officers later correctly identified it as a fanny pack.

The bloodhounds are not multipurpose and thus are not often a regular part of a police team. Roger Titus of the National Police Bloodhound Association said, "They are purely trackers. They don't do much of anything else. As a result, of every 100 police dogs, 2 might be bloodhounds."

Some bloodhound handlers claim their dogs can track a person up to three weeks after they have disappeared but Titus said that a few days is a more reasonable time frame if the conditions are right—cool and damp. Such conditions had been prevailing over recent days in the woods, resulting in scents—basically dead skin cells—remaining intact and low to the ground and enhancing a bloodhound's sense of smell.

However, a bloodhound does have limitations once they find a suspect, preferring a cookie rather than any sort of confrontation, making them perfect for search and rescue operations involving children or dementia patients. According to Riverside County Sheriff's Sergeant Coby Webb, "We have had success teaming a bloodhound with a 'bite' dog—one finding the suspect, the other catching him or her." She added that bloodhounds cost about $1500 to buy and then a further $5000 to train each year but, in her opinion, "They're absolutely worth it."

$\wp$

Mounting costs

Wednesday, September 21st, 2011

It was reported in various newspapers that up to and including Tuesday, September 20th, the Mendocino County Sheriff's Office had paid for 2,690 hours in overtime alone on the case so far. This amounted to about $133,000, or about $1.50 for every County resident— Mendocino County's 35,010 square miles being the home to 87,500 residents. This did not account for regular hours of work spent on the search. A statement released by the Sheriff's Office stated, "Long hours, rough terrain, insects, poison oak, weather, and all the things associated with this search are difficult. But knowing we have the support of our community strengthens our resolve to continue the search." At this point, agencies assisting the Mendocino County Sheriff's Office in the search for Bassler included the Fort Bragg Police Department, the Willits Police Department, the Ukiah Police department, the Mendocino County District Attorney's Office, Mendocino County Welfare Fraud Investigators, Cal Fire, California Highway Patrol, the State Department of Fish and Game, the State Department of Parks and Recreation, the Department of Justice, the F.B.I., and the U.S. Marshals Service.

"We cannot afford to walk away from this right now; we have a very dangerous person in the woods who is wanted for two murders," said Sheriff Allman when asked about the increasing costs. "We have a decent idea where he is and we're going to be continuing on this. If we need to change our tactics in a few weeks we will. We're evaluating this every day."

Allman notes that the previous day they had received reports of a "tent encampment" (a gathering place for the homeless) not far from where Melo had been shot. "It turned out to be just that and there was no sighting of Bassler around there. We thought we might have something because this was a little unusual as by that time even the homeless had evacuated the woods."

Message in a food bag

Thursday, September 22nd, 2011

Sheriff Allman recalls that around this time a bag of food was found hanging in the woods close to Bassler's mother's home. Captain Smallcomb had a good conversant relationship with Bassler's mother and asked her about this. "She told him there was food there for him that she had put out the previous day in a bag and underneath that she had left a note for Bassler saying, among other things, 'Please turn yourself in, we are all worried sick about you.' She wanted a resolution to this as much as any of us. No mother wants her son out in the woods, cold and alone, being hunted down. There's nothing stronger than a mother's love. Kurt Smallcomb checked the message and left it there under the food. We all hoped Bassler would come back and respond to the message but he never did return. Over the following week or so she left a number of messages in the woods for her son but he never responded to any of them; in fact I'm sure he never returned to that particular area to find any of them. Meanwhile, Bassler's father, Jim, did not hold the same hope as his former wife for their son's survival. He had told Captain Smallcomb that from the very beginning he was fairly certain what the final outcome would be—the death of his son. This was a pretty tough thing for any parent to swallow."

☙

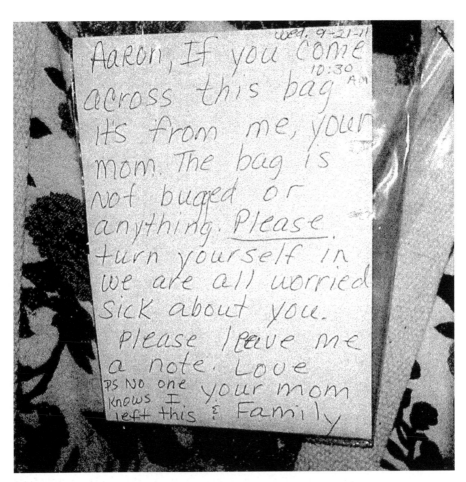

Message to Bassler from his mother

At one point midway through the investigation, Detective Sergeant Van Patten revealed to the press that Bassler had shown no inclination to surrender. They had brought Bassler's father into the forest with a bullhorn, traveling through the area on the Skunk Train and stopping at several locations and calling for his son to surrender. None of this worked. Meanwhile, it was obvious to everyone involved in the case that Bassler was clearly a very savvy woodsman with the knowledge of military flanking techniques for getting behind his target and gaining the advantage. The Sheriff Office's lead investigator in the Melo murder, Detective Bryan Arrington, concluded, "We're not dealing here with a suspect who possibly did something and may turn himself in. This is someone who isn't afraid of firing on law enforcement and is comfortable in this environment. This is his backyard."

❧

Bassler's friends

Friday, September 23rd, 2011

Law enforcement generally assumes that suspects will counter any moves they make in a rational way. About halfway through this case Sheriff Allman had wanted to start leaving messages for Bassler out in the woods, encouraging him to surrender. "At that point the U.S. Marshal suggested we wait before doing that. They were pacifying me because they had been waiting for an analysis of Bassler from their Behavioral Science Unit, a group of very experienced psychiatrists. This report basically stated that we 'cannot expect that Aaron Bassler will at all be rational in his thoughts and actions.' His thoughts would be very erratic—we had already learned that he thought the Chinese and space aliens were going to take over the world. On the suggestion of the U.S. Marshal we were advised to leave short and ambiguous messages for Bassler; handwritten messages addressed to him, with locations on them coupled with the words 'safe' or 'unsafe,' that might pique his interest and perhaps result in him visiting these locations."

Despite his obviously erratic behavior, it was thought that Bassler was still very capable of acting rationally in some ways. Just the previous February, following his arrest at the Fort Bragg tennis courts, he had been in jail and in his work in the kitchen there he had shown no irrational behavior of any note. In fact he had been particularly unremarkable and was not remembered by those who worked with him for that month. People around town did not know his name, he was often seen wearing all black, and some of his exploits had been noted but nothing that extraordinary. Sheriff Allman comments, "Somebody told us he wanted to remain anonymous to everyone and sometimes his solution for this would be to wear a black fishnet covering over his face, not the normal way to avoid attention obviously, but most people we talked to, including his schoolmates, thought he was odd but nothing more. He had very few friends but we did continue to suspect that somebody might be feeding information to him in the woods.

"One friend of Bassler's in particular, Jeremy James, wanted to give us lots of information. He claimed to have been a friend since they were about 20 years old and was still the best friend Bassler had to that day. He knew Bassler as well as anyone, he claimed, and informed us that Bassler had never had a girlfriend—another possible person who might help him. We were very wary of his motivation. Jeremy was buying infrared binoculars and camouflage gear, indicating to us that he was going out and looking for Bassler in the woods. He told us he had served in the U.S. Special Forces. This may well have been true but we are always cautious when such claims are made, as this is the branch of the military that most 'military service liars'* claim to have served in. He told us he and Bassler knew the woods better than anyone. He kept calling Kurt Smallcomb and became very frustrated with us, I'm sure. We did not follow up on much of what he said, believing his motives were perhaps not the best. We could not be sure whether or not he would pass on information to Bassler somehow. Perhaps Bassler had a two-way radio and [was] in contact with someone in town. Now, with hindsight, I think that Jeremy had the best intentions and was motivated to end this without further deaths, believing he could bring Bassler in without harm.

"Another friend of Bassler's, Jason Johnson, told us he was the one who had taught Bassler how to grow poppies and had convinced Bassler to do so. Like Bassler's mother, he too told us he would welcome Bassler into his home, feed him, and then call us."

☙

---

*"Military Service Liar" is an increasingly found phenomenon in which many are claiming extreme military service and the receipt of major awards for valor and bravery such as the Congressional Medal of Honor. For nearly a century, there have been laws that make it a crime to wear an unearned military medal. Congress then passed a statute in 2006 making it a crime to even lie about this, entitled the Stolen Valor Act. However, on June 28, 2012, in "United States v. Alvarez," the U.S. Supreme Court ruled that the Stolen Valor Act was an unconstitutional abridgment of the freedom of speech under the First Amendment, striking down the law in a six to three decision.

"Everybody's nervous"

As the length of time spent on the intense yet fruitless search for Aaron Bassler reached four weeks, local residents were becoming even more weary and worried. "We just want it to be over," said Fort Bragg Mayor Dave Turner speaking to the Press Democrat.

Local resident Randy Marler, who had a deer-hunting tag for the area under search, said, "Everybody's nervous. You see a lot of pistols and rifles coming out of the closets now." Logging had also obviously been significantly affected, with operations suspended periodically.

Law enforcement officials remained optimistic, however, with Detective Sergeant Greg Van Patten saying, "Every day I think we're closer." The thefts from the cabins in the woods had continued and it was believed that Bassler had two more weapons following a burglary at one of these remote locations. No ammunition was taken but it was thought that he had probably purchased it previously at local hardware stores. It was not known if the ammunition could be used in the guns he seized. Van Patten also revealed that law enforcement believed Bassler had an assault-style rifle among his weapons, adding that people with houses in the forests around Fort Bragg should secure their weapons before going out.

The calls were also still coming in about Bassler sightings. All were investigated; some were more reliable than others. A couple of days earlier, a logging crew working about 19 miles east of Fort Bragg, near Northspur, spotted a man matching Bassler's description but he was too far away to be certain.

SWAT at rest
Exhausted searchers take a quick break while they can.
(Christopher Chung/ The Press Democrat)

❧

The search teams were tired but Van Patten informed the press that fresh "troops" from outside the County were expected over the weekend, about 20 of them, and that the bloodhounds were still being deployed, although the extremely dense trees and brush meant that their effectiveness was somewhat limited.

❧

Warning the public

Sunday, September 25th, 2011

Sheriff Allman knew that the public was very restless and concerned, and it was time to give them something for their ailing morale and at the same time reemphasize the need for continued diligence. "As time went on, the arguments for not informing the public about the photographs were gradually outweighed by considerations to the contrary. A major one of these was the necessity of warning the public that Bassler was still around. There was a definite need for the public to know, with factual certainty, that Bassler was still in the Noyo Basin. We had been uncertain whether or not Bassler had been hit when Ian Chaney fired at him on August 27th, the day that Melo [had been] shot. Although he was spotted very briefly near his mother's house a week or more later, on the 4th of September, perhaps he was wounded and had died of his wounds by this point. There had been no sign of him: no campfires, no break-ins that could be conclusively attributed to him. When the photographs were taken on the 12th, we now had him on camera, in the Noyo Basin. That was the good news and we decided for a time to keep this under wraps. However, with deer season now in operation we did not want people going into the woods in the belief that he was not there. The photographs showed that he was still fully armed. He had his finger alongside the trigger—an offensive tactical position. He was still committing crimes. He appeared to be very healthy. We had to release the photographs, although as things turned out I don't believe that if we had released the photographs any earlier it would have helped."

❧

Cabin break-in
Following its release to the press and public on September 26th, over the ensuing few days the investigation's iconic photograph appeared in newspapers all over the country. The story also began to appear as a news item in other countries.

"Caught on camera..."

Monday, September 26th, 2011

The six photographs taken by the camera at the cabin over a 10-second period on Monday, September 12th and discovered by law enforcement two days later on September 14th were finally released to the public at the first official press conference at 3:00pm on Monday, September 26th. One photo in particular, shown again on the previous page, caught everyone's imagination. This photograph appeared the next day on the front page of the Press Democrat under the headline "Caught on camera—slaying suspect outside cabin carrying assault rifle." The ensuing article informed readers that, according to Sheriff Allman, speaking at the press conference, the picture had been taken within the past two weeks by 1 of 40 surveillance cameras placed in the woods by law enforcement. The exact location of the cabin was not given by Allman, who was quoted as saying, "We have every reason to believe he is still in the original area. Many people wonder if we are getting closer to a resolution on this, and I assure you that we are. There are many vacation cabins in that area that have been broken into. We're obviously very concerned about that."

During other burglaries, a rifle and shotgun had been stolen and the sightings of Bassler by citizens continued, but police could verify none of them. Allman confirmed that DNA evidence had placed Bassler at the scene of both murder scenes but confirmed that the suspect had at no point so far opened fire at law enforcement officials, adding, "We do not believe Bassler is hunting any individual. We believe he is trying to stay away from society."

Bassler's father, Jim, agreed. "He's very unlikely to come out of the woods. That's where he's been and that's where he'll stay. He's definitely not going to catch a bus out or try to hitch a ride because he's not comfortable with people."

The article in the Press Democrat, written by Cathy Bussewitz, went on to point out that in the photograph Bassler was wearing a light-colored, long-sleeved jacket or shirt, and light colored pants that could be khakis or jeans. His dark hair appeared to have been recently cut or shaved, and the seat of his pants appeared to have been ripped.

∾

Sheriff Allman remembers this day very well and has thought about it often. "In many ways it was just like any other during the investigation. We would have two teams on the Skunk Train, we would have guys checking on the camera footage, surveillance continued on Bassler's mother's house, the search teams would go out with equipment, supplies, and the latest weather update. Later, in the afternoon, and what made this a very significant day, was the first official press conference."

∾

Sheriff Allman recalls, "People had been asking, 'What is going on?'; 'Why can't the police get this guy?'; 'What is taking so long?'; 'Are these the Keystone Cops?'. On television shows they get the bad guy in an hour and we often solve a murder case in 24 hours, but this was now over four weeks since Jere Melo had been killed and the search for Bassler had started. We had to give the public something and we now

First Press Conference
This was the first official press conference. Sheriff Allman shows the
assembled members of the press and television news the photograph of
Bassler breaking into the cabin in the woods.
(Christopher Chung/ The Press Democrat)

felt that, if we released these pictures, people would understand why
we were not going in as storm troopers after this guy. He was not some
angry lost Boy Scout; this was somebody very prepared to do additional
harm to anyone.

"The photographs were taken at Camp Noyo Boy Scout Ranch.
The manager there, Bryan Hemphill, recommended that we put cameras there because that specific cabin had been burglarized a month
earlier. We studied the photographs for hours and hours. We noticed
his shaven head and so he must have had some grooming materials to
do that; there was a slight bump under his shirt on the right hip—was
this a handgun? The transients who had seen him a few days after the
photographs were taken had spoken of seeing a handgun in his posses-

sion. This bulge led us to believe it was a gun and that he had at least two guns. He was wearing a similar shirt that he [had been] seen wearing when the deputies had spotted him on September 4th; he had a rip in his pants which might explain why he had stolen a sewing kit from one of the cabins—perhaps to treat a wound that he had received in his confrontation with Dutch the dog." (It turned out that Bassler had not been bitten in this incident.)

"The release of the photographs was probably discussed more than any other topic throughout the investigation. Now it was agreed that this was the time to release them and inevitably everyone immediately wanted more information. We just told them we felt we were getting close to a resolution but it was not simply a case of going out and finding this guy. He was not selling Girl Scout cookies. He was very dangerous and he had an assault rifle and we believed he was prepared to use it.

"At that press conference I also thanked the wives of the law enforcement officers for everything, particularly their trust for allowing us to send their husbands into the woods to take care of this horrific situation. I became a little choked up during my remarks. After the conference, people remarked on my comments and the emotions I had shown. It was perhaps inevitable. There were young men (there were no women on the search teams) who were at risk every minute they were out there taking part in the search. We believed, and took very seriously indeed, the notion that Bassler had the ability and the desire to shoot law enforcement officers. Each time our guys went into the woods for a 12-hour shift, their loved ones would be in fear of a phone call or a cop car turning up at their homes with terrible news.

"Actually, two parents and about six wives had called asking me to exclude their loved ones from the mission. I could not do that. None of my deputies asked me at any point to not participate. Having said that, one of my continual thoughts during the entire case was of having to at some point kneel down before a grieving widow or parent and hand her a triangular-folded flag."

℘

As mentioned earlier, among the many law enforcement agencies assisting in the search for Bassler was the U.S. Marshals Service and, according to U.S. Marshal Don O'Keefe, who was at the conference, they had sent its "well-equipped, well-trained tactical group" out of Louisiana. Tiffany Revelle, reporting for the Ukiah Daily Journal, noted that O'Keefe emphasized that the Marshals Service has a long history of fugitive chasing, dating back to 1789, and said this search was unusual in its length and the difficult terrain facing law enforcement. The unforgiving terrain is marked by jagged, steep grades, rising swiftly from 400 to 1600 feet, said Sheriff's Office SWAT Commander Jim Van Hagen. "It's pretty much straight up on your hands and feet. It's very steep country. He could be sitting three feet away from you and you wouldn't be able to see him."

Sheriff Allman stated that the terrain was like home to Bassler, who had been traversing the woods for 30 years. He acknowledged that the use of bloodhounds in the search might help at some point but that they were having trouble distinguishing between the many places Bassler had been and where he might be now. At times the searchers were getting about 2 hours sleep in 48. "That happens a lot," said Marshals Supervisor Mike McCloud. "It depends on what information we are getting, what tips come in. In a rural operation like this it is very different than working in San Francisco or Oakland."

In concluding the press conference, Sheriff Allman said that the reward of $30,000 for information leading to Bassler's capture still stood but emphasized that for "deadly engagement of Bassler by citizens," it would be null and void. "The reward is for information, not participation," he added. "This is the largest search for any individual in the history of the Sheriff's Office. This last 31 days has presented a lot of information to us. I believe that each day we are getting warmer and warmer and there have been no discussions of giving up the search or whether Bassler will never be found. I do not see an end in sight in the search for Bassler until we get to a resolution."

☙

"I am so damn mad right now…"

Tuesday, September 27th, 2011

It had been exactly a month since the Jere Melo shooting and life in Fort Bragg remained far from normal. Bassler's whereabouts and the numerous sightings of him by local folks were daily topics of conversation among the residents, but they were increasingly frustrated that Bassler had not been caught. According to reports in The Press Democrat, folks were locking their doors and windows like never before. Furthermore, and perhaps inevitably, there was the fear of vigilantes taking matters into their own hands.

"We don't understand why it's taking so long. They have professionals coming in from all over," said Heather who owned a shop in the heart of Fort Bragg, but who was afraid to give her last name to Press Democrat reporter Cathy Bussewitz. "Everyone is definitely on edge. Bottom line, we're just scared."

It was not only the general public who were frustrated, perhaps even more so were the family members of Bassler's second victim, Jere Melo. In a Facebook posting on the Press Democrat website, beneath the photograph that showed Bassler outside the cabin in the woods with the rifle in his hands, Melo's son Greg expressed his anger and disappointment in the lack of progress with the comment, "This is the no good S.O.B. that killed my Dad! He's still holding the A.K. I am so damn mad right now you can't even believe it! GET IT DONE!"

Life for many in the community had been put on hold. Those working for the many timber companies were prevented from work in some cases. Hunters, who relied on deer meat to supplement food for the winter, were avoiding going to their usual areas to hunt; and those who were employed by land trusts, just as Matt Coleman was, found their stewardship work temporarily on hold. The woods remained a very dangerous place.

Other changes were also affecting community events. The Noyo River Run, a charity walk and run, had to be postponed, and the Skunk Train, while running every day, frequently made runs with law enforcement officers on board. "Chief Skunk," Robert Pinoli, was insistent, however, that riding the train was safe. "There is more security in the area right now than you can imagine," he said.

Despite their concerns, those in the community continued to keep the searchers well fed, thanks to the many volunteer cooks and food donors, and this was much appreciated by those in the woods. SWAT Commander Jim Van Hagen said, "It is pretty draining out there in the forests, the strain is unforgiving. The community is taking great care of us, feeding us and keeping us healthy."

Meanwhile, not for the first time, Jim Bassler, father of the suspect, expressed his frustrations to the press. These were of a different nature, concerning the lack of help in obtaining mental health treatment for his son after previous run-ins with the law. "This community has been afraid of him for months, but our family has been afraid of him for years. It's frustrating because it wouldn't have taken very much for this not to happen. Now he's getting everyone's attention. Why couldn't I get anyone's attention earlier?"

℘

Many unsolved burglaries—one obvious suspect

Wednesday, September 28th, 2011

Over the previous months there had been a series of unsolved burglaries in the Noyo Basin but now there was a sudden rash of them, and Aaron Bassler was the obvious suspect.

℘

This press release, written by Detective Sergeant Greg Van Patten, appeared on Wednesday, September 28th and Bassler's presence in the area was once again confirmed.

On Sunday, September 25th, 2011, Deputies form the Mendocino County Sheriff's Office were dispatched to a discovered burglary of a vacation cabin located in the 16000 block of Northspur Road, approximately 14.2 miles east of Fort Bragg and approximately 10 miles northwest of Willits along the Noyo Basin watershed. Upon arrival, the deputies discovered the person responsible had forced entry and appeared to have taken food items. At this time investigators are still attempting to obtain an inventory of the cabin's items from the owner who was not present at the scene.

Deputies collected various items from inside the cabin that were believed to be touched by the person who had committed the burglary. These were forwarded to the Mendocino County Sheriff's Office Evidence Bureau for processing of latent prints, which resulted in the recovery of a latent print. This was forwarded to the California Department of Justice (D.O.J.) laboratory in Sacramento for identification purposes.

On Wednesday, September 28th at approximately 1300 hours, a D.O.J. latent print criminalist contacted investigators and confirmed the recovered latent print was that of Aaron Bassler.

It should be noted that on Tuesday, September 20th detectives from the Mendocino County Sheriff's office were dispatched to discovered burglaries at one full-time residence and at two vacation cabins located in the 17000 block of Northspur Road. They learned that the structures were not occupied at the time of the burglaries, forced entry was used, and food items taken. It was also learned that a .22 caliber rifle and a 12-gauage shotgun had been taken during one of the burglaries. Detectives at this time believe Aaron James Bassler to be responsible for those burglaries.

As a result of the preceding information, the Mendocino County Sheriff's Department activated the Reverse 911 system* during the afternoon of September 28th, 2011, to warn the residents of Northspur of Aaron James Bassler's presence.

---

*As explained earlier, the "Reverse 911" call is a method that law enforcement uses to get the word out to the public at times when public safety is impaired. A police dispatcher can send out a message to every listed phone number in any given vicinity. This technique was used in the Noyo Basin during the investigation as a way of informing the public of various developments. All told, about six of these calls were made to alert residents to the dangers on different occasions during the search.

The Apprehension Operation for Aaron James Bassler continues with support from several local, state, and federal law enforcement agencies. The public is encouraged to be vigilant of their surroundings and to report any possible sighting of Aaron James Bassler by calling the Command Post at 707-961-2479 or 911 under emergency situations.

☙

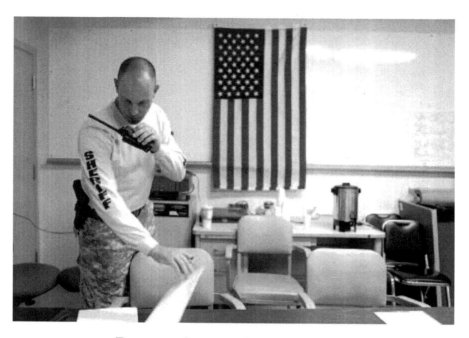

Detective Sergeant Greg Van Patten
Along with Captain Smallcomb, Van Patten was one of the
Mendocino County Sheriff's Office key decision-makers in the
investigation, leading the team of detectives throughout the 36-day
search as well as being previously involved in the Coleman murder
investigation. It was Van Patten who had downloaded the photograph
of Bassler breaking into the cabin on to his laptop computer while at
that scene. In this photograph, Van Patten is shown at work in the
Command Post that was set up in Fort Bragg for the duration of the
investigation.
(Beth Schlanker/ The Press Democrat)

Chapter 7
The Shootout

Photos go "viral"

Thursday, September 29th, 2011

Upon their release, the pictures of Bassler outside the cabin, gun in hand, went "viral" on the Internet and in the following few days they appeared in newspapers all over the country, from the Miami Herald to the New York Times to the L.A. Times. The investigation was even mentioned abroad, in the United Kingdom's Daily Mail national newspaper. "We hadn't expected it to ever be that big," recalls Sheriff Allman.

The article below, written by former Anderson Valley Advertiser reporter Tim Stelloh, appeared in the N.Y. Times on the morning of September 29th, underneath a photograph showing law enforcement officers searching for Bassler after his sighting near his mother's home on September 4th, in the early days of the investigation. The story led off by commenting on the now infamous photograph featuring Bassler breaking into the cabin, which was also shown.

164

FORT BRAGG, Calif.—*In this ominous photograph, Aaron Bassler's pants appear ripped and soiled. With his left hand, he is reaching through a window; in his right hand is a black semiautomatic assault rifle.*

The image, recently snapped by a surveillance camera at a cabin that the police believe was burglarized, is the latest sighting of Mr. Bassler, 35, a local man wanted in connection with two murders here. For the last month, Mr. Bassler, whom relatives describe as mentally ill, has eluded the police by nimbly traversing a large swath of forestland in Mendocino County, an isolated area three hours north of San Francisco.

It is the most intensive manhunt ever undertaken by the sheriff's office, Sheriff Tom Allman said. "Mr. Bassler has lived in this area for close to 30 years," said Sheriff Allman, who presented the photograph at a news conference at the Fort Bragg Police Department on Monday. "We are in his territory. He knows the trails. He knows the bushes. He knows the hiding spots."

The manhunt —which has sent aerial surveillance; K-9 units; and anywhere from 30 to 60 local, state and federal law enforcement officers daily into a 400-square-mile area that is marked by dense brush, towering redwoods and the occasional cabin — has shaken this coastal city of 7,000.

"The victims are gone, but the fact that he's still at large is driving people crazy," said Jim Muto, 64, the owner of V'Canto, a restaurant in Fort Bragg. "They're very uneasy about it."

Officers wearing camouflage are often seen around Fort Bragg, wanted posters hang in gas stations and convenience stores, hikers and hunters have been advised to stay out of the forest, and the city's middle school was locked down after the police received a tip that Mr. Bassler had been seen in the area (he was not found). "People are anxious," said Dan Gjerde, a City Council member. "They're waiting for resolution."

The manhunt began after Jere Melo, a prominent council member and a former two-term mayor, was shot and killed around 10 a.m. on Aug. 27.

That Saturday morning, Mr. Melo, 69, who had also worked as a forester since the 1960s, was walking in the deep woods as he often did for his job, said his son, Greg Melo: after being contacted by a property owner who believed someone was growing marijuana nearby on private timberland, Mr. Melo went to check on it. Once he had GPS coordinates for the garden, he planned on sending them to law enforcement, his son said. He did not find any marijuana. But Mr. Melo, who was accompanied by a friend, soon encountered Mr. Bassler, said Sgt. Gregory Van Patten of the Sheriff's Department.

Mr. Bassler darted from the brush, shouted at the men and then opened fire, Sergeant Van Patten said. Mr. Melo was killed by multiple shots from a high-powered rifle. "He didn't have a chance. He probably died before he hit the ground," Sergeant Van Patten said, adding that it was unclear why Mr. Bassler had attacked the men.

The friend, who knew Mr. Bassler and has not been identified because of safety concerns, escaped after waving down a service vehicle for a train that ferries tourists through the forest, said Mr. Melo's son, who spoke with the friend.

Shortly after, the police connected Mr. Bassler to a second killing: on Aug. 11, Matthew Coleman, 45, also a forester, was found dead outside his car on a rural property more than a dozen miles north of Fort Bragg. Mr. Coleman, who was working in the area, was killed by multiple gunshots. The authorities found Mr. Bassler's DNA at the crime scene.

After Mr. Melo was shot, Mr. Bassler disappeared into the rugged forestland, where, said his father, James Bassler, he had lived for several months. Officers have found possible evidence of Aaron Bassler's movements—burglarized cabins, ammunition caches and burned-out campfires. The authorities believe that a poppy garden that was discovered near where Mr. Melo was killed belonged to Mr. Bassler.

The only other confirmed sighting of Mr. Bassler, besides the photograph, was on Sept. 4, when the police spotted him near his mother's home in Fort Bragg, Sergeant Van Patten said. Though chased by a police dog, Mr. Bassler escaped into thick brush.

Last month's murders came after more than a decade of erratic and strange behavior by Mr. Bassler, his father said. Though Aaron Bassler seemed normal growing up—he played baseball and had a circle of friends—by the mid-1990s he had changed, James Bassler said. "He didn't have any empathy," his father said. "He just sort of flat-lined." He destroyed a vegetable garden while trying to kill gophers, his father said. He drew aliens on the wall. He stole sugar and liquor from his father. Distrustful of his gas stove, he began cooking outside. Though James Bassler does not believe his son has ever gotten a diagnosis or been medicated—because of privacy laws, he has not been able to find out—he believes such behavior indicates mental illness.

A string of arrests dating to the mid-1990s—many of them for minor, nonviolent crimes, his father said—includes one bizarre incident in February 2009: Mr. Bassler was arrested after throwing a bag containing a black jumpsuit with red stars over a wall of the Chinese Consulate in San Francisco, according to a complaint filed in Federal District Court there.

At the news conference, Sheriff Allman said revelations that

Mr. Bassler could be mentally ill had not changed law enforcement's approach to the manhunt. "The tactics are: safely apprehend a man in the woods with a rifle," he said.

ဢ

Later that morning, back in Northern California, Sheriff Allman was in Sacramento in a meeting with five other County Sheriffs being held with the Director of CalFire, discussing Northern California's fire camps. There are 38 such camps in California housing a total of 4,500 State prisoners who are called upon to help in times of flooding, fires, search and rescue operations, multiple vehicle accidents, etc.—an inexpensive labor resource for public safety situations. There are two in the Fort Bragg area, right in the center of the search area, Chamberlain Creek and Parlin Fork, with 120 prisoners in each, supplied by the State Prison system. These inmates are classified as not violent or dangerous. There are no fences, and they are housed in unsecured dorms, maintained by the State. With the search for Bassler taking place all around this area, having such facilities nearby was certainly not ideal and one more thing for law enforcement to take into consideration.

ဢ

Exchange of gunfire

Around lunchtime, Allman was on Highway 5, north of Sacramento, driving back from the meeting to his home in Willits when he received a call on his cell phone from Captain Smallcomb. "Kurt informed me that at about 11:50am there had been an exchange of gunfire between Bassler and the Alameda SWAT team in the woods. He immediately told me that the good news was that none of our guys were hurt and that he wanted to let me know before anyone else told me. That was a relief of course and, from the point of view of the overall investigation, this was the first time since the photograph of Bassler at the cabin [had been] taken over two weeks previously that we had definitive proof that he was still in the area. A spate of recent break-ins at the cabins had certainly led us to strongly believe that he was there and to concentrate our efforts in that vicinity."

After that phone call informing him of the confrontation in the woods, Allman took time to think things over as he drove back to Mendocino County. He concluded that another official press conference was necessary. "I wanted one that night at 6:00pm in Fort Bragg. We did not have these just for the sake of it. Each of them had a specific presentation that needed to be given out. I called the Alameda County Sheriff, Greg Ahern, to touch base and assure him his guys were safe. He already knew and was sending a lieutenant and a team to interview them for the full report that would be necessary. It was a little unusual as they were a team from Alameda County in Mendocino County but abiding by Alameda 'rules' because, in Mendocino, we always do a blood sample after a shooting to show that that the law enforcement officers concerned were clean and sober. Alameda doesn't do that— which is fine of course."

As Allman continued on his journey, a confusing few moments occurred when at 2:15pm the announcement of the press conference was sent out entitled *"Press conference at 6:00pm today—in regards to the apprehension of murder suspect Aaron Bassler."* By 2:28pm this had been changed to *"the attempted apprehension of murder suspect Aaron Bassler"*—a very significant change that was fortunately made after just a short time, otherwise the repercussions might have been very controversial not to mention embarrassing for the Sheriff's Office.

Sheriff Allman continued on his drive back to Fort Bragg, and after passing through Willits, he started along Highway 20, which runs through the Noyo Basin. "I immediately started seeing cop cars and must have passed about 12 and an ambulance at the side of the road over the next few miles before reaching Northspur. Having been to the meeting that morning, I was wearing a suit and driving my personal truck as I continued to drive westbound on Highway 20. I passed more cars past Northspur on my way to Fort Bragg, one every quarter-mile or so, and a couple of more ambulances. I acknowledged many officers by waving at them but did not stop and talk to anyone."

He arrived at the Substation in Fort Bragg and immediately confirmed that everyone was okay. Nobody knew whether or not Bassler had been hit. The CalStar helicopter unit had offered to help in any way but, as Allman recalls, it was not known if they were needed at that time. Meanwhile, he received the full account of what had transpired earlier that day in the woods.

಄

That morning three-man teams had set out for various places in the woods on dirt logging roads that they thought Bassler might use. The team involved in the shootout was comprised of a sergeant and two deputies. They had embedded themselves in the bushes near the junction of two logging roads. They parked their vehicle about 40 yards away, also in the bush.* They had only been at this location for a few

_____

*According to the DA Report: The Alameda County team had arrived at their assigned area in a van. Inside the van were stored two sniper rifles, ammunition, and other law enforcement provisions. While the two deputies were setting up camp at a tactically-advantageous spot

minutes when the SWAT team leader, Sergeant Wilhelm, decided he was not comfortable with how their vehicle was hidden. He put his rifle down, left the team's only radio with the other two men, and headed back down the road with his pistol at his side. He went to the van and began to camouflage it more effectively.

❧

"The Game Changer"

Sheriff Allman picks up the story, "While cutting branches to hide the car, through the bushes he saw a man he was immediately able to positively identify as Aaron Bassler, wearing all black clothing, walking very fast, and carrying what appeared to be an assault-type rifle. The sergeant had no radio and no rifle, just a handgun, which is not a 'tactical weapon.' As a result he chose to not engage the suspect. He waited until Bassler had gone on about 50 yards and then began to follow, moving from tree to tree, keeping a visual on Bassler all the time."

According to the District Attorney's report, based on interviews with the SWAT team members involved, events now began to unfold very quickly: *"As Sgt. Wilhelm stealthily tried to close the gap to get within pistol range, Bassler apparently sensed something wrong, turned and looked directly at Sgt. Wilhelm. Sgt. Wilhelm repeatedly yelled, "Sheriff's Office, get on the ground." Bassler raised his rifle and fired at Sgt. Wilhelm. In response, Sgt. Wilhelm dropped to a crouch, fired eight rounds, and quickly moved into the brush for cover. Likewise, Bassler moved into the woods for apparent*

---

they had scouted out, Sgt. Wilhelm returned alone to camouflage the van, which he had finished just before he first saw Bassler.

cover. Upon hearing at a distance Sgt. Wilhelm's commands being directed at Bassler, his SWAT team partners, Deputies Poole and Shannon, moved in that direction, with Deputy Shannon eventually bringing Sgt. Wilhelm his rifle. Sgt. Wilhelm saw Bassler come back up to the road, where it appeared to Sgt. Wilhelm that Bassler was trying to assume a tactical fighting position. At that time, more rounds were fired in Bassler's direction. In the hope of creating a perimeter, the discovery and engagement of Bassler was also transmitted over the air to all available teams. Not knowing how fast reinforcements would arrive, the three-man team formed a strategic 360-degree cover for one another."

☙

Sheriff Allman continues, "After the brief exchange with the sergeant, Bassler had jumped over a log at the side of the road and disappeared into the dense brush. All three members of the SWAT team went to the side of the road and listened. Nothing was heard. They thought Bassler might have been hit. It was completely silent, no sound of someone moving through the brush. Ten minutes passed, still nothing; no leaves, twigs, or brush being disturbed. Then suddenly, from their right, shots rang out and they were under fire. They returned fire towards where the shots [had come] from. The shooting stopped immediately and Bassler fled into the brush once again. He had flanked around them, creeping silently through the woods, and they had not heard a thing. Ten shots had been exchanged in total, seven by the S.WA.T. team and three by Bassler. It would appear that Bassler was very conscious of not firing too much to save his ammunition. It is also significant that Bassler had missed an open shot. They waited for an hour this time before feeling with enough certainty he was no longer

Alameda SWAT Team Shootout September 29, 2011

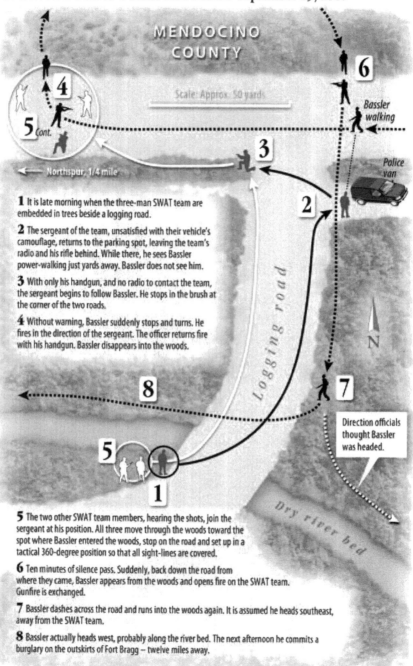

MENDOCINO COUNTY

Scale: Approx. 50 yards

4

5 Cont.

6

Bassler walking

3

2

Police van

← Northspur, 1/4 mile

8

5

1

Logging road

7

Direction officials thought Bassler was headed.

N

Dry river bed

1 It is late morning when the three-man SWAT team are embedded in trees beside a logging road.

2 The sergeant of the team, unsatisfied with their vehicle's camouflage, returns to the parking spot, leaving the team's radio and his rifle behind. While there, he sees Bassler power-walking just yards away. Bassler does not see him.

3 With only his handgun, and no radio to contact the team, the sergeant begins to follow Bassler. He stops in the brush at the corner of the two roads.

4 Without warning, Bassler suddenly stops and turns. He fires in the direction of the sergeant. The officer returns fire with his handgun. Bassler disappears into the woods.

5 The two other SWAT team members, hearing the shots, join the sergeant at his position. All three move through the woods toward the spot where Bassler entered the woods, stop on the road and set up in a tactical 360-degree position so that all sight-lines are covered.

6 Ten minutes of silence pass. Suddenly, back down the road from where they came, Bassler appears from the woods and opens fire on the SWAT team. Gunfire is exchanged.

7 Bassler dashes across the road and runs into the woods again. It is assumed he heads southeast, away from the SWAT team.

8 Bassler actually heads west, probably along the river bed. The next afternoon he commits a burglary on the outskirts of Fort Bragg — twelve miles away.

(Graphic by Loren Doppenberg)

there. Other officers soon arrived and bloodhounds were sent into the deep brush but they could not find any scent."

According to the DA Report, "*As expressed in each of their statements, all three team members were concerned that Bassler's final position of attack—after he had circled around—was very close to where the van had been hidden. Had Bassler discovered and been able to access the van, the officers were reasonably concerned that he might better arm himself and gain further tactical advantage.*"

Following these two brief exchanges of gunfire, Bassler had once again disappeared into the woods and it was not known if he had been hit or not. The members of the Alameda County team were each wearing soft body armor that would not have stopped the rifle rounds fired by Bassler. "In hindsight, one thing we didn't really talk about enough was how athletic Bassler was," recalled Allman. "Given what we had already dealt with in the previous few weeks, we should have reminded ourselves of that fact every day—he was fit, athletic, very determined, and, as I said before, knew those woods better than we did. Although many of the other SWAT teams out there that day had heard the shots ringing out, it is difficult in the Basin to determine from where they are coming. The team under fire had radioed that they were all okay and it was now thought that Bassler was somewhere inside an area about two miles across and three miles long. Smallcomb decided to close in the perimeter a little more. We were pretty convinced he was inside those six square miles but we could not be absolutely one hundred percent sure on this."

☙

Thinking back, Sheriff Allman regarded this contact with Bassler as a very significant event. "People had been asking how much money all this was costing when we could not be one hundred percent sure Bassler was still in the area. The shooting incident with the Alameda SWAT team changed the dynamics of the search in a big way. Simply put, up to that point our search had been defensive in nature, waiting for Bassler to come to us. It was very dangerous to do otherwise and we hoped that the whole thing would end with his surrender. We had thought of ourselves as the hunters-in-waiting, as it were, but clearly Bassler thought otherwise and we were now in fact the hunted. This changed things; in fact, from my perspective, it was the biggest game-changer to date. In my mind, I had still thought that quite possibly Bassler would give himself up and that would be how this all ended. As I have said before, every day I thought we would get him alive. Captain Smallcomb and I had had conversations with the jail commander, Tim Pierce, about jail transportation, the press issues with regards to this, and Bassler's isolation when inside the jail. I had said that when we get Bassler, his move to the jail must be done as quickly as possible. However, all along, the one thing we constantly said was that Aaron Bassler [would] get to choose how this is ultimately resolved.

"The incident with the Alameda SWAT team proved to us that we were conducting the right kind of search operation, and that we were in the correct area. Most importantly nobody was hurt and we had now had three sightings and we would continue to do what we were doing. However, as I just mentioned, we said many times that Bassler would be the one who decided how this all would end. The photograph at the cabin and now the contact with the Alameda SWAT team confirmed this.

"Before the press conference that evening, I talked to the three SWAT team guys involved—the sergeant and two deputies. Their whole team was one of the best I have ever come in contact with. In fact each year they host a contest called 'Urban Shield' in which various teams compete in a number of tasks to test their abilities as SWAT teams. The Alameda team was tactically brilliant for an urban setting. This was not an urban setting and after the incident that day I felt they would not be going into the woods again. I don't believe they were totally in agreement with our tactics of finding a spot and waiting for Bassler. I could be mistaken. Regardless, everyone must follow the operational plan and there could be no place for any lone rangers or loose cannons. As it turned out, the guys from Alameda left the next day. Their attitude towards the case had changed but their professionalism could not be questioned. They obviously felt they could no longer help although we certainly appreciated them helping as they did.

"Meanwhile, by this time, the whole investigation was teaching us that our Sheriff's Office could handle anything that was thrown at us. We were the nucleus of the investigation, the main coordinators of everything, and with help from other agencies this would soon end. The U.S. Marshal's plan was the one we had agreed to follow, and when each new SWAT team arrived the plan was made clear to them and they were expected to follow it. One of our Sheriff's Office guys would go through this with them—the background of the case, Bassler, the terrain, the communications, etc. In fact, when the Sacramento SWAT team arrived the next day, the Alameda guys also met with them, and informed them of what they had experienced the day before. They heard how this Aaron Bassler guy wanted to kill people like them— that certainly got their attention."

め

Second Press Conference
Following the shootout with the Alameda SWAT team, Sheriff
Allman held another press conference at which he expressed law
enforcement's belief that Bassler was within a six-square mile area.
On the left, Alameda SWAT Captain Dave Brady. On the right, US
Marshal Don O'Keefe.
(Photo courtesy of The Press Democrat)

With a Bay Area SWAT team now directly affected by the Bassler
case, the Bay Area news media were present in large numbers as the press
conference began at 6:00pm that evening. Sheriff Allman informed the
audience in attendance about the events of that morning and reiterated
that he was fairly confident that Bassler was still in a six square mile area
that Captain Smallcomb and his search teams had secured. The search
area had once been over 400 square miles. He maintained that they
were determined to bring in Bassler safely but acknowledged that this
latest incident was something of a surprise (having previously stated
that officers didn't think Bassler was trying to engage law enforcement).
He also noted that even though they were confident they had him
surrounded; it was a hard thing to maintain in the dense woods. "We
believe we've really and truly circled him and there are not too many

of our resources outside that area at this point. Tomorrow may bring a resolution—but I've said that for 34 days." (Later, Allman reflected on this comment—"Nobody laughed but, looking back, it was quite an amusing—and certainly self-critical—thing to say, but in the context of that meeting it was appropriate and it preempted anyone else saying it.")

That evening, after nightfall, a plan was discussed to send a team to the shooting scene and use blood-detecting lights to search for any sign that Bassler may have been wounded. But in the end this was not done, and instead it was decided to use the bloodhounds first thing in the morning. Meanwhile, outside the Fort Bragg Police department that night, Mayor Dave Turner let out a big sigh when asked if he was disappointed that Bassler remained at large. "I thought it was going to end today. They've basically flushed him out to where he felt he had to take action. I'm so glad nobody got hurt."

∽

"Bassler had escaped again"

Friday, September 30th, 2011

At daybreak on Friday, the bloodhounds had been sent out to locate any evidence to indicate whether or not Bassler had been injured in the gunfire with the Alameda SWAT team. Nothing was found. Over the next few hours many citizens around the North Coast and beyond were greeted by the startling headline "Shots exchanged in woods" on the front page of the Press Democrat, underneath which was a photograph of Officer Joe Hernandez and his bloodhound Willow of the Pomona

Police Department standing guard on the Skunk Train tracks at the Northspur station deep in the woods. The article, written by reporters Julie Johnson and Glenda Anderson, described how the SWAT team members had fired a total of seven shots at Bassler but it was not clear if Bassler had been hit. Sheriff Allman was quoted as saying, "We were very lucky that this situation was as it was, and no law enforcement officers were injured. We are somewhat hampered in the immediate search not only because of the dense brush but also because now he is shooting at the men with a rifle."

The article mentioned that the Alameda SWAT team had undergone interviews about the encounter and were all doing fine. They were all "highly trained" but their identities were not given. As for Bassler, Sheriff Allman informed the press that he was now wearing black clothing, obviously hidden somewhere previously, and this was apparently his regular M.O., according to people who knew him. Allman went on to say that enough of a perimeter around the area was now covered that they would know if Bassler had left the vicinity. Once again, the Sheriff emphasized the denseness of the forests, repeating that the heat-sensing equipment could not even detect officers whose positions were known and this equipment was no longer being used.

The newspaper report also mentioned that at one of the recently burglarized homes, those from which Bassler had been able to get food and more arms, it was believed Bassler was inside when the owner arrived. According to a law enforcement source, the owner, concerned about a break-in, was armed but then put his gun on a table after entering. He left the room but heard the front door close and when he returned to the room the gun was missing from the table.

Sheriff Allman recalls, "I had walked into the dispatch office the morning after the Alameda shootout with Bassler and asked the dispatcher, Tonya Van Camp, if anything else had happened the previous night. She told me that the drunken neighbor had been firing shots into the night once again. I said 'What?' Apparently, a man who lived in a remote cabin near the shooting scene of the previous day was in the habit of getting drunk and on several recent nights he had been yelling out into the woods and shooting his gun into the night. It turned out we had spoken to him about this but nothing [had been] done about it. Believing his gun had been stolen on this occasion, he called law enforcement and we made a major response to this call. He was intoxicated and found his gun behind the stove the next morning. Following the shooting incident involving the Alameda SWAT another 'Reverse 911' message had been sent out to the community warning them to be diligent and that public safety was a concern in the area. It turned out that the gentleman in the cabin had received the call and that was his reaction to it. This was a distraction we really could have done without at that point and it was a very expensive 911 call. We were dealing with more public safety issues than just Aaron Bassler with people like this out there in the woods. I don't believe anyone was around when Bassler broke into that particular cabin."

☙

The previous day, Sacramento County Sheriff Scott R. Jones made the decision to dispatch members of his SWAT team to provide mutual aid to Sheriff Allman to assist in the apprehension of a homicide suspect in the woods east of Fort Bragg. The Sacramento County team members arrived early in the morning hours of September 30, 2011. This team was briefed by Mendocino County law enforcement, U.S. Marshals, and the Alameda County personnel who had been involved in the shootout with Bassler the day before on the underlying evidence developed to date on the Coleman murder, the Melo murder, Bassler's tactics observed by Chaney during Chaney's death-defying escape, that Bassler was armed with a high-powered rifle with significant quantities of ammunition, of Bassler's familiarity with the area and terrain, Bassler's knowledge of military tactics, the descriptions and photographs of Bassler, and his tactics when engaged by the Alameda County apprehension team the previous morning.

Sheriff Allman vividly remembers the arrival of the 27 members of the Sacramento SWAT team. "They gathered in the Fort Bragg sally port, a secure area where prisoners are kept, and they were briefed primarily by the Alameda guys who had been shot at the previous day and by their commander. This team was now leaving the investigation. I went in, introduced myself, and said I wanted two minutes of their time. I thanked them and said we would take care of their needs. I went on to advise them to each think back to their time in the police academy and remember what the instructor talked about regarding 'Tennessee v Garner.' This is a Supreme Court case that resulted in the premise that an officer 'may use deadly force only to prevent escape if the officer has probable cause to believe that the suspect poses a significant threat of death or serious physical injury to the officer or others.' It is a very basic premise in law enforcement and in this situation we relied upon it. I went on to say, 'If you believe an arrest can be made without any shooting, then do it. If you believe it cannot, then base your action on your education.' I emphasized that this was not training; that the man in the woods was very dangerous and just yesterday he had shot at the guys they were replacing out there. I told them that Bassler would just as soon shoot you as look at you. The team now understood, particularly some of the younger ones who were perhaps not sure before. I then watched them as they listened to one of the Alameda guys talk about what had happened the day before. Here were 27 very experienced and highly trained SWAT team guys—all hanging on to his every word."

☙

Sheriff Allman comments on events to that point, "The citizens of Fort Bragg and the Noyo Basin had their quality of life significantly diminished for the whole period of this investigation in many ways. On top of that, deer-hunting season was affected, the tourist trade severely hit, and the vacation cabins empty. People made the right choice to stay away; I would have done the same in their position."

Detective Sergeant Van Patten was quoted as saying following the clash with the Alameda SWAT team, "I hate to say it, but Aaron Bassler has control. He's dictating where this goes." Van Patten's team was suited up in camouflage, bulletproof vests, and bug spray as they prepared to head into the woods on Friday afternoon to search for evidence of the encounter, including bullet casings. However, with the suspect known to ambush civilians, processing the scene required an additional team of about 30 officers to secure and guard the area so that detectives could collect evidence and search for clues without fear of being shot. "It's dangerous, but we have to get in before we lose any evidence," Van Patten added. "It's no secret that Bassler has the advantage here."

It was further reported that Melo's son, Greg, reached in Oregon, was now of the opinion that the search for Bassler was nearing its conclusion and that it was doubtful if that end would arrive without bloodshed. "The first language he decided to speak to them with was gunfire, and they spoke his language right back," said Melo Jr., referring to Thursday's shootout. "And that's appropriate." He went on to say that it would be difficult to endure a trial if Bassler was taken alive.

"My dad didn't get a trial. He's dead. I think there probably would be a certain form of justice if the same thing happened to Mr. Bassler that happened to my dad."

❦

On Friday afternoon, at about 4:30pm, a homeowner just outside Fort Bragg reported a break-in at his auto shop located on his property behind his house. It was reported that the workshop had been robbed of food, ammunition, boots, and other survival gear. This was a key break in the search according to Sheriff Allman. "The shop was only about four miles east of Fort Bragg, many miles from our main search area, but the break-in had Bassler's name all over it—door kicked in, and ammunition, food, beer, two compasses, matches, and size 12 boots were all missing. This burglary indicated that Bassler had slipped, undetected, outside the perimeter we had formed—one that we were convinced could not be breached. Investigators were immediately sent into the area and a team of bloodhounds moved into the surrounding area. These included Willow and her handler, Joe Hernandez, from the Pomona City Police Department in L.A. County. We had gone through the Office of Emergency Services to find her and she had been working with us for about three weeks or so at this point. She was the nearest bloodhound we could get that would suit this case because the search and rescue volunteers who own most bloodhounds are unarmed, but in this situation we definitely needed a dog handled by someone who could carry a gun. Anyway, soon Willow had picked up Bassler's scent and led searchers to a trail leading into the woods and it prompted us to dispatch a highly trained unit from the newly arrived Sacramento County Sheriff's SWAT team to the area."

This wooded area was a little east of where the burglary had occurred, and coincidentally was owned by Campbell Hawthorne Timber, Jere Melo's employers. Significantly, this latest search area was nearly 13 miles to the west of the previous search area—the six square mile stretch east and west of the community of Northspur that lies on the Skunk Train rail tracks, and in which the Alameda SWAT team had come across Bassler. This was thought to have been fully secured but Bassler had eluded law enforcement once again.

ↅ

Allman recalls, "It appeared that Bassler had escaped again. He managed to sneak outside the area we thought we had contained, probably very quickly after the confrontation with the Alameda SWAT team. He had slipped between many other teams, probably not even waiting for nightfall before making his move and starting on a long trek through the woods, heading west towards the outskirts of Fort Bragg. Meanwhile, as they had been doing every day in the search so far, that Friday afternoon Captain Smallcomb and the commanders of the various SWAT teams were already working on the plans for the following day so that at 6:00am, when the teams arrived for duty, these plans would be handed out to them and copies would be placed at the command center so we were all coordinated. Anyway, as I said, that day the plans were already in the making when news of this latest burglary came in. When information reached Smallcomb about the bloodhound following Bassler's fresh scent into this new area, he believed it was necessary to make a significant change in the plans. He felt we should move the vast majority of our resources to this area. This was based on facts and a very strong and educated hunch. I told Smallcomb that

Willow and Officer Hernandez

Bloodhound Willow, along with handler Joe Hernandez from the Pomona, California, Police Department, joined fellow law enforcement personnel as they intensified their search for Aaron Bassler a day after the double-murder suspect's shootout with the Alameda County SWAT team.

(Kent Porter/ The Press Democrat)

I would support him if he thought it was the right thing to do. His insights on the case at this point in time were second to no one.

"You could say we were putting all of our eggs in one basket by moving everyone away from the Northspur area, to a new location many miles away based on a bloodhound's work. A tremendously risky decision? Some might think that, but I'd say it was a very smart tactical decision by Smallcomb and, thanks to the critical role of Willow, that Friday evening saw some very experienced SWAT team members hot on Bassler's freshly made trail."

Some months later Sheriff Allman reflected on his reaction if,

Sac SWAT team member

Sacramento County Sheriff's Office SWAT team member Jeff Massagli
relaxes in the shade of a tree before being deployed from the staging
area at the Northspur train station. Later in the day all teams were
moved to the woods on the outskirts of Fort Bragg where bloodhound
Willow had tracked Bassler on Friday evening.
(Christopher Chung/ The Press Democrat)

having moved virtually all of their resources over to this new search
area, there had been a shooting or incident, or even another burglary,
involving Bassler the next day back in the six-square-mile area they
had been concentrating on previously. "Oh, my God, that would have
been difficult. I cannot imagine what the response would have been,
and our decision would have certainly been second-guessed by many.
However, I will defend the move and must stress that it was a very
informed decision. Having said that, given Bassler's abilities in the
woods, it was not one that came with a hundred percent guarantee of
success—very little did out there."

Chapter 8
The Final Confrontation

The 36th Day

Saturday, October 1st, 2011

Sheriff Allman was due to attend the funeral of his good friend, John Bogner, in Ukiah at 1:00pm. Bogner was a local realtor who had committed suicide a month earlier. He was a well-known local man and a huge attendance was expected. "He and I were both in the Rotary Club, had both performed as auctioneers at fund-raisers, and were often in the same circles. I had arranged to go and sit alongside District Attorney Eyster, and I was dressed up to go when at the last minute I felt that I just had to be out in Fort Bragg and could not go to the memorial. I just felt I needed to be there out on the Coast. I called the DA and told him what I had decided to do and he fully understood. I changed into civilian clothes and drove my own truck out to the Coast on Highway 20. I remember thinking that just two days earlier, following the shooting incident on the 29th of September when Bassler had shot at the Alameda County SWAT team, on that same road there had been perhaps as many as 20 law enforcement vehicles. There were none on this day."

Sacramento SWAT team
The newly arrived SWAT team grabs some rest after their first
experience of searching the woods for Aaron Bassler on Friday
afternoon.
(Christopher Chung/ The Press Democrat)

☙

That morning's front-page headline of the Press Democrat, under
the usual lead-in line "Fort Bragg Manhunt," quoted in large letters
Detective Sergeant Greg Van Patten as saying, "Bassler has advantage."
This was accompanied by a sub-headline emphasizing the point
"Dozens of officers tighten perimeter in forest after gun battle with
double-murder suspect; authorities say fugitive 'dictating where this
goes.'" Inside the front section was a photograph showing three of the
newly arrived Sacramento SWAT team taking a break after searching
for Bassler in the woods.

Reporters Julie Johnson and Mary Callahan went on to explain how Bassler was believed to be within a perimeter of armed and camouflaged officers but no evidence had been found to suggest that he had been hit in the shootout with Alameda SWAT team on Friday. That incident had certainly added to the increasing doubts that Bassler would be taken alive and, given what would transpire later in the day, the headline stating that Bassler had the "advantage" turned out to be somewhat ironic to say the least.

The DA's Report set the scene for the day's events: *On the morning of Saturday, October 1, 2011, the Sacramento County Sheriff SWAT team members, along with other law enforcement personnel, were assigned to three-man teams and each team assigned to pre-selected observations posts along travel routes that the operations commander believed Bassler may still be using, based on the locations of recent burglaries and canine alerts. Grouped as one team, Sacramento County Deputies Prehoda, Esty, and Owens were transported by Mendocino County law enforcement personnel after a 7am briefing to their assigned area at Sherwood Road and Mud Springs Road, arriving between 8:30 and 9am. Having quickly developed a defensible observation post, the men commenced 360-degree observation coverage from that post. As the team members would be looking in different directions, non-verbal signals were agreed-upon should one of the team observe the suspect. Following Bassler's fire fight with and escape from the Alameda County team, the Sacramento County team was concerned that any audible signal might be heard by Bassler, allowing him to immediately fire on their position and/or escape again into the woods. Of special concern to the Sacramento County team, as well as the other teams, was the report from the Alameda County team who had been engaged by Bassler that he had opted to flank, re-engage and fire on the Alameda County team with the knowledge that they were law enforcement officers, instead of disengaging and using his honed survivalist skills to disappear into the woods.*

Sheriff Allman inevitably recalls the day vividly—it is one he will never forget. "Earlier that morning we had decided to send in a highly trained SWAT unit from Sacramento to the wooded area within a mile or so from where the burglary had taken place the night before. The bloodhound had picked up Bassler's scent and we thought he was now in this area, many miles from where we had been looking in recent days. Meanwhile, I arrived at the Substation in Fort Bragg at around 11:00am and everybody was doing the things they had been doing for a few weeks now—watching camera footage, studying old pictures, the dispatcher being kept busy. That was Ember Koski, and Captain Small-comb was there too, as was a volunteer, a retired Captain from CalFire, Brian Kornagay, who had been a big help with the logistics so far. Brian told me that they were going to fly [in] a new dog to help in the search but the weather was not good at that time out on the Coast. They needed a weather forecast. I used my cell phone to call a pilot friend of mine in Willits—they would know. There was no answer, so I called the Willits Police Department.

"They were just telling me that it was quite clear inland, where they were situated, when suddenly the radio in the room crackled— 'C.P. (Command Post) Sierra Three—target down.' Everybody in the room just stopped what they were doing. We had been waiting for such a message for six weeks. None of us had really discussed how such a notification was going to be made. No room has ever been so quiet in my life. 'Sierra Three' was one of the several three-man patrols of Sacramento SWAT team officers, stationed out in the woods, not far east of Fort Bragg where the previous afternoon's burglary had taken place, waiting for a sight[ing] of Bassler. Nobody in the room had heard it exactly, and so finally I said, 'What did he say?' Our dispatcher Ember

Koski spoke into the radio, 'Sierra Three, C.P.—10/9,' which means 'Repeat.' There was no response. She repeated it again. The reply came back, 'C.P., Sierra Three—target down.' Ember asked about medical assistance and the reply was, 'Medical not needed.' This told us that death was confirmed. We then confirmed that all three team members were okay and, although we had a map showing us where 'Sierra 3' [was] supposed to be, we checked on their location. They confirmed that they were there—about half a mile from where the burglary had taken place the evening before, although they were in thick woods and not on an easily accessible road. At that point, Kurt Smallcomb and I did something not easy for either of us—we hugged!

☙

"It was a very emotional few minutes. My first thought was 'Is it really over—just like that?' To whatever conclusion this was going to have, we weren't sure how we would react. 'Are the guys okay?' was repeated a few times but, after about a minute or so, and once we knew they were, we could relax and it was handshakes all around.

"Shortly thereafter I called my assistant, Liz Evangelatos, and told her that it was very important for her to go to the office and prepare a press release to everyone involved. This was sent out later, at about 1:00pm. The wording was to be very specific, that Aaron Bassler had been 'located' and there [would] be a press conference at 6:00pm that evening. That was it. If I had said 'shot,' 'dead,' or words to that effect, so many questions would have been posed and we needed time to assess the situation and review the facts of what had transpired. I knew what I was doing by saying 'located,' and it proved to be the right decision given all that had to be done before that 6:00pm press conference.

"About 10 minutes later I called Madeleine Melo and said, 'Madeleine, it's over; he's been killed.' There was a long pause during which I could detect a catch in her voice before she simply said, 'Thank you.' I told her I'd see her later that afternoon.

"The next call I made was to Congressman Mike Thompson who had been very instrumental in getting a number of federal resources for us throughout the investigation, including the U.S. Marshals Service, that played a major role, and a Special Operations Group from New Orleans. He was a very good resource to have and he was also a friend of Jere Melo. He has a son who is a deputy with the Napa County Sheriff's Office, and Mike and I had talked regularly throughout this case, perhaps twice a week, as I kept him informed of major developments.

"My next duty was to call Sacramento County Sheriff Scott Jones and inform him what had happened—it was his guys who were on the SWAT team who had been at the scene. I got his voice mail. I wanted him to hear the news from me personally and not in any other way. I left a message—'Call me a.s.a.p.—your guys are okay; the situation has been resolved.' A few minutes later he returned my call and I told him that his guys were fine, they had been involved in the shooting, and that the suspect had been killed. I also told him that there would be a press conference at 6:00pm [here] in Fort Bragg if he wanted to attend. He thanked me and said he would come. I assured him that we would take care of his guys in the meantime. In shooting situations, my experience is that often the law enforcement officer feels like a suspect. We would not allow this to happen and planned to get the SWAT team out of the woods and back to their hotel where they could meet with their representatives.

"I called the county C.E.O., Carmel Angelo, and told her everything that had happened, and informed her of the press conference also. I also told her I would invite the Supervisor Chair, Kendall Smith, not just because of the position she held but also because the two murder victims were residents of her particular constituency. I also said the Mayor would be invited—it is very important to public morale that such people attend these events.

"My final call before leaving the Substation was to my wife. I was in jeans and a flannel shirt and, after telling her what had happened and that I had called a press conference for 6:00pm, I asked that she sort out a suit for me to wear and I would arrange for someone to come and pick it up. For such a serious and major event I had to wear something other than jeans and flannel shirt."

ᕫᕫ

Allman had made a decision at that point that he was not going to have a press conference until Captain Smallcomb and he knew all of the facts. "It was now about noon and, along with Smallcomb and U.S. Marshal Mike McCloud, we drove a Sheriff's Office truck out to the scene. As we passed Aaron Bassler's mother's house all three of us stared across. There was no activity and why should there be? Hardly anybody knew what had happened and certainly no members of the public apart from Madeleine Melo. There was a little confusion as to where the scene actually was, deep in the woods on a logging trail, and so a journey that should normally take 20 minutes actually took us about twice that. It was about 13 miles from where the exchange of gunfire had taken place with the Alameda SWAT team two days earlier, not far from the auto shop burglary and where the bloodhound had picked up his scent the evening before. Later, I reflected that this 'big break' in the case was not as a result of some FBI tactical suggestion, not from a SWAT team meeting and subsequent action, but from a regular patrol field sergeant doing his job, investigating a local burglary and deciding that this might be something important and calling for the bloodhounds before the crime scene was disturbed in any way by investigators looking for prints and evidence. It was brilliant—a police officer's instincts and a trained bloodhound's natural ability had led us to Bassler less than a day later.

∼

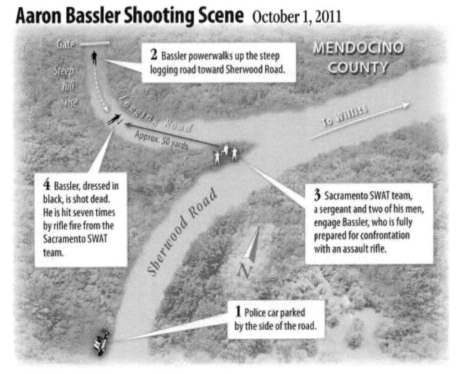

Aaron Bassler Shooting Scene October 1, 2011

Gate

Steep hill rise

2 Bassler powerwalks up the steep logging road toward Sherwood Road.

MENDOCINO COUNTY

Logging Road

Approx. 50 yards

To Willits

4 Bassler, dressed in black, is shot dead. He is hit seven times by rifle fire from the Sacramento SWAT team.

Sherwood Road

3 Sacramento SWAT team, a sergeant and two of his men, engage Bassler, who is fully prepared for confrontation with an assault rifle.

N

1 Police car parked by the side of the road.

(Graphic by Loren Doppenberg)

"On arriving near the scene I walked up to the deputy who had already put crime scene tape across the logging road. I asked him how he was and where the SWAT team was situated. He pointed up the hill and that was when I saw the body, lying in the middle of the 12-foot wide logging road about 50 yards up a very steep hill. The body, facedown, was dressed all in black—sweatpants and jacket, with a rifle alongside and a backpack. The SWAT team was a further 50 yards beyond the body. We walked up the road, on the upper side so as not to disturb where the suspect had walked, and stopped briefly and looked at the body. There was a lot of blood, particularly around the head area. I also noticed that the backpack was full and wondered if there was anything in there from the burglary he had committed the night before. It transpired that there were more of the eight of spades playing cards in the backpack—a mystery we never did solve. The pack also appeared to have been completely blacked out with a Sharpie felt-tip pen. It was originally in camouflage colors but that was all covered over by the black ink. It must have taken him hours and hours. It matched his black outfit—he looked like some terrorist. We later learned that the backpack contained a cut-down .22 rifle taken from the burglary in Northspur and a telescopic lens. He also had a fanny pack full of ammunition. Some ammunition was found later on the woods under some tree roots and I assume there is more ammo and some foodstuffs still out there somewhere.

"We stood there for maybe 20 seconds. It spoke for itself. Our mood was certainly not celebratory or giddy; we were very matter-of-fact and I personally felt no sense of victory. This was simply the 36th day of the manhunt and it would be handled in the same methodical way everything else had been done to that point."

Allman, Smallcomb, and McCloud continued up the steep hill and soon reached the three Sacramento SWAT team officers—a sergeant and two of his men. "We all shook hands and when we asked if they were okay, they told us they were fine. I asked them if they had called their wives and they had. In situations like this you do not want wives and loved ones to hear about a shooting or some sort of engagement without hearing that their husbands were fine. Also, law enforcement officers are entitled to full legal representation after a shooting and I made sure each of them had contacted their representatives on this."

At this point, Sheriff Allman asked the few deputies now around, plus the three SWAT team members, if anyone had used their cell phones to take any pictures of the dead body. "They looked at me and I said, 'I don't want these photographs on the Internet and I would appreciate it that if you took photos to now delete them.' I certainly did not want this to go viral on the Internet and we would get enough pictures of the crime scene by the investigators who were on their way and would do a complete documentation. Two of the officers present walked away and were looking at their phones. I assumed that they deleted any pictures they had taken at that time. As far as I knew everything was deleted. I did not check their phones as I believed they had complied with my request."

Allman asked the men to show and describe to him what had happened. "They had been there for about one-and-a half hours, settled in a redwood grove 'saddle' about 10 feet by 6 feet, in the middle of six second growth redwood trees, where the old growth tree had originally been. It was on the side of the road, about 40 yards up the hill from a bend in the road. They each had a backpack containing energy drinks and a granola bar. The decision to pick that spot had been made that morning as a possible spot where Bassler might walk nearby.

"We had been told by the Alameda SWAT who had confronted Bassler two days earlier, that he power-walked and so at about 12:20pm, when one of the SWAT guys caught a glimpse of someone marching up the hill around the bend, he immediately nudged the other two with his foot. There was no verbal communication. The suspect then appeared in full view in the middle of the road, walking very quickly uphill, a Norinco SKS 7.62-caliber assault rifle in his hand.

"He not only was carrying this in his right hand, he was completely ready to engage," Allman said. "His hand was on the handle and his right index finger was in an offensive tactical position—his rifle in his right hand, finger alongside the trigger. The officers did not hesitate. The first shot hit Bassler and he dropped to his knee and started to raise his rifle up towards their location. They fired 11 more shots in quick succession from their Colt M-4 .223 caliber weapons, with a total of 7 hitting Bassler in the upper torso. The suspect fell face down on the road. He died almost immediately. They watched for a full minute—there was no movement. They radioed in that the 'target was down' and then approached the body. They saw that the wounds were signs of

Bassler weapon
The weapon used by Aaron Bassler—a Norinco Mak 90 Assault Rifle

obvious death. They radioed again that there was no need for medical assistance.

಄

"In the time it took us to get to the scene I'm sure the guys could have come up with a different story had they wanted to—about how he had gone for his gun, etc. They told me the truth. That is what the public expects from me and from law enforcement officers. I had no reason to doubt them at all. One of the SWAT team guys pointed out to me a spot in the ground where the end of a rifle barrel had been stuck into the ground—this had happened when Bassler went down to one knee. Like everyone else involved with the investigation, I had been saying for weeks that I hoped it would end soon, but one of my biggest personal fears, one that I had dealt with many times over the previous month or so, was that I did not want to deliver a flag to the widow and children of a slain Deputy Sheriff or police officer and say 'I am sorry.' I felt a huge sense of relief."

಄

The DA's Report described the sequence of events thus:

> Rotating positions throughout the morning, around 12:30 Deputy Owens saw a white male dressed in all black "walking with a purpose," as had been described by the Alameda County team. Deputy Owens characterized the man as moving so fast that he seemed to "explode out of the gulch." The man was armed with a rifle at the ready. The

man was immediately recognized as Aaron James Bassler. Without giving a verbal warning,* Deputy Owens fired on Bassler. Despite believing that his shot had hit Bassler "center mass," Deputy Owens recounted that Bassler did not go down notwithstanding what Deputy Owens believed to be a hit. Bassler also did not release his grip on his rifle. Believing there still to be a risk, Deputy Owens fired again, joined now by the other two team members. Having a magazine filled to its capacity of 30 rounds, Deputy Owens fired a total of six shots, stopping when he perceived no further risk to himself and others. Having a magazine filled to its capacity of 30 rounds, Deputy Prehoda fired a total of three shots, stopping when he perceived no further risk to himself and others. Having a magazine filled to its capacity of 30

---

*Just as any law enforcement officer lacks authority under the law to use deadly force against a suspect who has affirmatively indicated an intent to surrender and does not pose an immediate threat of serious harm to anybody, a law enforcement officer is nevertheless well within the breadth and scope of the law, proper police procedure, and tactical response to fire on a well-armed individual at first opportunity who presents as a high risk fugitive, who has answered an earlier opportunity to surrender to law enforcement with a double engagement and gunfire, and who continues to pose a life-threatening risk as an armed, escaping fugitive. As mentioned elsewhere herein, after being told face-to-face by at least one person that he was a wanted man, Bassler ignored literally weeks of self-surrender opportunities and, instead, escalated tensions in the woods by focusing lethal attacks on members of an apprehension team. Again, the more specific and applicable criteria in this case are the deadly force criteria announced by the Supreme Court in Tennessee v Garner. In Garner, the Supreme Court held that: "Where the officer has probable cause to believe that the suspect poses a threat of serious physical harm, either to the officer or to others, it is not constitutionally unreasonable to prevent escape by using deadly force." The comments of one of the Sacramento County deputies, one who only secondarily engaged, are instructive. Had he been the deputy to first see the suspect fast approaching armed with a rifle with a high capacity magazine, Sacramento County Sheriff's Deputy Esty explained to DA investigators that he would have also fired on the suspect without announcing his presence because when Jere Melo tried to communicate with Bassler, Melo was immediately shot and killed. When Alameda County thereafter identified themselves as law enforcement, Bassler responded by firing on the sergeant, slipping into the brush to flank the team, and then coming out of hiding to again fire on all three team members. Had Bassler again escaped, there was concern on the part of at least Deputy Esty that Bassler would be a lethal threat to the other unengaged law enforcement officers in other observation posts spread throughout the area whom he may be able to take by surprise, especially given Bassler's recognized ability to move silently through the woods.

rounds, Deputy Esty fired a total of three rounds, stopping when he perceived no further risk to himself and others. A total of twelve shots were fired by the apprehension team as a whole. According to the results of the autopsy performed on October 4, 2011 in Ukiah, the pathologist was able to determine that seven of the 12 shots fired hit the deceased causing his death. The cause of death was determined to be multiple gunshots.

❦

Sheriff Allman recalls, "I called the District Attorney from the scene and updated him on everything that had happened, informing him that it appeared we had had a 'clean' shooting with no problems. His investigative team was on its way and he told me that if I needed something to just let him know. Then, just as I was leaving the scene, a deputy appeared and told me he had my suit in his car. I got that from him, thanked him, and headed for our vehicle."

The scene would now be processed by the Mendocino County Sheriff's Office and the District Attorney's Office, and at 1:00pm Sheriff Allman left with Marshal McCloud to go to the Melo home. "Again we passed the home of Bassler's mother and still there was no activity there. We arrived at Madeleine Melo's and by this time several family members had joined her. I told her what had happened in more detail and asked that if the opportunity arose to meet the Sacramento deputies who were involved in the shooting would she like to do that. 'Of course,' she said."

Sheriff Allman left the Melo house and by 2:30pm had returned to his office at the Substation to write up his notes in preparation for the upcoming press conference. "I needed time to get ready for this very

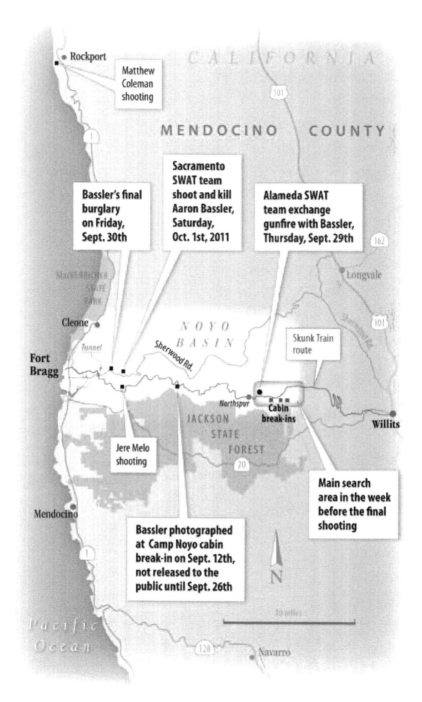

Noyo Basin—The Final Three Days
(Graphic by Loren Doppenberg)

important press conference. I would need to have my game face on and be fully prepared. The rumors had started to spread and the Sacramento Bee had contacted us and said that the Sacramento Sheriff Scott Jones had told them Bassler was dead. The local press had got hold of this too and said that the Sacramento Bee had confirmed the death of Aaron Bassler. The Santa Rosa Press Democrat was reporting on their website that Aaron Bassler had been killed by the Sacramento SWAT team. As I mentioned earlier we were very specific about the announcement of the press conference. It said specifically—'Murder suspect Aaron Bassler has been located.' Kurt Smallcomb and I had agreed upon our use of the word 'located' and stuck with that, informing people that the full story would be told at 6:00pm. We even heard one rumor that Bassler had committed suicide. 'You'll get everything at 6:00pm' was my statement."

"If I had to do it again I would make the same decision. Once Kurt Smallcomb and I had made that decision we were going to stick with it. It was a great help and it gave me the time I needed to prepare for the conference and it was imperative that I did not misspeak. We had chosen 6:00pm because the Bay Area news' folks who had been following the story needed time to get up to Fort Bragg and I knew that Sheriff Scott Jones was also trying to get there from Sacramento."

☙

That Sunday afternoon was very cloudy, and while it was not raining it was very damp and there was lots of moisture on the road. As Sheriff Allman prepared for the press conference news came in that four wrecks had taken place on Highway 20 between Willits and Fort Bragg. "I was concerned. I wanted to make sure everyone got there safely—after all, it was over. Fort Bragg Police Chief Scott Mayberry had designated the Emergency Operations Center (E.O.C.) room for the conference and there were about 40 comfortable chairs in there. The Sheriff's Office podium, used at previous press conferences, was still there also, so it was very convenient. The rumors continued to spread—maybe Melo's relatives told some people, perhaps cops' wives had spoken to family and friends; I heard that some U.S. Marshals were in Starbucks talking about it. That was all fine. I was not bothered by anyone between 4:00pm and 6:00pm and could do what I had to do.

"At about 5:15pm I was almost ready when I heard that the helicopter carrying Sheriff Jones could only get as far as Willits due to the weather conditions that had become very foggy further out towards where we were on the Coast. I instructed the dispatcher to request that a deputy go to the airport in Willits—Brooktrails actually, and pick up Jones, and to drive carefully. Meanwhile, I called in Lt. Greg Stefani of the local Sheriff's office and read to him what I had prepared. He is a very knowledgeable officer, a case law trivia expert. I went over Garner v Tennessee with him. This landmark case states that an officer 'may use deadly force only to prevent escape if the officer has probable cause to believe that the suspect poses a significant threat of death or serious physical injury to the officer or others.' The lieutenant confirmed everything I thought but I wanted to hear it from him—he knows that stuff as well as anyone. He suggested a few small changes, for which I was very appreciative, and we came up with the final draft. Among the many things that were not changed was my opening statement—'This is the third and final press conference with regards to the Aaron Bassler situation.' I put my suit on, which was very well coordinated by my wife, I must say. I had met Sacramento Sheriff Scott Jones maybe eight times and on every occasion he was the best-dressed person in the room. I had said to Laura, 'Honey, I believe that the Sacramento Sheriff

Willow at the Final Press Conference
(Beth Schlanker/ The Press Democrat)

is going to be there—I need to be well dressed.' Anyway, she had done a good job and I felt confident that all was going well. I headed for the E.O.C. room, which was packed, standing room only, media lining the walls, cameras rolling."

However, just before entering, Allman had heard that Sheriff Scott Jones was still 20 minutes away. Allman was making an announcement to this effect when people to his left started to leave the room, holding their noses. "The evening before, when Bassler had committed the burglary, we had sent in Willow the bloodhound to track him. She did a great job and it led us to believe Bassler was in the vicinity. If the burglary had not been reported and she had not been used I doubt if we would have had our men in the area at that point.

"Anyway, just as the press conference was to begin poor Willow had had a severe attack of diarrhea—it was terrible, all over the floor in the room, just at 6:00pm. Those not laughing were gagging. I had to maintain my game face and when I noticed Dave Brookshier of the public radio station KZYX & Z laughing, I responded with a stern 'Knock it off— it's not funny.' Looking back, I wish I could have chuckled too, but I was the one guy in the room who could not show any such levity. The Fort Bragg police chief, Scott Mayberry cleaned the mess up, sprayed some deodorant, and by 6:20pm we were ready to go again. I had just stepped outside for a minute when Scott Jones arrived. He was in casual clothes and, as we shook hands, I commented 'I can't believe that I out-dressed you' and we went inside to begin."

⁂

Those in attendance included Jere Melo's brother-in-law; Melo's friend Ian Chaney who had been with him in the woods when Melo was shot; Fort Bragg Mayor Dave Turner; Chairperson of the County

The Final Press Conference

Supervisors, Kendall Smith; and many members of the press—print, television, and radio, including Vickie Watts of the local radio station, K.O.Z.T The Coast, that was broadcasting live from the room with news director Joe Rigelski.

Flanked by more than two dozen members of the search team still in camouflage, Sheriff Allman laid out the ground rules. Conference call facilities had been set up so that the out-of-town press, in various places around the country but specifically for journalists at the Los Angeles Times and New York Times, could ask questions later. He would give his report, which was a matter-of-fact report featuring the timeline of events—the basic police blotter report, then take questions from the room and then questions by phone on conference call.

Allman confirmed that murder suspect Aaron Bassler had been shot and killed in the forest outside Fort Bragg. This had occurred at 12:23pm when Bassler was spotted as he walked down a logging road six miles outside Fort Bragg, one half-mile south of Mud Springs, near Sherwood Road, less than two miles from his mother's house. He explained what had happened and that there was no question in anyone's mind that Bassler was ready and willing to shoot any officers he came upon.

"The hardest part for me to explain to everyone was that Aaron Bassler had been killed without law enforcement saying 'Police—drop the gun.' The Garner v Tennessee case was very clear in my mind. That is what the SWAT team was following—this was the real world we were dealing with. No warning was given. The Sacramento team saw him, made a judgment that he was posing a significant threat of death to others, and he was killed."

Allman finished his statement and was about to take questions from the room when suddenly, on the conference phone, a voice said "Sheriff, this is the L.A. Times, was there a 'shoot to kill order' given?"

"I was not so much angry as surprised. I wanted to tell him that if

I had the ability to remove him I would. It was an asinine question—there is no such thing, unless in the military. In some SWAT situations there is something called the 'green light' where it is evaluated that future harm is going to happen and snipers will be called upon to kill a suspect. This was not a 'green light' situation. At no point in the investigation was there a 'green light' policy in effect. Each incident is treated differently in dealing with how the threat has to be neutralized. Whether that is by applying handcuffs or a shooting depends on the situation. We told the guys going into the woods they would get all the information they would need to get their job done. They would be expected to do what their agency policy allowed them to do. The SWAT team was only going to shoot first if it was felt that Bassler was in an offensive and threatening position. He was not asleep in his sleeping bag; his rifle was not on his shoulder. He was in an offensive position. It was all down to 'Garner v Tennessee' and the three SWAT guys made their decision based on that. It was the correct decision.

"The next question came from the audience in the room. 'How do you feel about how this ended?' As if I was in slow motion the following two seconds seem to take forever and then I answered, 'I want you to know that I fully support the manner in which this situation ended.' I think a number of people were surprised that I did not announce that there would be a further evaluation. There comes a point where you have to say 'that is what we did; this is why we did it; and I agree with the result. I had come to that point. Of all the many things that played through my mind, that question was the most frequent. It was a defining moment and most people in that room also felt, 'Yes, that was right'—'Yes,' knowing that Bassler had killed two innocent Mendocino County residents in cold blood already; 'Yes,' knowing that two days earlier Bassler had attempted to kill three Alameda County deputies; and 'Yes,' knowing that the SWAT team out there on the logging road knew that they were up against someone who was very capable of doing that again—what else was there to talk about?"

After about 50 minutes or so, Captain Kurt Smallcomb stepped in and announced that Sheriff Allman would take one more question. "I was very relieved but I actually took two more... The conference ended and I thanked several people and spoke briefly to Scott Jones from Sacramento. I then found Brian Kornagay, our volunteer logistics guy, and asked him to get me a hotel for the night. I was spent. At that time there were about 60 law enforcement officers in town—Sheriff Deputies, U.S. Marshals, SWAT teams, various law enforcement miscellaneous departments, and the Fort Bragg Fire Chief had arranged for an informal gathering at the fire station. Everyone was very appreciative of this and there would be no press there. Most went along, some wives showed up, and it was a case of 'letting your hair down.' I had two beers and decided I wanted to leave—nobody wants to hang out with the Sheriff! I thanked everyone, particularly Smallcomb for all his work, and left.

"I stopped at the local Safeway to get a toothbrush and razor, and drove to the Harbor Light Motel where Brian had booked me in. I called Laura and lay on the bed. I was totally exhausted but could not sleep. Relief was my underlying emotion. I can't actually describe how I felt because I had never experienced that feeling before—it was a combination of relief, accomplishment, and a huge appreciation for the effort by so many people."

જ

Chapter 9
Aftermath

Sunday, October 2nd, 2011

'Bassler shot dead' was the succinct headline in large black letters on the Press Democrat's front page that morning. Sheriff Allman was quoted as saying, "I've said many times that I wish this incident could have ended without another shot being fired. But I fully support the manner in which this ended. No more lives are endangered by Aaron Bassler."

Reporters Julie Johnson and Mary Callahan were at the press conference and wrote about Sheriff Allman's account of the previous day's confrontation with Bassler. Allman had said, "At 12:23pm, the first person saw Bassler and recognized him. They were situated about a quarter-mile from Mud Springs, near Sherwood Road." After describing Bassler's appearance and the weapon he was carrying, Allman went on, "He was not only carrying this in his right hand, he was completely ready to engage. His hand was on the handle and his right index finger was in a tactical position."

Investigators later found that Bassler had what appeared to be most of a 30-round clip loaded in the weapon. All the shots hit Bassler in the upper torso. Bassler did not fire and died immediately. He was about two miles away from his mother's home.

Word had spread quickly through the community and along with a huge collective sigh of relief came the feeling that things could get back to normal finally. As reported in the Press Democrat, at the monthly Grange breakfast more than 300 people gathered and conversation inevitably centered on the end of the 36-day manhunt in the woods. Several people expressed feelings that they wished the investigation and manhunt had not ended the way that it had, but one gentleman, perhaps sharing the view of the majority, countered by saying that he wished it hadn't started the way it did. Overall, there was a palpable sense that the community could now get back its regular routines, windows and doors no longer needed to be locked, weapons could be put away, and the fear of having an unstable murderer in the vicinity was at an end.

Most people seemed to agree with how the SWAT team had dealt with the situation surrounding Bassler's final moments. Naturally some were going to question why no warning had been given to Bassler, given that three SWAT team members had their guns trained on him. Nevertheless, being aware that Bassler had fired upon law enforcement just days earlier in the shootout with the Alameda SWAT team, this was a key factor in determining how the searchers would approach dealing with Bassler from then on, and it had been clearly spelled out to them by their commanders how they should proceed in the possible scenarios that they may face.

Sheriff Tom Allman maintained that there were few options given what confronted the Sacramento SWAT team on Saturday lunchtime— an armed Aaron Bassler, with the semi-automatic weapon in his hand in an offensive tactical position. "If he'd been walking down the road with the gun slung over his back, or we had come across him when he was sleeping, those are situations when we'd be able to announce who we were without him answering back with gunfire. I wasn't willing to risk the lives of these men. If he'd shown any signs of surrendering peacefully we could have used other tactics, but he didn't."

And what did he think would have happened if the SWAT team had announced their presence to Bassler as he walked along then logging road, gun at the ready? "I think we all know the answer to that. He would have immediately opened fire at the area from where the voice had come, and we could have been dealing with more deaths." He concluded, "I do have feelings for the Bassler family, they suffered a loss. But the other losses in this county were something law enforcement thought about every day for the last 36 days."

Greg Melo, the son of victim, Jere Melo, speaking from his home in Coos Bay, Oregon, had heard the news from a relative in Fort Bragg, and commented, "I heard what I needed to hear. None of our people got hurt and the threat is neutralized. I have so many friends in Fort Bragg who are breathing easier. Today is a good day."

❦

Monday, October 3rd, 2011

Two days after Bassler had been shot and killed in the woods, questions were being asked whether the whole episode could have been avoided. Mental health experts certainly thought it could have if Bassler had received the mental care his family had been requesting for many years. The Bassler family believed the 35-year-old had been suffering from various mental health issues since he was 19 years old. "It has been like watching a slow train wreck," Jim Bassler, the dead man's father, had said.

Sonya Nesch, author of "Advocating for Someone with a Mental Illness," and a member of the National Alliance on Mental Illness (N.A.M.I.), was quoted by Glenda Anderson of the Press Democrat as saying, "I believe that, had he been able to get the help his family had been pleading for, the deaths would not have happened."

Nesch, along with many others, including Fort Bragg officials, is now advocating for county supervisors to adopt the provisions of California's "Laura's Law," those that set up programs that in certain situations can force people with psychiatric problems to undergo outpatient treatment. The critics of this law point out that it infringes a person's civil rights. Advocates of Laura's Law claim that Bassler's behavior over the years, not to mention his obsession with space aliens, is consistent with schizophrenia. He refused treatment but advocates point out that he probably did so because of the illness.

Nevada County is the only one in the state to fully implement the law at this point and it is a county-by-county option. A judge in Nevada County, Tom Anderson, called the Bassler case "a glaring disappointment." The supervisors in Mendocino will need more information to move forward on this but they seem to think it is a good idea. Supervisor Dan Hamburg commented, "There needs to be a way for family members, when confronted with a severely mentally ill family member, to get some kind of help from the system."

Further developments with regards to the implementation of Laura's Law in Mendocino County continued for many months. In mid-July, 2012, the Board of Supervisors voted down its introduction. For a detailed examination of this issue see Addendum B.

☙

Tuesday, October 4th, 2011

A final press release was issued, written by Detective Sergeant Greg Van Patten of the Sheriff's office:

A forensic autopsy has been performed on Aaron James Bassler in Ukiah, CA. The preliminary findings of the autopsy showed Aaron James Bassler died as the result of multiple gunshot wounds. An official cause of death will not be determined until Blood Alcohol and Toxicology analysis results are received by the coroner's Division, within the next estimated 4-6 weeks.

⁊

Over the ensuing days the story inevitably appeared in newspaper headlines and articles all over the region and in many cases across the country. Two articles, which perhaps best summed up the saga, and offered differing perspectives, are reproduced below:

The Short, Sad Saga Of Aaron Bassler
by Bruce Anderson, publisher/editor of the Anderson Valley Advertiser

A loner, who had spent years in the woods by himself, Bassler was first arrested in October of 1994, the year of his graduation from Fort Bragg High School. The charge was receiving stolen property, specifically a pair of AK-47 assault rifles and another gun an acquaintance had stolen from his father. Bassler, in his first appearance in the famously lenient courtroom of Ten Mile Court Judge, Jonathan Lehan, was sentenced to 90 days in jail with 87 of those days suspended, plus two years' probation.

Three more arrests for a vandalism, a drunk in public and a DUI occurred in 1995. And on it went as the young man's mental health deteriorated, a deterioration expedited by heavy drinking and methamphetamines.

In February of 2009, Bassler was arrested by the FBI for tossing paranoid messages rolled up like dynamite sticks at the Chinese Consulate in San Francisco. He may have attended court-mandated therapy sessions in connection with his Chinese offensive but, as Bassler's despairing father has pointed out, no one knows for sure because the authorities, federal and local, inevitably cite patient confidentiality laws as they refuse to confirm or deny, let alone discuss, a subject's mental health history.

The Bassler family's repeated warnings to Mendocino County authorities that their son was quite likely a danger to others were simply ignored.

Bassler's arrest by federal authorities in San Francisco required him to get mental health treatment and, Bassler's father told the Santa Rosa Press Democrat, "fearful of being jailed, Aaron toed the line." One of the conditions of his federal probation was that he stays with his mother at her home on Sherwood Road, Fort Bragg. But when his federal probation ended, Bassler resumed drug and alcohol use and, according to his father, "became increasingly delusional and anti-social."

His parents couldn't help but see a steady deterioration in their son's rationality while his criminal record indicated an increasing tendency to life threatening behavior. In February of this year, careening drunk through Fort Bragg at speeds upwards of 80 miles per hour, Bassler lost control of his pick-up truck and, as students gathered for a dance looked on, hurtled onto the Fort Bragg Middle School tennis courts. He then had to be subdued by police when he resisted arrest. He'd been pepper sprayed and was still smarting from the spray's chemicals when his booking photo was taken. That photo, incidentally, is the one most often used by the media. It makes Bassler look quite maniacal although in ordinary circumstances there was nothing off-putting about Bassler's appearance.

The consensus, though, from everyone who dealt with Bassler, including law enforcement, is that Bassler presented a mental health dilemma not unique to him. Mental health staffers, not speaking for attribution, say that "drug induced mental illness" isn't, strictly speaking, mental illness as we usually think of mental illness.

'These people aren't crazy when they are off drugs' a Mendocino County Mental Health staffer has said. Prevalent in Mendocino County for years now, methamphetamine often leads its consumers into temporary psychosis. At any one time, there are lots of people pinballing around the County in varying states of self-induced mental illness because of methamphetamine. Off the drug, they function normally. Aaron Bassler was unwell on or off drugs, but off drugs he seemed quite resourceful and functioned well enough to sustain himself in the woods for long periods of time.

ᥱᤥ

The Extraordinary, Depressing,
Cautionary Tale of Aaron Bassler
by the Treatment Advocacy Center

In many ways, the Aaron Bassler story is depressingly familiar. Like twenty-five other California counties, Mendocino County has no psychiatric beds. It has failed to implement Laura's Law, the California statute authorizing court-ordered treatment in the community. Mental health services are being gutted—mental health staff cut, psychiatric first-responders eliminated, hospital admissions reduced, visits to mentally ill inmates by psychiatrists slashed. And Bassler's family had been pleading with county officials to get his son into treatment—without success.

Bassler's parents, from whom he was estranged, are separated but live in the Fort Bragg area. His own father says he keeps a handgun on his nightstand and commented that he'd unsuccessfully sought mental health services for his son who, Mr. Bassler said, exhibited no signs of mental illness until he began using drugs at about age 18.

"His family fears for his safety, their own safety and that of the community if this psychiatric disorder is not addressed," father Jim Bassler wrote in a letter that the Santa Rosa Press Democrat reported was sent to jail medical staff, the county psychiatrist and his son's public defender months ago. The elder Bassler says he never received a response, and no one connected to the case has admitted seeing the letter.

Two Mendocino County supervisors are now co-sponsoring a Board of Supervisors presentation and agenda item on Laura's Law. Amanda and Nick Wilcox, parents of Laura Wilcox—the victim of a 2001 rampage and namesake of California's assisted outpatient treatment (AOT) law—have written the county urging implementation of the law.

'The alternative to providing effective timely treatment, as we and Nevada County sadly learned the hard way, is to provide inadequate treatment and hope that there will not be a bad outcome,' the Wilcoxes wrote.

It's a lesson too late for Aaron Bassler, his victims, and the town of

Fort Bragg and surrounding Mendocino County. For thousands of other counties like them—in California and nationwide—the cautionary lesson is that betting on non-treatment can be not only costly, but, as in this case where three people's lives ended before their time, also deadly.

☙

And now…

A final autopsy report with an official cause of death would be made when toxicology reports were available, which could have taken four to six weeks.

Meanwhile, the County District Attorney's Office would be reviewing the shooting and Bassler's confrontation with the Alameda SWAT team a few days earlier. State law requires that the DA's Office take such steps in all officer-involved shootings to determine "Does the evidence at hand support what the officers say happened?" It is a matter of protocol and the officers involved in both incidents went directly to the DA investigators for debriefing. The investigators then prepare a report that goes before the DA and the process can take a couple of months or so.

That final autopsy, completed on October 4th, 2011, with a blood alcohol and toxicology report following on October 11th, stated that Bassler had died from "multiple gunshot wounds to the abdomen, the upper torso, and the head from high-caliber rifles."

The toxicology report stated that traces of T.H.C., the principal psychoactive ingredient of marijuana, were found in Bassler's system, along with small and not significant quantities of amphetamines, not necessarily cocaine or methamphetamine and quite possibly from the prescription drugs Bassler may have taken from the vacation cabins. There was no significant level of alcohol in Bassler's system that day.

☙

At the Mendocino Sheriff Office's annual "Officer of the Year Dinner" in May of 2012, Ian Chaney, the man who had accompanied Jere Melo into the woods on that fateful August day, was in attendance. Sheriff Allman introduced the 32-year-old to the crowd. "I thanked him for what he did on that August morning, and for being able to give us some very necessary information in those early days of the investigation. I also commented that his brave conduct ultimately resulted in the prevention of other deaths. He was emotional, as was Madeleine Melo who was also there, and he received [a] standing ovation from the audience."

At the meeting of the Fort Bragg City Council on Monday, August 13th, 2012, Mayor Dave Turner honored Ian Chaney for his bravery and actions on August 27th, 2011, when Chaney and the late Jere Melo came under fire from Aaron Bassler. Melo was shot to death; Chaney narrowly escaped. The proclamation read as follows:

> *Whereas, on August 27, 2011 Fort Bragg City Councilmember Jere Melo, working as a security contractor for a local timber management company, headed out into the woods with local resident Ian Chaney to document the existence of an illicit trespass grow operation on private property on the outskirts of Fort Bragg; and*
>
> *Whereas, after forging their way through dense brush, Jere and Ian entered a recently cleared area, looked up the hill and saw logs piled into a makeshift bunker; and*

Whereas, with no warning, 35-year-old Aaron Bassler jumped out of the bunker and fired a semi-automatic rifle at them; and

Whereas, Jere fell to the ground fatally wounded, while Ian managed to return fire while running for cover; and

Whereas, Ian raced towards the Skunk Train tracks and flagged down a maintenance car to get help for Jere; and

Whereas, subsequently, Ian was able to provide valuable information to local law enforcement officials that allowed them to locate Jere Melo and to identify the suspect.

Now, therefore, I, Dave Turner, Mayor of the City of Fort Bragg, on behalf of the entire City Council, do hereby recognize and honor Ian Chaney for his heroism during this tragic event.

᜶

Finally, in late July, 2012, almost 10 months after Bassler's death, the Mendocino County District Attorney, C. David Eyster, announced that his much-anticipated report on the case was complete and would be presented to the Fort Bragg Council meeting mentioned above on August 13th, 2012. (For the DA's Report in its entirety, see Addendum A.)

In summation, *"Based on the combined investigatory efforts of all involved, when reviewed and evaluated under the mandates of applicable law, it is hereby the findings of the District Attorney that:*
1. *The evidence is clear beyond reasonable doubt that Aaron James Bassler murdered Matthew Roger Coleman on August 11, 2011 in cold blood while Bassler was trespassing on private property in Mendocino County.*

2. *Between August 11, 2011 and August 27, 2011, the evidence is clear and convincing that at least one of Aaron James Bassler's immediate family members withheld critical information that would have reasonably warned and focused law enforcement—prior to the death of Jere Lynn Melo and the attempted murder of Ian Philip Chaney—that Bassler should be considered an armed and dangerous suspect in the murder of Matthew Roger Coleman.*

3. *The evidence is clear beyond reasonable doubt that Aaron James Bassler murdered Jere Lynn Melo on August 27, 2011 by lying in wait, ambush and in cold blood while Bassler was trespassing on private timberlands in Mendocino County.*

4. *The evidence is clear beyond reasonable doubt that Aaron James Bassler attempted to murder Ian Philip Chaney on August 27, 2011 by lying in wait, ambush and in cold blood while Bassler was trespassing on private timberlands in Mendocino County.*

5. *The evidence is clear beyond reasonable doubt that Aaron James Bassler attempted to murder members of the Alameda County Sheriff's Department, who were assigned to and deployed in Mendocino County to provide mutual aid.*

6. *The evidence is clear beyond reasonable doubt that the lethal use of force applied against Aaron James Bassler causing his death was objectively reasonable given the totality of the information known to law enforcement and objectively reasonable given the circumstances and information personally known and observed by the Sacramento County law enforcement officers assigned to and deployed in Mendocino County to provide mutual aid."*

❧

Blame and responsibility?

With regards to the second finding above, DA Eyster said there was no criminal misconduct on the part of Aaron Bassler's mother, Laura Brickey. "There is no affirmative duty to report these things because she really didn't know," Eyster said. On the day following the release of its report, The DA's Office stated that, while Aaron Bassler's mother's "judgment might raise questions," there was no indication that she committed a crime in withholding information.

Nevertheless, the Report's finding has not prevented many people close to the case, and those reporting on it, from taking the position that it is not unreasonable to assume that had she done this, or indeed had Jim Bassler decided to go to the authorities himself after receiving such information, then on Saturday August 27th, Aaron Bassler may well have been in police custody, or at the very least, Melo would not have been in the woods looking for Bassler's illegal garden.

In the final analysis, Bassler's mother did not believe her son was capable of murder so she did not want to be responsible for focusing law enforcement on him as a possible suspect, an unfortunate decision in hindsight. Bassler's father claims he had encouraged Brickey to report her concerns, and during the search was often outspoken about his suspicions that his son was mentally ill. Following the publication of the DA's report, Bassler said Brickey simply "couldn't believe her son could do that." He did not comment on why he himself did not come forward with the information he had learned from his ex-wife regarding her dropping off their son and his rifle in the remote area where the next day Matt Coleman was murdered.

During the week prior to the release of the report, Eyster and Sheriff Tom Allman had met with Madeleine Melo at her home and handed over a copy of the report to her. They chatted for an hour or so and then, a few days later, just before the report went public, Allman received a phone call from her. "She was very upset. The fact that the report emphasized that Bassler's mother had known for some time that Coleman had been shot very near to where she had dropped off her son yet failed to mention this to the police was most upsetting to her. I am not sure how this is going to move on from here. I do know that the mother may have to face some charges with respect to a civil wrongful death suit. As for the father, he told us that he had tried to get his ex-wife to go to the police. She refused, but he failed to act also. For this whole investigation we treated him like a victim, not as a suspect."

Had the authorities been aware of this they would have taken Bassler into custody, or at least tried to if they could have found him. Failing that, the Sheriff most certainly would not have allowed Jere Melo to go in to the woods on that fateful Saturday morning over two weeks later in search of a possible marijuana grow that was being maintained, according to the email sent by Melo to the Sheriff's Office, by a man by the name of "Aaron."

The Anderson Valley Advertiser's Bruce Anderson summed up this situation:

> "It's clear now that both of Aaron Bassler's parents could have prevented Jere Melo's death with a phone call to the Sheriff's Department telling the police that Aaron had been in the area of his first shooting victim, Matt Coleman. Bassler's mother had driven her son, armed with an assault rifle, to the Rockport area off Highway One and dropped him off shortly before and in the immediate vicinity of Matt Coleman's murder on August 11th, 2011. Prior to driving him to Rockport, Mom had taken Aaron shopping at Safeway and Purity stores in Fort Bragg where Aaron, an isolate who roamed the forested vastness between Fort Bragg and the Humboldt County line

where he grew marijuana and attempted to grow opium poppies, used his food stamp card to re-supply. On August 11th of 2011, Matt Coleman, a property manager for the Mendocino Land Trust, was found shot to death near where Bassler's mother had dropped her son off.

"Did Bassler's mother know that Coleman had been murdered? Did it occur to her that her odd son may have done it? Even the most ill-informed Mendo Person is invariably aware of the more atrocious local events, and Mom must have known, at a minimum, her mountain man son would have been suspect number one. But she didn't relay her suspicions to the police. If she had, Aaron probably would have either been arrested or killed before he murdered Jere Melo.

"On Sunday, August 21st, at a Bassler family barbecue, James Bassler, Aaron's father, was informed by his former wife that she'd dropped Aaron off near where Coleman was murdered. According to the DA's report, James Bassler suggested to his former wife that she should tell the police that Aaron had been in the area of the Coleman shooting and that he had been armed. But neither James Bassler nor his wife took that information to the police and, a week after the family barbecue, Aaron Bassler murdered Jere Melo. Another family member, not identified in the DA's report, had given Aaron the assault rifle he used to commit both murders.

"James Bassler has since said he'd sent a letter to his son's public defender warning that his son's apparent mental health was deteriorating, but that his warnings had been ignored. While he was incarcerated on prior drugged/drunken encounters with law enforcement, Aaron did not exhibit signs of mental illness, a solid indication that he was not mentally ill when he was away from drugs and alcohol, and not mentally ill in the clinical sense.

"So, then, this is the sad chronology:

August 11th: Aaron Bassler shoots Matt Coleman to death near Rockport.

August 21st: Bassler's parents agree that Aaron may have murdered Coleman but don't inform law enforcement.

August 28: Jere Melo is shot to death by Bassler.

September 29: Bassler exchanges fire with an Alameda County [SWAT] team.

October 1st: Aaron Bassler is shot to death by a Sacramento-based [SWAT] team."

Another point of view should most certainly be mentioned at this time. Jim Bassler has recently written, following further study of the DA Report, that California Fish and Game interviewed him in the spring of 2011 with regards to the issue of an elk shooting near to Westport, not far from where Matthew Coleman was killed. (See Thursday, September 1st.) Jim Bassler comments, "Law enforcement was very aware of the fact that Aaron spent lots of time in the area and apparently he was an obvious suspect in the elk shooting. I told them he was not a hunter and that particular investigation soon faded out, but not before I had spoken to law enforcement a few times and had shared information about Aaron's behavior with them. I assumed they would share the information they had about Aaron's frequent presence in the area where Coleman was shot with the Sheriff's Office."

This is an issue that Jim Bassler feels should have been brought up if the DA was to do a balanced report. Given that Fish and Game had interviewed him with regards to the suspected elk shooting by his son, an incident that occurred near to the Coleman murder scene, perhaps Aaron's name would have been expected to surface after that murder had taken place. Therefore, and with the benefit of much hindsight,

224

with his name known to the Sheriff's Office, upon receiving Jere Melo's email two days before Melo's death, in which he mentions his plan to go into the woods to search for a man by the name of "Aaron," they would certainly have told Melo not to go ahead with this plan.

Mendocino County Supervisor Dan Hamburg offers his support for the position held by Jim Bassler. "Like Jim Bassler, Aaron's father, I'm not criticizing the decision made by law enforcement to end the life of the young man suspected of killing two citizens of our county. But I am critical of both the DA and certain members of the press for insisting that the perpetrator of these crimes was suffering nothing more serious than excessive use of drugs and alcohol. Aaron Bassler's pattern of substance abuse may well have added fuel to the fire, but to dismiss his symptoms of severe mental illness is to dangerously miss the point.

"Letters were sent to county officials by Jim Bassler and by Aaron's mother and sister. These were pleas for help from desperate family members who had no idea how to handle their son and brother's increasing dysfunction and hostility. For example, Natalie Serrano, Aaron's sister, wrote: 'We believe Aaron has some type of mental disorder that is the underlying cause for his alcohol abuse and reckless behavior in general. All members of his immediate family have witnessed Aaron behaving, writing and speaking in a delusional manner that leads us to believe that he suffers from a psychological disorder or disease. He has proven to be incapable of functioning socially and productively within society and among his family.'

"Jim Bassler, in a letter to jail psychiatrist Dr. Doug Rosoff, wrote: 'My son Aaron Bassler is currently in the Mendocino County Jail and I believe he needs a psychiatric evaluation and medical treatment for his psychiatric disorder which appears to be schizophrenia. His behavior changed when he was 18 or 19 years old. His symptoms are: bizarre delusions, paranoia, marked personality change, denial of obvious problems, strong resistance to help, out of touch with reality, strange ideas, significant changes in sleeping patterns, social withdrawal and isolation even from family, increased irritability and anger, uncharacteristically poor judgment, risk-taking behavior, [and] anger and hostility out of proportion to the situation.'

"Jim Bassler goes on to describe Aaron's arrest by federal authorities for harassing the Chinese Consulate in San Francisco. 'He was apparently acting out on his delusions dealing with space aliens and the Chinese.' The distraught father ends the letter with a plea that his son be diagnosed and put on medication that 'will stabilize him.'

"These letters were hand-delivered and faxed to county authorities in February of last year [2011], a full six months before the murders of Matt Coleman and Jere Melo. During part of this time, Aaron was in custody. Needless to say, the letters went unanswered and unheeded. Due to an errant procedure at the jail, Dr. Rosoff never even saw the letter from Jim Bassler."

At the time of writing, this issue continues to cause concern for many, particularly those directly affected by the tragedies that resulted.

❧

The DA's Report also addressed the issues raised by Laura's Law. *"Some have attempted to use the crimes and tragedies described herein as a lightning rod for sparking a public debate on mental health policies in Mendocino County, in particular as those policies may relate to a local interest of some to implement Laura's Law. Having reviewed the Laura's Law criteria and compared it against the facts and background of the person in question, the District Attorney hereby finds that Aaron James Bassler would not have qualified for Laura's Law intervention pursuant to then-existing* eligibility criteria. On the general topic of mental illness, it also should not go unmentioned that the Chinese-made rifle used by Bassler to commit his crimes was recently given to him by a family member. It is patently unreasonable for a family, even a broken one, if they truly believe that their son suffers from any form of a significant mental illness, to allow anybody, let alone another family member, to give that mentally-ill son a lethal assault rifle. If that was being contemplated, it seems reasonable that aggressive intervention to prevent such gifting should have taken place. It is also noted that even hidden mental frailties are often revealed and manifested in jail settings where staff is trained to look for such things. Having reviewed all jail records applicable to Bassler, there are no notations by trained and vigilant jail staff suggesting any suspicion of mental illness. It is strongly believed that Bassler's situational mental instability was primarily driven by alcohol and/or illicit drug abuse, both of which the local criminal justice system attempted to address at various times.

"As an aside, when Bassler was arrested by the Fort Bragg Police Department on September 13, 2010 for public intoxication and transported to jail, he requested during the jail screening process (while intoxicated) that he not be housed with other inmates. The reason he gave for this request was that he was a former police cadet. As with all his other bookings at the local jail, he was not perceived as an inmate needing to be referred to Jail Mental Health for evaluation. When Bassler was back in jail in March 2011 following his DUI and resisting arrest, he again requested during the screening process (while intoxicated) that he be housed separate from other inmates. However, in the morning after he had sobered up, Bassler told jail staff that he had no problem being housed in a shared housing unit, which is where he was ultimately housed without incident. Again, during this last screening process and thereafter, Bassler was not determined to be an inmate who needed to be referred to Jail Mental Health for further evaluation."

See Addendum B for further analysis and discussion on Laura's Law.

Recognizing the passing of one year since the two murders and the ensuing hunt for Aaron Bassler, the Press Democrat sent reporter Julie Johnson to the Coast in August, 2012. This resulted in an article featuring memories, thoughts, and comments of the citizens of Fort Bragg on the tragic events that had taken place on the edge of their town in the late summer and early fall of 2011 and the community's slow but gradual recovery from them.

On August 27th, 2012, one year to the day after the death of Jere Melo, his family decided to hold a small memorial ceremony for family and close friends during which they placed a rock and picnic table at the site where he had parked his car on the edge of the woods on that fateful day.

✍

Chapter 10
Questions for the Sheriff

(Beth Schlanker/ The Press Democrat)

1. When did you first hear the name Aaron Bassler?

"A few days before the Jere Melo murder, Mr. Melo had emailed me saying that someone by the name of Aaron was apparently growing poppies and/or marijuana on a small part of the timberland he was overseeing. Then, on the day of the killing, I met Melo's friend, Ian Chaney, who was with Melo when the shooting took place, and he told me the person who had fired the shots at Melo was Aaron Bassler, someone Chaney knew from the local area and who he had chased off the property at some point before.

"Bassler's mother lived less than three miles from where Melo was shot and Bassler was known about town, by sight, if not necessarily by name. He always wore black and found conversation with people to be very awkward, often shielding his face as he spoke. A few months earlier it was reported that he was in town with netting over his face. He was certainly known as an odd, quirky guy and after two or three minutes of conversation with anyone he would just walk away. I had heard of someone fighting with the Fort Bragg police earlier in the year at the high school tennis courts. A situation where the suspect was pepper sprayed but kept fighting until a taser was used. I probably heard the name Bassler then but it had not stuck in my mind at all. Prior to a few days after the Melo murder, I had never heard of the stuff he did in San Francisco, where he threw fake bombs at the Chinese Embassy."

❦

2. At the September 26th press conference in Fort Bragg, the surveillance camera photo of Aaron Bassler with the assault rifle near the house where he was "committing a burglary" was displayed for the first time. When was that picture taken? And why wasn't it released sooner? [The press reported that it was taken about two weeks earlier.] Was the release of the picture supposed to at least have been partially timed to prepare the public that it was even more likely that Mr. Bassler would probably have to be shot rather than arrested?

"It was taken on September 12th. We had kept its existence hidden as we did not wish to alert anyone who might be in contact with Bassler that we had cameras in the woods. However, eventually this was outweighed by the need to inform the public that he was armed and dangerous and that they should not go into the woods. It never occurred to me to release the photographs (there were six of them) as some sort of message to the public that we would shoot Bassler rather than arrest him. That reasoning never came up. We were prepared for all eventualities but, as I've said many times, we discussed many, many times how we could take Bassler alive.

"The timing was more in line with the fact that the public was getting very concerned that no progress was being made in their mind. Furthermore, there was an upcoming watercolor painting seminar due to take place for a group of artists in the Noyo Basin and there had already been a Fat Tire Bike Race. With the deer season also open, there were too many circumstances where the public might be in danger, so we felt that by putting out the photograph we were reminding the public that there was a very, very dangerous person out there. We did not say that the Noyo Basin was closed but the warnings were out there. Once the $30,000 reward was offered on September 22nd, we felt people might be tempted to go into the woods and look for him. I don't think anyone did."

⁊

3. a. Many people wondered why Bassler killed Coleman and why he was so far north of his usual habitat.

"He and a friend of his, Jeremy James, had grown marijuana up that way at some point but we do not know for sure why he went there at that time.

3. b. When will the ballistics be released on the bullets that killed Mr. Coleman and will that tell us whether they match Bassler's gun or the bullets that killed Mr. Melo?

"Rifle bullets pass through the body—this was not a handgun he was using. We were unable to perform any ballistics as the bullets were not located."

℘

4. *Without using the word "hope" in your reply, given what we see in the booking logs on a regular basis and how many other drug-addled and/or untreated mentally ill people are obviously out there going through the same type of circular catch-and-release process that Aaron Bassler did, and given the department's experience with what some call "frequent flyers," what do you think the chances of another Bassler-type murder or assault happening are? (I.e., the actual numeric odds, not the hope.)*

"This is a statewide issue. If any county thinks that they are outside the circle of Bassler-like situations then they are wrong. We as a society have not prioritized mental health with our resources and money. The last big change in the state was in the '70s when then-governor Ronald Reagan closed down many state hospitals. I believe our counties must come up with a solution to identify the Basslers of tomorrow among the 20 percent of county jail inmates who should be mental health patients. Bassler had been through our jail system but we do not have the resources or the ability to identify who might be the next Bassler.

"Hopefully some good things will come out of this in the form of a significant increase in that ability to spot those outside the norm of mental health needs. We have to begin to properly fund mental health service. It is a Catch-22, though—if the proper funding gets approved the problem will go away for a time and people will start to ask if it is really still in need of funding. There is an ebb and flow in terms of mental health interest. The National Alliance for the Mentally Ill

(N.A.M.I.) consistently reminds us how fragile the mental health safety net really is.

"A 5150 citation is police code for persons judged to be a danger to themselves or others because of mental illness, or they are 'gravelly disabled.' I know a lot of people who qualify for such citations but mental health releases them because they don't have the money to keep them. To put a person in a properly locked and secure place costs about $1000 a day. Mental Health pays that now, unless the person is already incarcerated, in which case the Sheriff's Office pays. In fact from 5:00pm on Friday until 8:00am on Monday morning we are the de facto Mental Health.

"The system failed Aaron Bassler's parents. As a society we have the belief that government will take care of these problems—they don't. When uninsured mental health patients become adults they do not get the help they need as nobody is going to pay for that. The government did not assume responsibility for Aaron Bassler after there was a huge 'billboard' warning when he did the Chinese Embassy 'bombing' in San Francisco. The responsibility was punted away."

❧

5. *What do you think the County can do to minimize the likelihood of another Bassler-style murder or murders?*

"There have to be options for family members of mental health patients other than doing nothing. Jim Bassler had repeatedly said his son needed help but his voice might as well have been silent because it was ignored and people did not listen. There must be better mental health communication."

ↂ

6. Would you at least recommend to the DA that the Mendocino Courts institute a policy where people who come to court with symptoms of mental illness (or a family statement to that effect) AND a gun related incident on their record be automatically referred for a mental health evaluation, even if the arrest/charge is not a felony? Why did the crimes of Bassler continue to be judged as misdemeanors and not felonies?

"I would recommend that we have a mental health court—other counties do."

ↂ

7. What was the precipitating event or reason for the change in tactics from searching to lying in wait in the last few days before Bassler was shot? Was it the arrival of the Sacramento SWAT team?

"We did not change tactics after the first week. The idea to wait for him was developed in that time. Unless we had a dog with every search team he would remain concealed so we had to wait for him to make a move. If he had chosen to remain hidden it would have been tough to find him, and if we did he would have shot at us. The U.S. Marshal's tactic was to predict where he might be and in the end we had nine teams out there, each with three SWAT team members. I heard that some people thought these guys looked like Navy Seals or a team of Special Forces from Afghanistan. All the SWAT teams looked like that to me—trained officers in great shape ready to go out and do their job.

"On a side note, on September 24th, a week before Bassler was shot, there was a memorial in Ukiah for local man Jesse Pittman, a Navy

234

Seal killed in Afghanistan. The whole of Seal Team #6, those who had taken part in the operation that resulted in the death of Bin Laden, was in attendance. I was asked if I would consider sending those guys to Fort Bragg to help in the search for Bassler. Well, even if I could have done so constitutionally, which I couldn't, I did not even consider this. I fully supported the tactics of Captain Kurt Smallcomb and the search teams. Besides, the military is trained to neutralize their enemy, that's it. In police work we ask, 'Can we arrest the suspect, or do we have to shoot him?'"

℘

8. *In the* Ukiah Daily Journal, *reporter Tiffany Revelle stated that you said you were waiting for autopsy results before talking about where Bassler was shot and how many times. But reports from the final press conference say that you said that Bassler was shot seven times in the torso. Can you clarify?*

"We have to wait for the autopsy for definitive results. However, I can tell you again that twelve shots were fired at Bassler and seven hit him."

℘

9. *The "Tennessee v Garner" Supreme Court case says that an officer "may use deadly force only to prevent escape if the officer has probable cause to believe that the suspect poses a significant threat of death or serious physical injury to the officer or others." Even so, given that the SWAT team was hidden and camouflaged, why not first say, "Police! Drop your gun!" with guns poised, then, if there was no immediate dropping of the gun, fire?*

"I can say unequivocally that if we could have taken him alive then we would have. Absolutely that is the truth. Captain Smallcomb and I spoke more about that than any other topic—'Is it possible to take him alive?' If we found him in his sleeping bag? Yes... If we found him without his rifle in his right hand? Yes, quite possibly... But he was ready to engage when we finally did encounter him. We did not know if there was a bullet in the chamber or if the safety was off. It turned out there was a bullet and the safety was off. I believe in all my heart that he was ready to engage. He was going to shoot at any authoritarian figure he saw or heard.

"The conditions which the courts have given law enforcement in such situations are reasonable. I was not going to require any additional conditions, outside what the court has issued, that would have increased the danger to any officer. In a perfect world, the SWAT team would have been behind a bulletproof shield with a loudspeaker. They made a decision that I will not second-guess. I can only add, once again, that from the start of this whole event, it was Aaron Bassler who was going to get the opportunity to choose how it would end."

☙

10. *What was the cost of the whole investigation?*

"Approximately $266,000. Or $3 for every citizen of the County."

☙

11. *Do you think Bassler's mother was an enabler? She drove to Rockport and dropped him off knowing he had a rifle.*

"I believe she wanted him away from the house where he was a burden and was having conflicts with her new husband. She did not want to lose touch with him altogether and wanted to hear from him from time to time. He called her after the Coleman shooting to check in but no mention of that was made according to her. She saw him for the last time when she dropped him off near to Rockport, at the place where Coleman was shot the next day. She did not contact us at all after the shooting became public knowledge, despite dropping him off with the rifle so close to the crime scene. He actually phoned the house the day before the Melo shooting and spoke to the house-sitter. His mother was away. The next morning he went to the house and did some laundry and a little later that day he shot Melo in the woods."

❧

12. What things would you do differently if the case began tomorrow?

"I would certainly have called an earlier official press conference than the one we did—on September 26th, almost a month after the Melo shooting. We did meet with and talk to the press on many occasions in that month and kept them reasonably well informed of what was going on, but a formal press conference probably should have been held earlier, perhaps after three days or so.

"Due to the nature of this search, with hindsight we should have called in the U.S. Marshals Service after three days, not one week. They are the experts at this kind of thing, the ones who specialize in looking for fugitives, and they have all the latest equipment. Having said that, they had not experienced anything like the terrain and environment we had in this case.

"Other than those two significant changes, I imagine there are many little things I could come up with, but none that would have significantly changed the search or its outcome."

❦

13. You mentioned several times that you had some questions that you would have liked to ask Aaron Bassler had such a situation arrived. What are some of those questions?

"Well, I know what I would not ask him. That would be 'Why?' I don't think for one minute that he would give me a rational answer of why any of this happened.

"I would certainly want to know what the significance the eight of spades playing card was. And the 'crosshair' signs too. May be there is nothing significant about either but I spent enough time wondering what both of these 'messages' were trying to convey or represented.

"I would also like to know if at any time he had encountered law enforcement out there in the woods and decided not to engage. Given his abilities to evade us and move knowingly and stealthily through the brush, I suspect that he may well have but simply did not want to confront the searchers. It was only in the last few days that he seemed to change his mind on this.

"I would also want to know if there was anything we could have done to encourage him to give up and turn himself in, although I tend to think there was probably nothing we could have done to make this happen."

❦

Chapter 11
The Thoughts and Reflections of James Bassler
—Father of Aaron Bassler

A conversation with Steve Sparks on Friday, August 24th, 2012

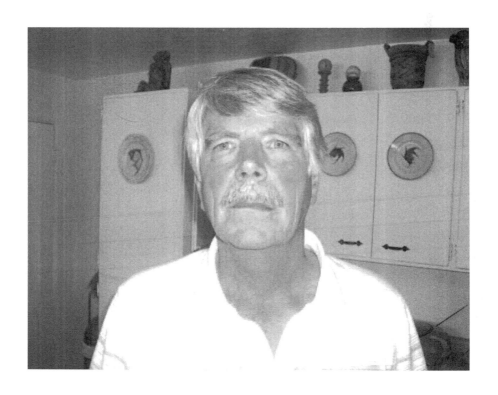

Upon meeting me for the first time in person, and sitting down for what would be a lengthy conversation, Jim Bassler's initial comment was that he had been disappointed that the first he heard of his son's death came from reporters calling to ask how he felt. He believed that since he had done everything he could to help with the apprehension that he at least deserved a phone call between the "high fives" after the shooting of his son, but of course it was too hot of a story to handle. Overall, he was satisfied the Sheriff's Department did what it could to end this without another tragedy.

Bassler is convinced that while alcohol and drugs were certainly used by his son and compounded his problems, the main reason for his son's behavior was mental illness. "He was a schizophrenic—all the evidence points to that. It would have been very evident to any professional early on if someone looked. Many people in town knew he was very strange. Even Jere Melo, in his email to the Sheriff, had said 'eccentric,' which is a polite word Jere used in forwarding Ian Chaney's description of the 'crazy man, Aaron.' He was not described as the 'drunk' or 'meth-head' that was trespassing on timberland; it was his mental state that was the most obvious problem."

Both of Aaron's parents come from long-time Fort Bragg and Mendocino County families, 100 years-plus. On his mother's side, Aaron's grandfather was the mayor and a city councilman in Fort Bragg—as was Jere Melo.

Aaron Bassler was born May 1st, 1976 and, according to his father, Aaron grew up in Fort Bragg as "a really happy and energetic kid who played with friends in the neighborhood and at school. He has a sister three years younger and, while they were not close, their sibling rivalry was normal. He played outdoors a lot; climbing trees, hiking, playing sports and a lot of Army games. He was well behaved in class and generally got good grades in school, A's and B's, for which I gave him some financial reward up until he was about 15 or 16 years old. His mother and I separated when he was 5 but I saw the two kids almost every weekend. He was doing well and had some good buddies in those years all the way to high school. In his early teens he had an interest in the military and law enforcement and joined the Police Cadets. He liked snow skiing but we didn't get to take him often enough. He also became interested in baseball; I remember one vacation to Santa Cruz where he spent almost the whole time in the batting cage. His future looked good; I had no reason to think things could go so wrong.

"I remarried when Aaron was about seven and my second wife was quite strict with the children. This was a hard adjustment for everyone at first, because his mother didn't always have the time to supervise the kids very rigidly. When they came to see me it was always a bit of a surprise for them. His stepmother softened as she understood the situation more, and the kids developed a lot of respect for her."

✍

As Aaron moved through Fort Bragg High School, his father saw Aaron less and less. Jim Bassler recalls, "The fact that he quit coming to stay over on weekends didn't surprise me. I don't remember wanting to hang out with my parents on weekends when I was a teenager. It did bother me that he started playing baseball and would not tell me when he had a game. According to his mother, she was kept in the dark also because he would be too self-conscious if we were there. I would have really liked to have coached him like my father had me. It's very hard being a part-time dad and getting left out so much. We did still get together on holidays and vacations, which we all enjoyed, but much of his life was a mystery to me. I knew that the single parent home he grew up in was hard in many ways, but there was little I could do about it.

"His grades started dropping around the age of 15 or16, and he got kicked out of the Police Cadets. Aaron and his friends were caught target practicing with guns borrowed apparently without permission. He was making new friends, some not my first choice, but he seemed to stay out of trouble with the law all through high school. I did see potential trouble coming and did what I could to put him on a better course. I discovered he was growing marijuana at his house. When I destroyed it, there was a traumatic confrontation. He said I was trying to ruin his life and was very upset. It was like I had done something he hadn't expected and could not understand. I think we both came to an understanding on that day. He came to understand I didn't think this was in his best interest and if he was going to do this, he better not do it in front of me. I came away with the understanding that I had limited control over what he did.

"Aaron was shy and had a tough time with girls. He never had a girlfriend. Some pursued him but he never had a date that I know of. Others in the family were concerned about this, but I didn't think it a problem, I had been like this at his age and I overcame it. What is sad for me is to look at this and remember how hard it was for the teenage me. Being so interested in girls but unable to get close because of my shyness. When the illness struck him at 19 it stopped his progress on all social levels and actually threw him backwards. As this was one of the hardest things in my own life, I can't imagine what a hell this must have been for Aaron, with his illness, [to] not only be unable get close to girls, but be unable to communicate and socialize with anyone, and with just a thin connection with family and old friends. In his senior year we took a family ski trip. He brought a very nice friend. His sister also brought one of her friends. He had a blast, and we all had a lot of fun. That was the last time he went anywhere with me, or we had any

242

fun together."

Toward the end of Aaron's senior year he gave up his shy profile of earlier years and started to party. He discovered alcohol and started to socialize more, and drugs were part of the party. After graduating from school he received an auto insurance personal injury settlement and with Jim's help bought a pickup truck. He got his first job delivering newspapers with it and seemed to be doing fine at this time. The job lasted several months and Jim is not sure why Aaron quit, but it was around this time things started to go wrong. Trouble with the law followed. He had three or four arrests over the next year or so. He moved into an apartment in Fort Bragg with three of his friends after graduation.

"Aaron had talked about joining the Army and I learned later that he went with a friend to a recruiter, but backed out at the last minute, leaving his friend to go on without him. I had discouraged him from joining; but I don't think he listened to me any more than he did about growing [marijuana]. I think he was already starting to have serious problems being around new people. I suspected they were all involved in marijuana growing and were all into having guns. My earlier fears of Aaron's involvement in growing came true when one of them invited up some black gang members from the Bay Area. The story I heard was that they came in friendly, but it turned into a home invasion when guns were drawn. The boys were locked in separate closets and rooms, and at least one of them was pistol-whipped. This went on for at least an hour, while they searched the apartment and tried to extract information, all the while each of these kids didn't know the fate of the others. After the gang members left, one of Aaron's roommates was smart enough not to follow instructions and called the police. They were caught before they got out of the County. I hoped this traumatic experience would make him change course."

The boys lost their apartment, and he moved into a tiny cabin at Jim's sister's on Highway 1 outside Fort Bragg. Trouble followed when he was arrested for keeping some guns for a friend that had been stolen from the friend's father. Very soon after that came the arrest that Jim believes resulted in the end of any chance Aaron had for a normal life. "I only know what led up to the arrest from his friends and his mother. He would never talk to me about it. They said he had been drinking and did some kind of drugs. He was found walking down the road, had misplaced his truck, and was arrested for being under the influence of alcohol or drugs and taken to the County Jail. His mother informed me of his arrest. We called the jail, but got the runaround and no answers at all. I don't think I've ever been treated that rudely. The attitude was he's an adult in jail so it's none of your business.

"Sometime after the arrest I went to his cabin, to look around for clues. It was unbelievably destroyed, as if wild dogs had been left there. It shocked me because he always kept his rooms so orderly. It didn't look like a break in, since the damage was more than anyone looking for something would do. I became far more worried about him; something was terribly wrong. If he was just drunk, he would have been released in the morning, but here we were into the second day. They wouldn't tell us why they were holding him or when he would be released. They soon released him but didn't tell us before [they did] and he disappeared onto the streets of Ukiah. A few more days passed before I got a call from a relative that he had just showed up at my mother's house in Ukiah, which was close to the jail.

"His mother and I went to pick him up and found him in a condition that is hard to explain and harder for us to understand at the time. He was zoned out like he was not entirely there anymore. They must have turned him loose like that, because the normal Aaron we knew would not have gone wandering around lost in Ukiah. It was as if this was not Aaron, or rather it was Aaron with something missing. There was a lack of connection or feeling at a basic level. We of course [were] thinking drugs but why would they release him still under the influence? Did a drug he took cause permanent damage? We stayed there and tried to talk to him to learn what was going on. It was so strange trying to communicate with him. He was there, but in a way he wasn't. We finally took him back to his cabin and I went to check on him the next day. I remember he wanted a ride to the library, and was excited about reading something on physics or quantum mechanics. He was also interested in the predictions of Nostradamus, and had some theories he wanted to check out. The next day I saw him again and asked about his research. He told me everything checked out, that he had already known it all along. I didn't know what to make of this, Aaron was never interested in the library before and it all sounded crazy.

"I contacted the Mental Health Department trying [to] figure out what to do. They needed to see him, not me, and he didn't want to go. I was frustrated by the fact he wouldn't go, but also that I could get no information as to what might be wrong or how I should handle this. With no help the best I could figure was that the drugs he'd taken [had] caused some damage that hopefully was not permanent.

"Looking back, two symptoms, 'delusions and detachment,' never went away. In his early 20s, you could see Aaron come back some to his normal self, only to fade away again. In his 30s, there was only a flicker of his old self. Those two symptoms we saw 16 years ago would come to dominate his life. He was detached from the normal range of emotions that connect us all to the ones we need. His delusional thinking created a separate world he lived in more and more, and under pressure his mind finally left the world the rest of us shares."

Aaron had a few minor arrests in his early 20s but then had no contact with the law for seven or eight years. Jim feels that this did not mean his mental health was any better. "His behavior was contained by his connections to his two separate families. His housing and employment record were both very telling in how much his illness disabled him. During this period I knew something was wrong but didn't understand it was the severe mental illness 'schizophrenia.' We were all just trying to help him get by."

❦

From an early age Aaron had helped Jim in his fishing business but in his 20s he quit helping. Jim moved Aaron into an old farmhouse owned by Jim's mother, across the street from Jim's own house. The plan was for him to help Jim put a new roof on it and remodel it. "My plans literally went up in smoke one day when he caught the house on fire. It was a warm but windy day, and he had a roaring fire going in the wood stove. The old dry redwood roof caught fire. Why he needed a very hot fire on a sunny day is the type of question I asked both him and myself over and over again, the rest of his life. The unexplainable things he did became more and more bizarre. The roof and second story were burned, but the Fire Department saved the rest. I found a large drawing of a space alien on the living room wall. In the days to come the neighbors reported lights in the house late into the night. When I investigated, I found melted wax and evidence of many candles having been burned in front of the drawing.

"I put him up in a small outbuilding on my place for a while, and

246

then got a large trailer for him back on my mother's property. His on and off again strange behavior destroyed that in a few years. Next he lived in a tiny cabin built on the same spot. After that I moved him into my mother's small rental house on the same property. That house became a big part of Aaron's story."

By the late 1990s, and now in his early 20s, Aaron did odd jobs for Jim and cut some firewood when he needed money—that was about it. Jim thought it was obvious he was growing marijuana but trying to keep that fact from his father. He would leave the property almost every day, saying he was going to his mother's or to the gym. The money he had to make truck payments, and to buy rifles, pistols, and many other things told Jim what he was up to. "I kept reminding him I didn't want to see anything illegal on my mother's property, and he knew better. At 25 he started to fish with me again, but it was very frustrating for me. He would come in, work very hard, and seem satisfied, but the next day he had some excuse and could not come. Sometimes his excuse seemed plausible, but over the years I came to realize that his delusional life became more important, or the real one too difficult. This strange sequence played out over and over, every time he needed money. Delaying payment had no effect. His mother found work for him cleaning a local theatre. It was in the morning with no people to deal with. His mother could help see that he showed up and could cover for him if he didn't. Aaron worked a few hours a week for four years. About the time this employment ended he told me he was retiring from his marijuana business. I never knew why. I think he just lost focus, and couldn't keep it together to continue. The reason growing worked for him up to this point was that he could do it alone and [had] learned it in his teens before his illness severely damaged his brain. He was like this in many ways; for a long time he kept his old friends but never made a new one and finally couldn't keep it together with the old ones either."

By his mid-20s that flat emotional response his mother and Jim saw in him when he was 19 became locked in. He would come to the house if he needed something but would never stay or sit down for dinner. They would talk for a short time and then he wanted to go. Once in a while he would ask Jim about the fishing business, but even then it often seemed phony to Jim. There was only the faintest hint that he cared about Jim or what Jim did. He visited his mother more frequently and went into her house, but he wasn't really there to visit. He was comfortable taking advantage of the food and other things, as he had since childhood. To Jim, he became like a wooden boy and for years Jim hardly ever saw him laugh, but neither did he see him sad. Most of the time Jim could not identify what mood he was in, except for when he was angry. Aaron just didn't show a normal range of emotions.

"The last place he lived has a story to tell. He moved out of the cabin and into his grandmother's rental on the same property. It was my decision and since he had maintained employment at the theatre and was working for me some, he deserved a chance to have better living conditions. It was a small house but his first real house and I think he was very happy, excited, and proud, though he had a hard time expressing it. I was surprised how much money he had. He soon furnished it with a big screen TV and fairly expensive furniture. Things almost looked normal for a while but about a year later he was fired from the theatre job over talking back or yelling at his boss. He didn't work for me anymore and at some point told me he retired from everything. During that first year he hired someone to build a six foot wall around the house. He told me he didn't like the neighbors looking at him. He covered the windows with black curtains, the furniture was all black, and he put black flooring in the kitchen. There was a gas stove in the house that he unhooked because he smelled gas. The propane guys came out, hooked it back up, and checked for leaks. Everything was fine except you could not convince Aaron. We had to remove it and the old electric service wouldn't handle an electric stove. Looking around at his kitchen, it was clear anything with heat or flame endangered the house anyway.

"He became very reluctant to let me in the house, but I kept telling him as landlord I had the right to check on the house. I wanted to check for marijuana, although the old wiring would never support an indoor grow. Over the next few years I checked less and less. He was unable to maintain his living space even close to resembling normal and it was hard to look at. Places to draw and do arts and crafts had come to dominate the living space, including a four foot by eight foot plywood sheet covering the counter and half the kitchen. He hid the artwork whenever I was coming or else wouldn't let me in. There didn't seem to be anything I could do about this craziness but try to figure out what was wrong with him, so I quit going in. At some point he hired someone to build a basement. His mother's family knew and even helped him design it, but they all kept it secret from me. I felt like Colonel Klink and that Hogan's Heroes had dug a tunnel right under my nose. When I learned of it and investigated, I was surprised at how large it was. Behind a bookshelf I found a hidden steep stairwell that led to a standup room about 8 feet by 12 feet, with only a mattress and a small desk. Why the secrecy? It wasn't wired or ventilated enough for a grow room."

Jim believes that Aaron must have been very successful during his last year of growing marijuana because his money lasted a long time and he had no trouble paying his rent for the next few years, but later he began to sell his possessions in order to pay rent. Jim recalls, "The first thing to go was the furniture; he didn't have a use for it anyway. What made my family happy was when he sold all his rifles and pistols. His strange behavior was a lot easier to live with when that was all gone.

When he couldn't pay his rent, I know it put stress on him. The family tried to find work for him, but he couldn't handle any job where he needed to be supervised more than a short time. He couldn't handle being around people. He would work hard if you found a simple job he could do alone, without supervision. He soon fell over a year behind in the rent he owed his grandmother. She didn't have a problem with that and didn't really know what was going on. She was in her mid-90s and I was managing her property on the Coast and felt some guilt towards the rest of the family for letting Aaron freeload. I couldn't afford to pay the rent for him so I did everything I could to make him productive."

∽

In 2007, at the age of 95, Aaron's grandmother broke her hip and the family began providing 24-hour care for her in her home in Ukiah. After recovering from surgery, it was decided she needed someone there 24/7 because dementia was setting in. She could do a lot for herself, but needed someone to help her and just be there "in case." Most of the family traveled from Fort Bragg and stayed a few days at a time. Jim thought that if Aaron could fill in overnight and a few hours in the day when there was little to do, it would help the rest of the family. He could cover his rent and be paid a little so he'd have some spending money. This worked well for a long time but eventually Jim realized Aaron couldn't handle the job as his mother's mental and physical health worsened. "People may wonder why I would let a crazy person take care of my mother. By this time I was getting far more familiar with what science actually calls his problem, but other than that I knew how he felt about his grandmother and was very aware of his behavior and what to expect of him. It worked out okay for a time. Moreover I knew my mother, in her right mind, cared about him and would have given him the same chance. He loved his grandmother and his behavior was strange but not threatening toward anyone at this time."

Early in 2009, Aaron was arrested for "terrorizing" the Chinese Consulate in San Francisco by throwing bundled messages over the perimeter fence at least three times. Each time this required the building to be evacuated and a bomb squad response. These bundles turned out to be very strange messages that dealt with the Martian military, its weapons, and the Chinese. Aaron was finally caught by the federal authorities and put in jail. "I went into his house while he was still in jail. I can best describe it as heartbreaking. I had found some strange artwork there before but now it was in volume. There was no furniture except some drawing tables; everything was in disarray and the walls, doors, and ceilings beat up. There were large world maps all through the house, not on the walls but scattered on the floors, along with books on military aircraft, submarines, and even a foreign language dictionary. The most interesting thing I found was a large art book filled with drawings and some of his writings. The drawings were of space aliens, maps of landing sites, aircraft, and other strange weapon systems. These drawings were not very sophisticated and quite child-like. His writings rambled and I couldn't follow them except one that talked about an upcoming meeting with an alien named Rea. The drawings and writings weren't describing what he had seen but what he knew was coming. His writing rambled about battles and other events, but I couldn't figure out who was fighting who or where he fit in.

"His mother gained his release by making bail and taking full responsibility for him, including Aaron living in her home for the duration of [his] probation and mental health counseling. She soon realized she got more than she bargained for, as Aaron was not the same as he was when he lived with her as a child. Her husband couldn't understand why he was so dysfunctional when it came to employment. His bizarre behavior continued and strange things happened late at night or when he was home alone. She told me they were close to divorce over Aaron's stay."

Jim believed that at least everyone now knew that Aaron had a mental health problem and that now he was going to get some help. This was not the case. "I was way too confident in the system; really nothing was done. He surely got a diagnosis but we were not allowed to know, because of privacy laws. We couldn't get any information from anybody. His mother was trying to make sure Aaron got to more of the appointments and Aaron simply told his doctors his meeting dates were his business and not hers so she could never remind him and encourage his attendance. I know now that by law they couldn't do much. He was required to see the doctors, but can't be required to get treatment, [or] take advice or medication. That can only happen if the doctor determines he is an immediate danger to himself or others. I don't think he was an immediate danger to anyone then but he was certainly a possible future danger. I do think treatment should have been pursued in a more assertive and collaborative way. The local mental health system and local law enforcement should have been at least notified of [his] arrest record. When a delusion is acted on in as deliberate a way as Aaron did, and weapons and military themes are a large part of the delusion, a little more attention should be given. I feel they just dumped the problem back on the family and community. After his probation played out with no answers, I went back to the books. I needed answers."

☙

Aaron's grandmother died about a year after the Consulate incident and her estate was settled in the summer of 2010. Aaron inherited several thousand dollars. He bought monster tires and did deferred maintenance and repairs on his truck. This was the last time Jim got to praise him with a compliment on how good his truck looked. The money didn't last long.

What Jim found interesting here is that Aaron did not go out and buy any guns. "Apparently he didn't think there was any need to arm himself. For me, there is a clear turning point sometime after he had spent most or all of that money. He had learned he needed to move out of his house because someone else inherited it and they needed to move in. I noted a slow increase in agitation, drinking, and drug use in the months before he needed to move. I didn't put two and two together at the time. The substance abuse was definitely a factor in his behavior, like throwing gasoline on a fire. In the last several years his illness was there always, but you could recognize when alcohol or hard drugs were present. I don't think I could really tell when he was using marijuana but the others got my attention."

The increase in alcohol and drug use brought Aaron into contact with Fort Bragg city police that fall. He was arrested after being refused liquor and scaring a store clerk, who then called the police. Alcohol was the reason for the arrest but Jim believes that any sort of interview with both the clerk and arresting officers would have shown there was something a little more bizarre going on.

"The City Police weren't the only ones having to deal with the new Aaron. He [had been] a problem for us but now he was starting to get scary. Before a lot of the strangeness took place inside his house, now it was outside and more visible. My sister saw behavior she couldn't believe. The scariest times were when he was abusing drugs or alcohol. The rest of the time it was just crazy nonsense. He threatened my life after he argued with me about an unsafe cooking fire he started near tall dry grass. He apologized later but that didn't make me feel better as I understood there was a lot of anger ready to blow given any little spark. He was scaring the hell out of my sister, not by threats but by just doing weird things all the time. She told him she needed that building he was living in for storage, leaving him no place to go. By this time he was causing trouble all over and different Fish & Game officers spoke to me on three different occasions about Aaron and his drinking and suspicious activity on the Coast, north of Westport. I wanted to find him a place to live but I didn't have many choices. I was trying to decide whether to buy him a little trailer and put him up on some wooded land I had some right to. But he would be a fire danger and a little too close to people [who] were afraid of him. If it was just me, I would have, but I didn't have the right to put other people at risk. I knew I was powerless to do anything on my own. I needed help and he needed help. The County had always been a dead end and I had heard of a support group for families dealing with a mentally ill family member."

ℝ

This came about in February, 2011, after Aaron had tried to drive through the school tennis courts at 80 mph after drinking a fifth of schnapps. "He wasn't hurt except for when he resisted arrest. He was in jail and my family was relieved. Everybody felt at lot safer with him in jail. I was sure this was my chance to get some help. I found the NAMI (National Alliance on Mental Illness) Family Support Group and told them how desperately I needed help and asked what to do. At this point I was already sure that what he had was schizophrenia. The group was very helpful with my education on the illness. Most importantly,

254

they helped me write a letter and instructed me about where to send it. Aaron's sister also sent me a letter to forward to Aaron's judge. She [had been] living in Arizona for the last year and didn't realize how volatile he had become recently but knew he needed help for his mental condition. Her letter was addressed to the Judge but I hand delivered it to Aaron's Public Defender with the belief that he would share it with both the Judge and the District Attorney. My letter addressed to the Jail Psychiatrist was faxed to the Jail Medical Department on February 25, 2011 and also faxed that same day to the chief psychiatrist at the Mental Health Department. The letter clearly stated that I thought Aaron had schizophrenia, and I listed specific symptoms, that he was a danger to others, had had previous arrests because of his mental health, and I asked for a psychiatric evaluation and treatment in the jail. I got no response! The case went on as if it was dealing with only a person driving drunk with no thought that he may be a drunken schizophrenic who was potentially dangerous to others. There seemed to be no concern for my family's safety or anyone else's. I could not believe it. There was no way I could keep him near home with no help at all. I had to let him go. I felt like I had called the fire department and they had hung up the phone.

"Mendocino County assumed that this accident was only about alcohol but I read much more into it. To me, drunken driving accidents are different than this. Usually a driver swerves off the road because they can't follow the line or they aren't able to judge their speed going into a turn. Simply put, they are unable to drive with any precision. Aaron's accident didn't look exactly like that. It [looked] more determined, he was said to be going 80 mph on a straight road, and one he has driven along all his life. He didn't swerve and hit any parked cars and 80 mph is awfully fast on a city street for anyone, let alone a drunk. If there was a brick building at the end of the road I'd say he was trying to commit suicide. But there is not and he was not. He knew where he was and what was at the end of the road. He knew he couldn't make a 90-degree city corner at 80 mph. He drove into a giant steel mesh net. I looked at the tire marks on the curb he hit and there was no evidence of him turning at all. Why was he so determined? What was he trying to do? There are many possibilities given the fact he had so much delusional thinking. He could have been performing some kind of Evil Knievel stunt. He may have thought he was in a rocket and might go airborne. He may have thought he was in a DeLorean and that if he went fast enough he might time travel, and if none of that worked he had the net to catch him. There are lots of possibilities but forever I'll believe it was a cry for help, and I couldn't help him."

Following the tennis court incident, Aaron's sentence was reduced and he was ordered to go to AA meetings. Jim knew this was not going to happen, that the symptoms of his illness would prevent him from meeting with any group of people. "No one was concerned when he didn't show up." Over the next month or so he completed his move out of his house. He then spent a little time on some other family property near Jim's home in some brush. Jim told him he was very welcome on the property, but to not come around if he'd been drinking. Jim also remembers a very rare talk they had when Aaron actually came into Jim's house and sat down for a few minutes. "He told me about his jail stay, as though it was a scary adventure, and he was a little excited about telling me. It was an adventure for me just to have him want to talk to me. We also talked a little about where he was going and all he could tell me was that he was going to live in the woods for a while and get his head together. I knew that wasn't entirely possible but I thought he meant he was going to get away from drugs and alcohol. I'll always look back on this conversation as a missed opportunity for me. I saw him briefly a few more times not knowing one of them would be the last."

256

During Aaron's time in jail and after, Jim tried to educate himself more on the illness, trying to understand how to best handle his son, and help him, and where the illness might be headed. Jim also tried to educate his former wife's family, but with limited success. "When I learned how little hope there was for much recovery from this illness, after it had gone untreated for this long, I went numb. I hoped that being in the woods might keep him away from alcohol and the worst of the drugs, though he may have had access to marijuana. I didn't know he had acquired a gun and I foolishly hoped that being out in the woods, away from people, would be safer for everyone. No one could or would help him and he [had] exiled himself to the deepest part of the forest.

"I have to shamefully admit at some point here that I gave up on trying to figure this out. I gave up on Aaron. I gave up on the medical profession, I gave up on my government, and I gave up on my community. It was too much for me. I was completely worn out.

"Looking back, my education on his illness was always one step behind events, always a little late to effect a significant change in the course of things. Understanding his illness a little better now, the biggest mistake I ever made was not understanding how hard it was on him, in his diminished capacity, to handle that move from his home. At the time I thought living in the woods wouldn't be much different than living in the house. He cooked outside, didn't use dishes or furniture, slept on the floor, [and] had no phone and no TV. I felt bad about his eviction as you would with anyone in a similar situation. The problem here is Aaron was not just anyone, he was a paranoid schizophrenic. He had designed the house himself for his own safety. He [had] built a six-foot wall around the house, covered all the windows with black shades, and dug a secret basement. He slept down in the basement. What was he hiding from behind the walls, the shades, and way down in a hole?

Whatever it was, when he had to move out into the woods without any walls for protection, he dug a bunker and armed himself. He went from a place in which he was safe to be crazy and where nobody bothered him to a place where he was vulnerable."

Aaron picked up the last of the things he needed in early spring and Jim never saw his son again. "I kept in contact with his mother on what he was up to, knowing she might not be telling me everything. She told me she saw him about every week and took him to the store to shop. It was one of the wettest springs I can remember; it rained until summer. I often thought about him out there alone in the cold wet forest. I tried to convince myself he'd do well out there; after all, he always liked the woods and the weather had never seemed to bother him much. I'd seen him in tank-top shirts when everyone else was bundled up in coats."

❧

When Jim read in the local newspaper about Matthew Coleman's murder on Thursday, August 11th, 2011, he didn't think of Aaron at all. There was talk in the reports and around town about a drug cartel being involved and that didn't fit Aaron in any way. Jim thought more about an incident 25 years previously when there was a missing person and another unexplained death north of Westport. At the time he had suspected some marijuana growers he knew of in the area, and that's where his thoughts went. "Several days later something reminded me of the conversations I had had earlier in the year with three different Fish & Game Officers concerning Aaron and what he might be up to on the Coast north of Westport. The first talk was about the possibility Aaron had shot an elk near Usal. The second two conversations were simply an inquiry as to what I thought Aaron was doing in the coastal area north of Westport. Aaron had been trespassing and observed acting suspiciously in the area. Both Westport and Usal were mentioned, and I asked how often, and the reply was all the time. My answer to their question was that Aaron may be doing something illegal but he may also be up there secretly meeting a spaceship because he's crazy. Those conversations made it seem to me that a number of people in law enforcement were well aware that Aaron was in the area of Coleman's murder often and that his behavior had been suspicious. Aaron's recent arrest record and my letter sent to the Sheriff's Jail Medical Staff should have made him an early suspect. I suspected they had ruled him out or they'd be looking for him."

Jim and his wife had rarely socialized with Aaron's mother's family before there was a grandchild, but now that Aaron's sister had had a baby they were invited to a family barbecue at Cleone Lake on Sunday, August 21st, 2011. "This was about two weeks after the Coleman shooting. Just before we left the party, Aaron's mother told me she had dropped Aaron off with a gun somewhere north of Westport. This information stunned me and I tried to get her to pinpoint what day she [had] dropped him off. It may have been the day after the shooting, she thought. There was alcohol at the barbecue and, from our long history, I knew it was not a good time to talk. Before I left, I told her she should call the Sheriff. I left thinking I would get together with her the next day and straighten out what day she dropped him off, and talk her into calling or call myself if I could be sure of the date. My head was spinning about many things. If I threw out my uncertain suspicions, and in fact it was the day after the shooting that she dropped him off, and therefore he was innocent, it could be a likely death sentence for him. Police have been known to shoot the mentally ill if they are holding a bat or knife, let alone a rifle. The zero response I got from officials six months earlier gave me little confidence in anyone giving a severely ill person a chance. I also had conspiracy theories; the cartel mentioned as suspect in the reports had to be more than one person. He had made a call to his mother at some point when I thought he had no phone. If there were other people involved, they may have called him up there to take the rap. The next day I made a very bad decision. I hesitated, the weather turned good, I went fishing, and by the time I tried to reach my ex-wife, she had gone on vacation.

"Yes, I made some mistakes, and should have made more effort six months earlier to communicate, but communication is a two-way street. It doesn't work if it is only in one direction; it soon breaks down. Any look at this tragedy reveals that the reason these men died was because of a lack of communication and not just on my part. There was an unbelievable lack of communication from every corner of our government. The absolute inability among us so-called sane people to work together allowed a crazy person to outsmart us as a group."

☙

On August 27th, 2011, former mayor and current Fort Bragg council member Jere Melo was shot and killed in the woods east of the town. The news of a shooting near the Skunk Train tracks spread quickly. Jim Bassler recalls, "There was a lot of false information but Aaron's name came up enough for me to realize my worst nightmare had come true. This was worse than my worst nightmare, how could this be my real life? After I picked myself up from a hellishly low place, I realized that I couldn't change the reality of what had happened but I could let people know the whole story of what did happen. Reporters soon came to my door and I hoped they wanted to know the how and why of this story. We can learn from the past and apply that knowledge to the future."

After a few days into the search for Aaron, no one from the Sheriff's Office had contacted Jim so he called them. "By this time it didn't matter if someone else was involved in the first shooting, Aaron was likely directly involved in the second shooting and should be suspected in the first. I think everyone in both families cooperated in every way they could; nobody had any secrets. I had told them early on that Aaron had mental problems but that was not going to hamper his ability to hide. He was good at it and it was part of who he was. I had plenty of personal experience looking for him. I also told them it would be unlike him to come to town or leave the area he knew, the Pudding Creek and Noyo River watersheds. He might, if pressured enough, try to get to the coastal area north of Westport, but he didn't know how to get there other than the road and he had a hard time doing or learning anything new and complex."

This was the beginning of "five traumatic weeks" for Jim Bassler. "I opened up to the press quite often and talked to many people involved in the mental health field. Aaron's mother meanwhile closed up and would not talk. I can understand that but for me the whole story had to come out.

"Detectives interviewed me several times over the next few days and were looking for some way to get Aaron to give himself up. I met with Captain Smallcomb of the County Sheriff's Office to talk about Aaron's state of mind and what he might do. The U.S. Marshals were also present at some meetings I had with Smallcomb. The press constantly wanted to talk. I agreed to many of their requests but not from television. Some of my experience with the press was not good— they got a lot of important details wrong and I was better off making my own statements, although having said that the majority were good in getting the message I was saying out.

"I am sure Aaron thought he was going to win this battle in his 'army game.' I doubt very much if he was ever afraid—he'd lost that emotion. He would not have been afraid out there. I imagine he probably just observed the searchers at times and chose to not attack them on those occasions. There had to be mutual contact for him to fire. He was pretty deep into his delusion at that time and I'm not sure if anything could have pulled him out of it.

"At first I was nervous about him showing up at my house, armed and out of his head, or just looking for help. After a little time passed, I realized he wasn't going to come that far out of the woods. A week into the search Aaron showed up at his mother's house and officers quickly pounced but Aaron was able to escape. I think this really confused them and gave Aaron a mystic quality for the rest of chase. The story I heard was that Aaron [had come] out of the woods behind his mother's house. The family in the house was aware something was happening because their dogs started barking. Someone came out to investigate but didn't see anything because a redwood stump blocked the view. At the same time, officers pulled up and released a dog. Minutes later the dog returned with Aaron's fanny pack. That same day I talked to a young Deputy Sheriff and he could not believe Aaron had gotten away from their best dog, one that had always gotten their man. He talked like Aaron was some kind of ghost or had some power over dogs. A week or so later they got a picture of Aaron breaking into a cabin and they saw the seat of his pants ripped and assumed that the dog had ripped them. This made his escape even more mysterious. I knew Aaron's capabilities as much as anyone and I have my own theory. He simply outran the dog.

"Aaron was physically capable and who knows for sure; he may have had some mystic capabilities—he certainly thought he had some, but what bothers me to this day is the people who think he was too smart to be crazy because his apprehension was so difficult. Aaron was

262

smart in some ways but much diminished in others. He was certainly smart enough to run and hide like an animal and, with the hounds after him [not having] much luck, you might as well say he was smart like a fox. That falls far short of fully rational human though. He, like a fox running from the hounds, kept doubling back to familiar territory, with a predictable outcome, given time and the number out to get him. He had only one human advantage over an ordinary fox; he was a fox with a rifle.

"From the very start I didn't think he had much chance at survival. His delusions were always locked in and he had crossed a line; I don't think there was any way to bring him out of it by talking. I did want to try though, so I rode out on the Skunk Train and tried to call him in. His mother was going to go but backed out. I don't blame her; it was very emotional. From my experience, it was impossible to get him to come out if he was hiding. Many times I'd go over to his house looking for him and surprise him outside with something he didn't what me to see. I'd get a glimpse of him bounding away into the woods. If I looked and called I could never find him. Even if he had time to hide whatever it was, he would not come out. If I didn't look for him, but waited a while and returned to his house, he'd be there and greet me. When I ask why he ran away, he told me he didn't know I was looking for him. I think his first instinct was to remain hidden and [not] give his position away. He wouldn't have shot at anyone if he wasn't discovered. Try as I would, I could not come up with an idea to get that gun safely out of his hands. I just didn't want him to hurt anyone else. I'm not sure he had much of a life left if he survived. I think we let him get too far out of this world and he was all but gone already.

"It was not going to be easy for law enforcement to get him but I knew they would cross paths at some point. Aaron would be in the wrong spot and they would shoot him. I was certain that this was the most likely outcome."

If you ask Jim who he thought Aaron was and why he would do this, the simple answer you get is that he believed his son had never "grown up." "The untreated illness didn't allow him to develop an adult mind. When he reached the age when you start to develop the thought processes required to function as an adult, the illness kept beating him back. He approached everything in his adult life as a child would. He didn't look like a child and no one bought him toys but he improvised and spent most of his time playing as a child with a limited attention span would, moving from game to game. He would try to pretend to be an adult for your benefit, like a child does when they think have to. Although he gained knowledge through most of his teens, the illness eventually drove him back into an even younger mind. His delusions were childhood dreams, locked in for life by the illness. The delusional thought expressed in the writings and drawings I saw were clearly very similar to my own dreams as a child. As a child anything is possible, we can be Captain Kirk or John Wayne or any hero we want to be. Sometimes his dreams turned scary and didn't go away when he awoke. It's normal for a child, but called paranoia in an adult. The only thing the illness brought on that was different than childhood is that he could no longer express a full range of emotion[s]. He became an unhappy child because everyone expected him to be an adult and he couldn't because the illness damaged the circuits in the brain necessary for that. If the illness tortured him, we as a society tortured him more. When he couldn't perform as required as an adult we humiliated him over and over, [then] we finally cast him off to the wilderness, a child totally unsupervised. Even though Aaron could not function better than a child, he was expected to make his own medical decisions. The final answer to the question "Why?" is that he was just playing army—in the same place he had for years and years as a child."

On Saturday October 1st, Aaron Bassler was shot and killed in the woods by members of the Sacramento SWAT team. By the time the search had entered its final week, Jim Bassler had played out all the possible outcomes and they were all bad, and some much worse than others. Most likely he thought his son would make a mistake and walk in to the wrong place at the wrong time and it would be over. "The only good outcome that I could hope for was a fantasy that his alien friends would beam him up and no one else would be hurt. But this was reality; no one had toy guns and he was gunned down.

"Was he a monster? No. Aaron was just a person with an illness. He was confused and needed more love and supervision than most of us. He was unable to get either once he became really ill and then dangerous to a level that we could not give care to him.

"I was surprised and lifted by the many cards and condolences the family received. After all that had happened, many people still had a heart. We very much appreciated and needed to know this. These good people got me to thinking that their good feelings might be better spent on helping to prevent this from happening again. The humanity and safety of this community [demand] that we develop a mental health system that does not depend solely on a mind, disabled by an illness, to make the right medical choices for themselves.

"I do not think Aaron's illness is any excuse for what he did, but I know there is no excuse for our society to be so ignorant, casual, and uncaring about this disability. At least our communities have risen above allowing the blind or physically disabled people from dragging themselves around the streets begging. But the majority of us don't mind ignoring the mentally ill in the same sad shape.

"I am having lots of trouble letting go of this. It has also crossed my mind to slam the door on this and move on or away. I looked at everything in Aaron's life up to those final developments. I [don't] see what I could have done differently. The government certainly could have done things differently. Families need help. I have a lot of respect for N.A.M.I. (National Alliance for the Mentally Ill)—they have more answers than anybody. I am glad that they will receive some money from the proceeds of this book.

"I believe I understand the feelings of loss that the Melo and Coleman families are enduring and support their efforts to put an end to the marijuana growing activities in the woods. I believe that legalizing it would be a big start. However, I think this whole series of tragic events centers around mental illness."

In October, 2012, Jim Bassler was moving forward with his efforts to work with various people and organizations to improve the treatment available to the mentally ill residents of the County. When I spoke with him he was planning to meet with County Sheriff Tom Allman to collect his son's personal belongings. It was a meeting Jim told me he needed to have, and finally receiving these items that belonged to Aaron would be another step towards closure.

∽

Chapter 12
Recollections of the "Chief Skunk"
—Robert Pinoli, Owner/Operator
of the Fort Bragg Skunk Train

Friday, August 3rd, 2012

When I called Robert to set up our meeting he had commented that he and his staff at the Skunk Train had not talked to anyone about their role in the investigation and hunt for Aaron Bassler, but almost a year had passed and perhaps it was time for him to share his thoughts and memories of that remarkable couple of months in the late summer and early fall of 2011. He also informed me that he had a fairly complete diary of his many years at the Skunk Train and that obviously included notes on the time in question. This would turn out to be very useful.

I met with Robert in his wood-paneled office in the historic Skunk Train Building in Fort Bragg. We sat down at his desk and his first comments were with regards to the fact that the previous day, in preparation for our meeting, he had gone through his diary from exactly a year earlier and had read that on that day, August 2nd, 2011, he had sat down in that very office for a conversation with Jere Melo about the problem of drug grows in the forests east of town, specifically near the Skunk Train tracks in Alpine at the 171/2 mile marker.

Robert Jason Pinoli, or "Chief Skunk" as his business card states, is the principal owner and operator of the Skunk Train, a North Coast institution that has been in operation for 127 years. "I am its caretaker in time and this is my 20th year here. During our peak season we have four departures a day from this station, each going to the Northspur station at the 21.3 mile marker, approximately the mid-point of the 40-mile track, which then continues to Willits, 18-plus miles further on. Trains also come into Northspur from there and all of our trains turn 'round at that point and return to their original destination. It is about a four-hour round-trip, with an extra hour if passengers elect to have the barbecue lunch. I have about 40 employees, part- and full-time, in the office, the shop, engineers on the trains, track maintenance crews, etc. We own all of the real estate through which the tracks run and that includes 2 tunnels and 30 bridges."

Robert recalls that meeting with Jere Melo. "Someone out there had been having campfires and on one occasion a significant fire had started in that vicinity. Jere, in his position as property manager for a timber company, had been out that way and heard gunshots from a high-powered rifle and soon after had spotted someone fitting the description of Aaron Bassler walking along the tracks before that person simply vanished into the woods."

Robert and Jere talked about this situation and Melo informed him that he had also had another recent encounter out in the woods. One was a man by the name of Allegro who was a recreational tree climber who told Melo that he had recently come face-to-face with Bassler, dressed all in black and carrying a semi-automatic weapon and a bottle of alcohol of some sort. They met on the tracks and exchanged pleasantries before Allegro headed down the hill to the river and Bassler continued along the tracks. Allegro remembered looking back and Bassler had gone from a spot on the rail tracks that could only have been either straight up or down.

∾

What are your recollections of the Matt Coleman murder on August 11th of last year? "I did not know him and had not heard his name until that day. At the time, like many folks around here, I was very sad to hear of such a tragedy. I soon learned he was another person, like Jere Melo, who loved the forest and taking care of the land. There was not much information in the press, and after a week or so the story seemed to disappear from the newspaper."

What are your recollections of Jere Melo? "I had known Jere for about 20 years, both in connection with my work with the railroad and outside that. I think I originally had seen him as one of the organizers of the annual salmon barbecue event in town and then over time we got to know each other well through our railroad connections. His office was right near to here at the end of the tracks; he worked at the division of the Georgia Pacific Mill Company. The Skunk Train had carried freight for them. When he became mayor and later [a] city council member we interacted a lot and it was not uncommon for him to call me with any problems he may have had or with a request for help in some way. He was involved with every facet of this town's activities and in our community.

"On that day, August 2nd, 2011, around train departure time—10:00am, I remember walking back to my office and seeing him there. He had come in through the back door of our building and greeted me with the words, 'Well Robert, we have a problem in the woods.' We chatted about the fires in the woods and marijuana grows, and he talked about his brief encounter with Aaron Bassler and then later with the 'really nice tree-climbing gentleman.' He finished by saying he was not asking me to do something, but if anything odd was reported to me by my guys on the trains, then could I call him."

℘

August 27th, 2011 was a Saturday and most unusually Robert was not in his office. "I had to drop off some stuff at Campovina Winery in Hopland and then my partner and I were going on to do some shopping at Costco in Santa Rosa. The Skunk Train had left Fort Bragg as usual that morning at 10:00am with 333 passengers aboard. At about 10:35am, as it was approaching the old station at South Fork, a little east of the five-mile marker, the conductor and a number of passengers heard gunshots in the woods. Shots were not unheard of, deer hunting took place in the woods, but these shots were distinctive—Pop! Pop! Pop!—semi-automatic gunfire, which is uncommon. The train continued its journey—what else were they to do? However, 10 minutes behind the train came the Speeder car—a sort of go kart that follows the train along the tracks checking that no fires have been started as a result of a passenger dropping a cigarette butt. On this occasion, as the Speeder passed the spot close to where the shots had been heard, the lone operator encountered a guy tumbling down the steep hillside with a pistol in his hand.

"Now we have certain protocols that are followed, as set out by the U.S. Department of Transport's Federal Railroads Administration. The operator immediately called the railroad office and initially it was 'heard' that the man who had appeared had shot Jere Melo. Everything reported is repeated fortunately and on the second hearing this was corrected—someone else in the woods had shot Jere Melo. The office called 911 with this information. The man who had tumbled down the hill was Ian Chaney. We never referred to this name throughout the ensuing investigation. He was always 'the person with Jere Melo' and we were very careful on this.

"We were in the tasting room at the winery when I received a call on my cell phone. The office told me what had happened and I was informed that 911 had been called. I did not really hear the details and as we continued on to Santa Rosa there was a huge cloud and sense of burden hanging over me. 'I should be in Fort Bragg' I kept thinking, 'but everything will be okay.' My cell phone now began to ring nonstop—The County Sheriff's Office, The Department of Fish and Game, the Fort Bragg Police Department. One call came from a relative of Ian Chaney's who worked for us. He told me I must get the people out of there. The train was now in Northspur, 16 miles [farther] on from the scene. The train from Willits, with 38 passengers, was also now at Northspur. I decided I needed to be in Fort Bragg to support my staff and to help in the evacuation of the passengers and crews out of Northspur, and started on my way."

Initially the plan was to send the train further east, on to Willits. There was no way that the train could return along the tracks to Fort Bragg. Lunch is served at Northspur as part of the regular ride so the passengers had food, drinks, restrooms, picnic tables, shade. "They were comfortable there, and safe. Lunch was served to them around noon. Later that afternoon, realizing that the passengers might be there awhile, and with our evening barbecue train having been canceled, we fixed everyone an early dinner of barbecue tri-tip and chicken, baked beans, corn-on-the-cob, green salad, potato salad, and a blackberry sundae for dessert. We made the passengers comfortable—the last thing we wanted was any kind of 'mutiny.' It was a great group and we had no issues. Our communications with them were good, something we believe we are very good at, and we had announced to them what had happened. We told the whole truth as far as we knew it—that former mayor Jere Melo had been shot, that the train was in a crime scene area, and that they were being asked to remain here for their own safety, with plans to either get them east to Willits by train or out of there and back to Fort Bragg some other way. It was then decided to organize buses to go and get the passengers out.

"I called the M.T.A. [Mendocino Transit Authority], the Willits Unified School District, and the Fort Bragg School District, asking each for buses. I told them what had happened and there was a need to evacuate the passengers and crews. I emphasized that it was a matter of emergency. The first two agencies said 'Yes, without question. When and where?' The Fort Bragg School District administration said they would not help us, despite the willingness of the drivers. In my mind that was inexcusable."

272

The buses were lined up in Willits when word came from the Sheriff's Office that this plan was being changed. Law enforcement officers would be going to Northspur where they would board the trains along with the passengers, and move the train a couple of miles west, to Camp Mendocino, a much easier place for the buses to get in and out of. "I was driving west along Highway 20 on my way to the office in Fort Bragg and saw many law enforcement vehicles flying by. Meanwhile, the 323 passengers boarded the trains (10 had been previously dropped off at the Holmes summer camp a few further miles west of Northspur where they planned to stay for a few days), and at around 4:30pm they were taken the two miles west to Camp Mendocino where they were met by law enforcement, loaded on to the buses, and driven via Highway 20 to Fort Bragg, with armed agents on every bus. The last passenger drove away from our depot at 6:30pm. Refunds had been given out with some people refusing them, saying our guys had gone beyond the call. The 38 passengers from Willits were taken back there while my crew members drove the train back to Northspur where it was left and police officers put them in the back of their vehicles and transported my guys back to town. Now the real work began."

Robert decided that night that the trains scheduled for the next day would be cancelled. Law enforcement had still not gotten to Jere Melo's body. Robert decided to go home, knowing that even though the Sheriff's Office had not yet asked for his assistance, the only way in and out of the Noyo River drainage area, the hundreds of square miles where the search for the suspect would begin, was either by helicopter, with landing zones not easy to find, or by the Skunk Train. The terrain was extremely unforgiving, something most of those who would be involved in the search had not seen before. As a result, before he headed home, Robert and his staff got out the very detailed maps of the area, with the bridges and tunnels and every culvert shown. They made copies and made sure they were ready for the Sheriff's Office who would find them a huge help. Later that night Robert received a call from the 10 people who had been dropped off at the Holmes summer camp asking if he was sending out another train to get them. He told them absolutely not and that they should stay where they were—"I said 'it is the safest place for you to be'—there were so many law enforcement officers in the surrounding woods."

℘

On Sunday morning, Robert received a call from the Mendocino County Sheriff, Tom Allman. "I had already had several conversations with Sheriff's Office Captain Kurt Smallcomb prior to this. Sheriff Allman told me that later that day there was to be a confidential conference call with various people and he wanted me to participate. I readily agreed and joined the conference with the Sheriff; Dave Turner, the Mayor; Linda Riffing, the City Manager; the County C.E.O., Carmel Angelo; two County Supervisors; our local representative, Kendall Smith; Supervisor John McCowen; a representative of Campbell Timberland, Jere Melo's employer; and owners of the land where his body lay."

During the meeting it was confirmed that Jere Melo was dead. "The Sheriff told of an email he had received from Melo a few days earlier, talking about his planned trip into the woods. He also shared that the person with Melo that morning in the woods had returned fire before scrambling through the woods down towards the Skunk Train tracks. Many agencies were now getting involved and Campbell Timberland [was] closing all of their forest areas. The SWAT team had been out in the woods all night and had confirmed that Melo had received a number of direct hits and that they knew that the suspect, Aaron Bassler, had acted alone. I now remembered that name from the previous conversation with Jere Melo. I pledged to the Sheriff that whatever they required, where possible, we would provide uninhibited access to."

Following the meeting, Robert cancelled all operations of the Skunk Train. "My staff seemed to be on top of everything and were dealing efficiently with the cancellations, refunds, etc., and I told them to call me for anything they may need to talk about. I was supposed to be at a pool party and barbecue. I also now recalled that Bassler had been the man who [had been] encountered by my caretaker at Northspur earlier in the year. Bassler had been with some other guys who had metal detectors. They were respectful but quickly disappeared. Apparently, Bassler and his friends [had] spent time at Lost, an old retreat about one mile west of Northspur. Apparently, I was informed later, some of my guys had met Bassler on the tracks in mid-August. It was nothing significant at the time and [it] was not reported to me. One of my staff, a former school teacher, had taught Bassler and told me that he had been spending much of his time since childhood out in the woods. He believed that nobody knew the woods as well as Aaron Bassler and to this day I am convinced of that."

Robert was extremely busy over the next few days. While [the Skunk Train was] closed to the public, he and his staff were coordinating the trains to fit with the requirements of the searchers as they were transported in and out of the forests. "On Tuesday, August 30th, one of our employees, who lives at Northspur, was reported missing and for a time we were concerned but it was a false alarm and he showed up late. In those first few days I had many conversations with Captain Smallcomb and Lt. Van Patten of the Sheriff's Office. They told me that all of the camps and residents were being evacuated. The residents could not be forced out but it was strongly suggested by the police and the whole area was sealed off. We had closed on Sunday of Labor Day weekend, our busiest day, then Monday also. The middle of the week is always a little quieter and we reopened on the Tuesday, with both uniformed and plain-clothed armed agents inside the cabs of each train. The search continued but, knowing the woods and the terrain quite well myself, I could not help but think they were searching for a needle in a haystack."

❧

On Saturday, September 3rd, which was the Labor Day weekend, the Skunk Train office received a call at about 11:45am from the driver of the morning train who reported that there was campfire smoke at the nineteen-mile post, near to Four-Point Lodge. "As far as we knew nobody was supposed to be out there. I immediately called the owners of the property there and they told me they had left days ago. I called the Sheriff's Office and informed them. They were very busy with their own plans for the ongoing search and decided not to investigate. However, we know the surroundings better than anyone and felt this was very unusual. It later turned out that there had been a burglary at the house, along with more break-ins at a number of cabins in the vicinity, all attributed to Aaron Bassler who was clearly restocking his supplies. What was amazing to many was that he had started a campfire at Four-Point Lodge on the Friday night/Saturday morning and then [had] made it all the way back to his mother's house in town, 19 or so miles, by Sunday morning!"

The following day, at around 9:00am, the Skunk Train office received a call from the Sheriff's Office telling them to cancel all trains for the day. "There had been a sighting of Bassler by law enforcement officers near his mother's house, followed by a brief encounter with a police dog in the nearby woods. This led to a large number of officers going into the woods not far from town and we had to cancel our trains on what is our busiest weekend of the year, with 700 to 800 people riding the trains per day... On [Wednesday] we received a radio call from the locomotive engineer informing us that the Holmes Camp, around the ten-and-a-half mile marker, had been the scene of a break-in. I reported this to the Sheriff's Office and an hour or so later, at 1:45pm, they called me back to say that about six cabins there had been broken into. Clearly Aaron Bassler knew the woods all too well and was stockpiling his supplies as the searchers tried in vain to pin him down."

The next day, Thursday, September 8th, Robert remembers being very busy with the "new" logistics of his operation when he received a request from the Sheriff's Office for a train to be ready to go into the woods. "The way things had changed had become the 'new way of things' around here. I was told the searchers needed a train to be set aside for them at 8:00am on the following Sunday and that Aaron Bassler's father, Jim Bassler, was going to be on that train and taken into the woods with a bullhorn and would be trying to contact his son and hopefully get him to give himself up.

"At 3:15pm that Thursday, after we had been transporting agents in and out of the woods all day long, I received a call to contact the engineer and conductor on the regular scheduled train and to tell them to return to the terminal a.s.a.p. The searchers were focusing the area around the tunnel once again, not far from the mother's house. This was just another typical day and we continued to do what we could to help when and where we could."

☙

For the next three weeks this was how things were, day in and day out. "This became our 'normal' and we now had plain-clothed and uniformed officers on every train. Every day was a huge flurry of activity—it was what our 'new normal' had become as we continually rotated our crews often on 12-hour shifts. We were now into our fall schedule of one train per day out of Fort Bragg, although we had two or three more ready to go if requested, and they often were. On one occasion the request came for an extra car to be added to the train going out from town. We set this up for them and then at the last minute they changed their mind and so I told my guys to take the car off. Then they changed their mind again and the SWAT teams suddenly showed up at the station, in full camouflage and painted faces, all standing alongside my regular passengers on the platform. I remember vividly an older couple came over to me and said they wanted to go on the ride but were hesitant. I told them I [understood] but to be honest, if there was any day to pick in the last hundred years or so of rides on the Skunk Train, this was probably the safest day of all. There was more security that day than the President travels with! I believed that there was no reason for people to think they were in danger at any time, not just that day. Full-uniformed officers were on every train. This was a crime scene and quite frankly the suspect did not want to be seen.

"By mid-September the search had narrowed considerably and the teams were focusing on the area to the east of Northspur, in areas known as Crowley and Shake City. Frankly, I felt this was an area where he would not be. There [were] many year-round residents in that vicinity and, given what was happening, these people [would] shoot anything that [moved]."

Personally, this had been a tough few weeks for Robert. Quite apart from the loss of friend Jere Melo and the toll of dealing with the "new normal" of the Skunk Train operation, another good friend, John

Bogner, had committed suicide. "We did things with a smile on our face because that's what we do, but I have to say it was trying at times, being asked to repeat trips into the woods when we had just returned and other such inconveniences were at times difficult to accept, but we did and would no doubt do the same again. This was a working railroad built in the late 1800s by the Mayor of Fort Bragg, C.R. Johnson, who was a true visionary when he built this logging railroad as a standard gauge railway. He did so to serve this community and I don't want us to ever lose sight of that. We had none of the extra hours our staff worked scheduled or budgeted for; we had to pay for all of the extra costs incurred."

℘

On Thursday, September 29th, the morning train had just arrived at Northspur when word came that Bassler had opened fire on three members of the Alameda SWAT team not far from there. "We were told to get the passengers back on the train and for it to return to town. This was done without further incident and we learned that Bassler had once again disappeared into the woods east of Northspur. It turned out that he not gone east and had in fact doubled back, because the following evening he broke into a property on the edge of town here, 14 miles or more to the west!

"That Friday evening, September 30th, I was in my office working on food and supply logistics and the crew were waiting to go out into the woods once again. Captain Smallcomb called and gave the go-ahead for the train to leave with its cargo of supplies and search teams. As I was on the phone with him, his other phone rang and he asked me to hang on. I'd been there that day from 4:00am and it was now 8:30pm and dark. I could hear Smallcomb and whom I assume was a detective of some sort talking about somewhere being broken in to. I [thought I] heard the words Sherwood Road mentioned but wasn't sure. He got back to me and told me to hold the train until further notice. I went home and was unwinding there when the phone rang. It was Captain Smallcomb again. He asked me to have a train ready at 8:00 in the morning but to wait for his call. I said 'Yes' and went to bed.

☙

"The next morning, Saturday, October 1st, we heard nothing. Then just before 10:00am the Captain then called to say he did not need the train. Shortly afterwards he regular scheduled train went out and I headed home—I was due to attend the funeral of my friend John Bogner at which I was to give a speech. As I was driving home, at about 11:00am or so, I experienced what I can only describe as a surreal moment. It was very odd. A cold shiver struck me and yet I was sweating. I didn't know what to think. Sure, I had been overdoing things for 36 days or so, as had my staff and crews and many others. I felt completely off-kilter. I reached home, showered, changed, and at 12:15pm I left for the Lake Mendocino Clubhouse and the service, picking up some friends on the way. We arrived at about 12:35pm and there were hundreds of people there. I still felt odd but was used to public speaking so knew that was not what was causing this.

"People were sipping martinis, Manhattans, and other cocktails, [and] even though I could do with one, I didn't as I wanted to maintain my composure. John was a close friend and I was upset. A friend of mine had a martini in her hand and she said 'We are going to be just fine' and gave me a sip. I then went to the restroom and realized that my cell phone had been vibrating in my pocket. I missed the call and it went to voicemail. The District Attorney, David Eyster, came into the bathroom behind me and said, 'We're done.' I didn't really take it in as I was retrieving the call on my phone. I listened to the message from Captain Smallcomb—I still have it on my phone. He said, 'Robert, it's Kurt, call me on my cell. Life is going to be a little easier for you now. I can't thank you enough for what you have provided for the Sheriff's Office over the past 34/35 days. You have been a great friend. Call me.' I knew exactly what he meant. I went and made the speech and that night had quite a few of those cocktails."

✧

The following day, Robert was in his office with various members of his crews and staff. "It was odd, the activities were different; the 'new normal' was done. What would we do with all of our free time now?!

"There wasn't a single person I was aware of who did not like Jere Melo. It was a time of great sadness in town but people wanted to do everything they could to help and make sure nobody else got hurt. As for our customers, many were very complimentary of how we handled the situation and were very understanding. We received many wonderful cards in the mail and this all helped us as we dealt with the situation.

"The financial burden was something we accepted. What else can you do? As a result of some of the expense I have had to lay some people off. I do not like screwing with people's lives in that way. It was very hard to do and I hated it.

"In terms of the effects on our operation, on any given day our security measures are in place, the crew's safety comes first, then that of the passengers. This event made us more aware of the possible threats,

God forbid, but we have not made any really significant changes."

❦

Robert wanted to share his thoughts on a few things...

Jere Melo—"A nonviolent, non-confrontational, man with a mission. He was a real gentle giant, a lumberman, and a gentleman. He was just in the wrong place at the wrong time."

The law enforcement operation—"Fantastic. Captain Smallcomb may come across as very unapproachable but actually, in reality, he is actually one of the most approachable people I know. He was no-nonsense; black and white, no grey—a skunk who was very sure of his color."

The press—"I had some interaction and my style is to treat everyone the same. I was the same with the press and was always straight with them. I told them to not misquote me and to be reliable with the facts. If they were going to do a shoddy job then we were not going to talk. For the most part they did a fine job. Frankly, most press these days are sloppy and I have no problem in letting them know that. I had a fine rapport with them through this investigation and they never painted the Skunk Train in a bad light. I thought some of their photographs were great, my favorite being the one of police dog Dutch on the front of one of our locomotives."

Sheriff Tom Allman—"A fantastic person to work with and to have in the service of our community. He has to be 'the Sheriff' but you couldn't ask for a fairer or more understanding person; such a giving person. I attend many charity events and he's always there, giving back to the community. He is very professional yet fun to be around. He was here in my office on countless occasions as the events unfolded.

I remember he was in here on Friday, September 30ᵗʰ, the day after the shootout between Bassler and the Alameda SWAT team, and the day before Bassler was shot. I offered him a beer and he said he'd love nothing more but couldn't. We had a good talk that day. He was always very good at checking in and finding out how the staff and I were doing. We were very appreciative of that.

"At this point I still think about the events, just about a year ago now. I feel bad for Jim Bassler. He wanted to help his son but at some point previously I believe he needed to do more than just raise his hand. As for Aaron Bassler's mother, she earned the right of place next to her son as a result of not informing the police of her dropping off Bassler with a gun and not reporting this when she heard that Matt Coleman was shot and killed right there the next day. She would surely lose a civil court action against her as an accessory in the murder of Jere Melo by her son a couple of weeks later."

❦

Chapter 13

Searching for Bassler
—Mendocino County Sheriff's Office
Detective Sergeant Greg Van Patten

Thursday, September 13th, 2012

At the time of the investigation, Greg Van Patten was a Detective Sergeant who led the Mendocino County Sheriff's Office team of detectives in this case. He was promoted in April, 2012, and I met with Lieutenant Van Patten at the Sheriff's Office in Ukiah. He had previously helped on this project with the maps and diagrams, for which his unique knowledge of the four shooting scenes proved to be invaluable.

జ

In the middle of the night of Thursday, August 11th, 2011, Detective Sergeant (D.S.) Greg Van Patten was woken by a phone call to his home in Ukiah, He was informed that a body had been found out on the Coast, 20 or so miles north of Fort Bragg and, as the leader of the Sheriff's Office Detective Unit, he headed that way.

Before he arrived he had heard that it might be an animal attack and then that it was a possible suicide. He was told that the deceased was Matthew Coleman, a conservation worker, and within a very short time of his arrival he knew that it was a homicide. "It was very obvious, and I also knew, given where we were in a very isolated spot, that a lot of investigative work was going to be needed in this case. The victim was possibly trying to get into his car during the shooting and the fact that the body had been defecated on suggested that the killer was making some kind of message or warning. With regards to this being a marijuana-related crime, I was thinking that was a possibility, but anything could be under the circumstances. Something was not right and many theories needed to be explored."

Within a few days, Van Patten and his team had arranged for overflights of the area to be made and nothing to suggest a marijuana link was seen. The search and rescue teams had also come up empty in this regard. "Our focus was to find out more about Matthew Coleman— what he was involved with and whether or not he had enemies. By all accounts he was a decent human being with great passion for his work on preserving the environment in this area. There was no obvious reason at all for his murder."

℘

A week into the investigation, on August 18th, the search and rescue team had still not found any shell casings, but, very significantly as it turned out, they had come across a tin foil pipe, or "blunt," and wrappers from Hershey's Kisses chocolate candy. "These were not fresh, they had been there for a week or more, and based on the bullet trajectory investigation conducted by a criminalist from the Department of Justice, these items were found to be in the area from where the shooter had fired. Two shots had hit Coleman's car, with one of those going through the bumper and into the tire, while two more shots had hit Coleman, one fatally separating his aorta. We believe the killer fired these shots in quick succession."

The items discovered were found to not belong to Matthew Coleman. "He did have a regular small pipe with him, with which he smoked marijuana, and he did have cigarettes, but he was very particular with the butts from those, always taking care to put them in his pocket after smoking.

"We never did find any shell casings whatsoever. We went back to the scene with the Department of Fish and Game who have specially trained canines who sniff out gunpowder. The handlers were very confident of finding something, even though it was a few weeks later, but we had no luck. We tried metal detectors and were down on our hands and knees searching the undergrowth. It was very hard to see and it's no exact science where those casings might land.

"As for the fecal matter on the body and the driver's side door of the car, it was sent to forensics but found to be too contaminated and its consistency not suitable for DNA recovery."

During the two weeks following the murder of Matthew Coleman, three detectives worked on the case but only one remained full time— Detective Andrew Porter, who would pull in others as and when needed for certain tasks. Little further progress in terms of a suspect in this murder case had been made and it disappeared from the newspaper headlines. But that was all to change very drastically on August 27th.

☙

On that fateful morning, D.S. Van Patten was with his two young children preparing for one's soccer team's picture day in Ukiah. "I received a call and was told that all units were responding to Fort Bragg where there had been a shooting in the nearby woods. There had been a fatal injury and reports stated that another person was fleeing the scene, calling into 911 while under fire. Homicide detectives were on their way, along with the Sheriff's Office SWAT team and the major crimes task force. I soon learned that the former mayor of Fort Bragg and current councilman, Jere Melo, had gone into the woods that morning and [had] been shot while searching with another man, Ian Chaney, for illegal marijuana gardens on the timberland he was managing. I headed out to the Coast once again.

"Our initial task was to get to Jere Melo's body and assess what we could do to save his life if possible. Although we thought the shooter had probably left the vicinity, we could not be sure, and had to proceed with great caution out there. It was a very thickly wooded area with heavy brush and many natural hiding places. We were unable to get any closer to the body than 100 yards or so by nightfall and we had to stop the search, although SWAT teams did stay out there all night.

"During the afternoon we interviewed Ian Chaney and, based on what he told us—that Melo [had been] hit three times and fell to the ground without any attempt to break his fall, we believed that Melo was dead. Chaney identified the shooter as Aaron Bassler. I remember the dispatcher broadcasting that name and the Fort Bragg Police Department Sergeant, Brandon Lee, commenting, 'That guy's a nut.' That evening I was kept very busy organizing our resources and processing the situation for the continuing investigation."

The detective team stayed out in Fort Bragg that evening, and by first light on Sunday, August 28th had been joined by various other law enforcement agencies. The SWAT team reached the crime scene and the bunker that had been built there by Bassler by about 11:00am and confirmed that Jere Melo was dead. "We were taken out on the Skunk

Train to mile marker six, and from there my team and I hiked to the scene where others also gathered, including the Medical Emergency Unit and the Mendocino Major Crimes Task Force. The area was secured with a perimeter covered by the SWAT team, even though, as I said before, there was a high probability that Bassler had fled.

"We knew the name of the person we were dealing with, we knew he had committed an ambush-style killing, that he had a high-powered assault rifle, and quite possibly was wearing body armor. Also, at the scene that morning, I remember thinking that there was a strong possibility of a link between the Melo murder and the shooting of Matt Coleman. We found more candy wrappers and a blunt—that was a very unique piece of evidence found at both murder scenes."

❧

During the following few days, Van Patten and his team of detectives sent off the blunt that had been found near Bassler's bunker for DNA testing. They also continued to work on intelligence gathering, which included interviewing Bassler's parents. All of this was gathering momentum in the same direction, and with a 7.62mm rifle round found at the Melo crime scene, which is a round from a high velocity rifle that would have resulted in the bullet wounds on Matthew Coleman, they firmly believed that Bassler should be considered as "a person of interest" in the Coleman murder also. These thoughts were further validated after a further interview with Bassler's mother.

"Bassler's mother told us that on the day before the Matt Coleman shooting, she had driven her son to Cape Vizcaino on Highway 1 where she dropped him off with a scoped, high-powered rifle. Meanwhile, we also interviewed Bassler's friend, Jeremy James, who told us that he was aware that Bassler knew that area well and had spent time there. We also learned from the mother that he had phoned her a week or so after the shooting from Shelter Cove, north of the Coleman crime scene. We traced that call to a woman's cell phone and we interviewed her. She told us that she was parked on the highway and a man matching the description of Bassler had approached her and asked if she knew where the nearest phone was. She offered the guy her cell phone which he accepted and used. The man told her that he had walked to the location from the Usal area, which she noted was perhaps 40 miles or so away. After using the cell phone, he asked for a ride and the woman agreed. After about 15 miles she dropped him off at the Shelter Cove/Whitehorn junction and he began walking in the direction of Shelter Cove. At the interview, she viewed the wanted poster of Aaron Bassler and was almost 100 percent certain that the man she had given the ride to was him.

"Once we knew the name of Bassler from Ian Chaney, we checked our records and, following an incident at the Fort Bragg Middle School earlier in the year, when he had crashed his vehicle into the tennis courts there and was arrested, we had his DNA from a sample of his blood. Given that he was our suspect in the Melo murder and, now, following the interviews, that there were reasons to suspect he was involved in the Coleman murder, we compared the DNA on record to the DNA we processed from the blunt at the Coleman murder scene. We got a match.

"I believe that Jere Melo possibly would not have been killed if Aaron Bassler's mother had done the right thing and reported what she knew after hearing about Coleman's murder occurring and its very close proximity to where she had dropped her son off with his rifle. After that first murder, Melo's company, Hawthorne Campbell Timber, was asking us if they should tell their employees to not go into the woods near to Fort Bragg, and we said we could not strongly advise them either way.

Had we known that Bassler had been dropped off at Cape Vizcaino and was therefore "a person of interest" in the Coleman shooting, we would have investigated him, and then knowing that he frequented the woods where Melo worked, we would have certainly said he should not go there.

"Bassler's mother told us she didn't think her son could have been involved and did not want us to harass him. She felt he was not capable of doing such an unprecedented act of violence. In the following weeks of the search, she did go on to help us many times and we certainly needed her on our side as she was the one person he might contact. However, thinking about the fact that she had failed to act on what she knew was in my mind wrong, it led to Melo's murder, and it took everything inside me to stop myself from calling her out on that."

∽

On Sunday, September 4th, after a week of searching the unforgiving terrain deep in the woods, contact with Bassler was finally made—by the Sheriff's Office best "bite dog," Dutch. Van Patten recalls, "It was pretty amazing that he got away from Dutch that day. He had made a visit to his mother's property on the edge of the [forest] and ran off into the woods when law enforcement approached. The dog got close and we believe he may have made contact. We will never know. [Dutch returned] with Bassler's fanny pack that contained a blunt. The searchers were not far behind the dog but heard nothing. That terrain was very rough and overgrown and yet they could not hear anyone scrambling through the woods. Nobody heard a thing. It was very eerie.

"Dealing with that terrain was one of our biggest difficulties. It was pretty dark due to the thick tree cover, the brush was deep and difficult to walk through, there were many natural bunkers and downed trees for the suspect to hide in, and the poison oak was everywhere—a big issue for the searchers. We felt [Bassler] might be 10 feet away and we'd still not see or hear him. In fact, in some ways, it was almost a good thing that we didn't know if he was watching us. Even the very experienced guys from the U.S. Marshals Service had never experienced terrain that dense and they had been on many fugitive hunts.

"I felt for the handlers of the bloodhounds who were out there at the front of the search parties. They were certainly very vulnerable. Watching what their dogs were doing as they sniffed the ground meant that the handlers were not always completely aware of their surroundings. They did weeklong tours and one of them, after his tour, had said, 'I have never been so scared in my whole life. I'm leaving and not coming back. I wish you all the luck in the world—you will need it.'"

℃

As time went on, the investigators learned more and more about Bassler's abilities and tendencies as a man on the run in the woods. "He was tactically very savvy. The shootings of Matt Coleman and Jere Melo showed us that. He was only ever going to engage us if he thought he had the advantage. I believe he probably watched us quite often but chose not to confront us. He would know the prime spots but, as the operation moved forward and the area where we thought he was became smaller, I believe he got more desperate. He would eventually have to go on the offensive.

"His survival skills would be more tested as winter approached and they would not be as effective. In September he was still able to sleep outside, on a blanket somewhere, committing burglaries at the cabins in the woods and stealing provisions but not staying inside for any longer than he had to. He was very smart and only ever started small warming fires, less than a foot in diameter and under the cover of trees. The overflights never detected any. We never thought he'd leave the area. He had spent his entire life there—it was his comfort zone. This meant we seemed to be always two steps behind him and, in the early days, his moves were very hard to predict. This changed over time as we felt we were learning more about what he'd do next, but it remained very difficult.

"I don't believe we questioned the tactics we had developed but it did become apparent that tracking him was not going to get us the result that we wanted. He was just too good out there. In modern-day law enforcement you are on the chase for the bad guy. That is what we know and what we do. That was not going to work in this case. Intelligence-gathering was helping us better predict his tendencies and we began to set up posts where we thought he might come across us. This was certainly a more efficient way for us to operate. Bassler was also evolving his tactics and no doubt gaining confidence in his ability to go unnoticed. He was using some of the bigger roads in the woods and also the dry creek beds, enabling him to move around very quickly. It was him against the world and he probably had a sense of invincibility. He was overconfident in the end.

"We were working smarter and became more hopeful as time went on. The mantra became 'Today is the last day' but the sheer size of the search area meant it was always going to take time. As I said, each day were gained more understanding of his tendencies and behavior. He had a sense of purpose to everything he did, and getting food from the cabins was a big part of his efforts. We watched those areas closely, and we had a bloodhound out there not long after one burglary and for 20 minutes he was on his scent. Suddenly there was nothing for him to follow. It was very unusual. Even the dog seemed dumbfounded.

"There were emotional highs and lows and many of us worked for weeks on end without a break, 12-plus hours every day. But morale was high, nobody wanted to be off duty if there was a break or big lead in the case, and people had to be ordered to take some sleep."

☙

The discovery of the photographs, one in particular, of Aaron Bassler breaking into a cabin at the scout camp deep in the woods on September 12th, was "a huge part of the investigation.

"We were thinking, with no confirmed sighting of Bassler for over a week since the Dutch incident, that one of our biggest assets, the U.S. Marshals, might be leaving us. We could not say with great certainty that Bassler was still in the vicinity and they had other cases to deal with. Those photographs, depicting an armed suspect still around in the search area, rejuvenated the searchers' morale and ensured that the Marshals would stay. It gave us a second wind and was a huge lift. I think the Marshals might have been moved on to other projects in just a few days if we had not got that break."

The game camera had been set up at the camp on the advice of the caretaker there. There had been break-ins earlier in the year and it was thought this might have been Bassler, so the caretaker offered his camera, and it was set it up overlooking the porch of one of the cabins. "Many of the 40 or so cameras we had positioned in the woods were motion activated. When that [happened], it worked like a cell phone and a call was automatically made to the command post, the GPS reading given and tracked, and a check on the camera in question would be made by searchers and detectives. The U.S Marshals had set up a cell phone tower to get better reception after we had been having some problems. However, this camera was not cell phone-activated and so it was checked every couple of days in person.

"On this occasion, along with five or six others, I went out to the cabin to check if anything had been spotted. We stood on the porch and downloaded the disc in the camera onto a laptop computer. A few grainy images appeared and then—a person standing right where we were standing, holding an assault rifle, and appearing to break into the cabin. The hair on my neck went up as I realized this photo sequence could have taken place just minutes before we arrived—he might still be right there nearby. We froze and were silent. We could hear something knocking, a sound on a nearby corrugated roof of one of the cabins. I thought it might be him moving around... I glanced at the date and time on the computer and saw that the pictures were from 36 hours or so earlier and then the noise turned out to be acorns falling from the trees. Still, it was a very scary moment and we were all a little shocked. We had no cell phone or radio service there and had to hike out not knowing if he was watching. That was a moment I shall not forget. When we reported what we had seen there was a great deal of elation at the command post—we had confirmation that he was still around."

❧

Two more weeks of searching passed by with no further sightings. There was, however, the slow but steady process of gradually narrowing down of the search area from the original 400 square miles, plus more insights to the patterns of Bassler's movements and behavior. By Thursday, September 29th, the search area was down to about six square miles and it was in this area that the Alameda County SWAT team encountered Bassler in the woods, an engagement that saw two separate shootouts occurring in a period of about 20 minutes. Nobody was hit and Bassler eluded law enforcement once again, retreating into the woods without trace. The Alameda team was very experienced but more so in urban areas, and they left the following day, a development that was repeated by a number of the many law enforcement agencies assisting in the investigation. They were only available for a relatively short time before they would have to withdraw and resume their regular duties.

"This was our backyard and even we were out of our element. We knew the dangers and accepted them. We hoped for the best and expected the worst. However, by the time of the shootout with Alameda SWAT, we were pretty confident that [Bassler] was now boxed inside an area of about six square miles. We were very aware of his ability to move quickly and had been told that he could go from Fort Bragg to Rockport, 25 miles or so, in a day of power-walking. We also knew he had supplies in various camps in the woods. However, we were still surprised when the next day we heard that there had been a burglary 12 miles or so to the west, on the outskirts of Fort Bragg. The circumstances of this new break-in seemed to point to Aaron Bassler as the suspect but it was almost inconceivable."

Bassler had indeed escaped from the "six square miles." This new break-in was reported at about 4:30pm on Friday, September 30th, and operations were moved almost entirely to this new area. "That morning we were told it was unsafe for us to conduct our investigation of the previous day's shootout scene as it was thought Bassler might still be around. The scene had to be fully secured by the SWAT teams before we could go in and so we had [to wait] until the afternoon to begin. We had been working on that when we were told that everyone was moving west to this new crime scene where the bloodhound had hit Bassler's scent and was moving forward, nose to the ground, on his trail. However, as darkness fell, it was decided to call off any further pursuit that night. It was a huge gamble to move everyone out there. We did not know how he had got through the perimeter but, based on the bloodhound's reactions and other factors at this burglary scene, we were sure he had."

ↀ

On the morning of Saturday, October 1st, D.S. Van Patten was picking up his niece from her S.A.T. test. "I received an email from dispatch stating that Captain Smallcomb advised that 'the situation was resolved.' Aaron Bassler had been shot by members of the Sacramento SWAT team and was dead. I began to call my people and when I arrived in Fort Bragg there was a sense of relief in everyone's faces. We had all been constantly aware that someone from law enforcement might get injured or killed. Once again, my job was just starting, and we headed into the woods and assisted the DA's team in processing the scene where Bassler had been shot and killed. Throughout the investigation, our prime responsibility was intelligence gathering, although I should say that at times my guys and I did assist in the actual search, too. We got to work on the shooting scene; a huge sense of relief was felt by us all."

ↀ

Van Patten's experience with the press was very positive. "Apart from their continued use of the phrase 'manhunt,' we had no problems with the media. We wanted the press to emphasize that we were not out there to kill Aaron Bassler. Our goal was 'suspect apprehension.' On that final morning, the Sacramento SWAT team was faced with a decision based on their training and knowledge. Bassler was dictating how the situation went. He had shown just a day or so earlier that he was willing to take violent action."

As for their dealings with the public, Van Patten thinks of that as an even more positive experience. "It is easy to get jaded at times but this is a profession, not a job, and I feel I want to make a difference in the community. I was in contact with so many people who respected what we were doing, and their support continually rejuvenated us and maintained our sense of purpose. That sense is better than any paycheck I get. I never thought we'd get the kind of support we did with all of the community fundraising, food donations, lodging provided, cards sent thanking us and asking us what they could do. I am very gracious and grateful for that."

As for anything that he felt could have been done differently, D.S. Van Patten thinks their organization of resources might have been a little bit better but overall not much more could have been done. As for the right calls? "Getting the U.S. Marshals was critical. They were a huge resource and were very respectful of us local guys. They did not treat us like some 'Podunk' country cops and were very down-to-earth. They had to be busy every day and if they were not out there in the woods they would be mopping the floors at the post or taking out the garbage. They were top-notch guys among many top guys and we established so many positive relationships as a result of this investigation."

Looking back a year later and now a Lieutenant, Van Patten reflects, "It was a very tough time on our families. Not only were they neglected but also wives would pack our bags and not be sure if we would be coming home. I have a 10-year-old, and she had many questions expressing her fears and concerns. I answered them truthfully. Other than that, the ripples from that time are still surfacing. Any time I am in the woods now I think of those days and the hairs on my neck go up. There are many little triggers from that time that still have that effect. They probably always will. Apart from that, I do miss all those wonderful cookies, baked goods, and great burritos—we had such great community support.

"As far as the big picture and other 'Aaron Basslers' are concerned, I think some things need to change. I don't get too involved in that discussion but I believe in nothing ventured, nothing gained. We should certainly work on whatever can be put in place that may have helped in preventing this case from happening."

∾

ADDENDUM A

Aaron Bassler: The District Attorney's Final Report

The following is the official inquiry into the murders committed by Aaron Bassler, and Bassler's death at the hands of law enforcement. The report is the work of Mendocino County District Attorney David Eyster, Assistant DA Paul Sequiera, DA investigator Tim Kiely, and DA spokesman Mike Geniella. These events began with the murder of Matt Coleman on August 11th, 2011 and ended with the shooting death of Bassler by law enforcement on October 1st, 2011. We have omitted several footnotes not necessary to the narrative, and have renumbered and appended those notes that seem crucial to a full understanding of these locally unprecedented events. (All notes appear at the end of the transcript.)

DA Determines Fatal Officers-Involved Shooting Of Serial Killer[1] Outside Of Fort Bragg Was Legally Justified

The Mendocino County District Attorney's Office has completed its full and rather exhaustive review of the officers-involved fatal shooting of Aaron James Bassler, age 35, formerly of Fort Bragg. Senior members of the District Attorney's Office, particularly District Attorney David Eyster himself, have carefully reviewed the entire investigation relating to allegations of Bassler's criminal misconduct, law enforcement's response, and Bassler's ultimate demise on October 1, 2011 in the immediate presence of members of the Sacramento County SWAT team.[2]

As determined by the United States Supreme Court, the standard for review of any use of force during any manhunt is objective reasonableness. According to the U.S. Supreme Court, that reasonableness should be determined based upon a reasonable officer's assessment of four factors:

(1) the nature of the crime at issue,

(2) whether the suspect is an immediate threat to the safety of the officer or others,

(3) whether the suspect is attempting to evade arrest through resistance or flight,

(4) the degree to which the situation is tense, uncertain and rapidly evolving. This last point acknowledges that officers must act with little time to analyze and consider circumstances, rather than with the luxury of 20-20 hindsight.

Based on the combined investigatory efforts of all involved, when reviewed and evaluated under the mandates of applicable law, it is hereby the findings of the District Attorney that:

(1) The evidence is clear beyond a reasonable doubt that Aaron James Bassler murdered Matthew Roger Coleman on August 11, 2011 in cold blood while Bassler was trespassing on private property in Mendocino County;

(2) Between August 11, 2011 and August 27, 2011, the evidence is clear and convincing that at least one of Aaron James Bassler's immediate

family members withheld critical information that would have reasonably warned and focused law enforcement—prior to the death of Jere Lynn Melo and the attempted murder of Ian Philip Chaney—that Bassler should be considered an armed and dangerous suspect in the murder of Matthew Roger Coleman;

(3) The evidence is clear beyond a reasonable doubt that Aaron James Bassler murdered Jere Lynn Melo on August 27, 2011 while lying in wait, in ambush and in cold blood while Bassler was trespassing on private timberlands in Mendocino County;

(4) The evidence is clear beyond a reasonable doubt that Aaron Bassler attempted to murder Ian Philip Chaney on August 27, 2011 by lying in wait, from ambush and in cold blood while Bassler was trespassing on private timberlands in Mendocino County;

(5) The evidence is clear beyond a reasonable doubt that Aaron James Bassler attempted to murder members of the Alameda County Sheriff's Department, who were assigned to and deployed in Mendocino County to provide mutual aid to the Mendocino County Sheriff's apprehension effort;[3]

(6) The evidence is clear beyond a reasonable doubt that the lethal use of force applied against Aaron James Bassler causing his death was objectively reasonable given the totality of the information known to law enforcement and objectively reasonable given the circumstances and information personally known and observed by the Sacramento County law enforcement officers assigned to and deployed in Mendocino County to provide mutual aid to the Mendocino County Sheriff's apprehension effort.[4]

The Murder of Matthew Coleman

On August 11, 2011, Matthew Roger Coleman,[5] age 42, a former Fish and Game Department employee and current land manager for the Mendocino Land Trust, was found shot to death beside the driver's door and partially in his vehicle on private property in the area of Cape Vizcaino outside of Westport. Those who directly viewed the crime scene believed that Coleman had either tried to use the vehicle as cover or was trying to get into the vehicle to escape an attack.

Coleman had worked as a conservation steward, volunteer coordinator and wildlife population surveyor for the Mendocino Land Trust during the past six years. Coleman had been clearing brush near a 400-acre ranch owned by the Save the Redwoods League north of Westport in coastal Mendocino County. While some members of the local community and media immediately speculated that Coleman's death may have been the result of trespass activity by illegal marijuana cultivators, no evidence of marijuana cultivation was found at or near the crime scene.[6] However, clues found at that crime scene and other evidence would ultimately identify Aaron James Bassler as the individual who murdered Coleman.

An autopsy performed on August 15, 2011 determined that Coleman had been shot in the lower abdomen and right upper arm, with the bullet traveling through the arm into the torso, wounds inflicted by what authorities believed to be a high-powered rifle. The cause of death was declared to be gunshots to right chest and right flank. At the crime scene, law enforcement investigators did not locate any shell casings that could later be used to trace back the casings by ballistics to a particular firearm. However, on August 18, 2011, a Search and Rescue Team member located a piece of aluminum foil in the crime scene that had been rolled up and fashioned to smoke marijuana.[7] Burnt marijuana was still in the device. This item was found at a location where it was believed the person shooting at Coleman would have been positioned. A wad of foil from Hershey chocolate Kisses was also located. These evidentiary items, along with DNA testing and witness statements, would eventually positively identify Aaron James Bassler as the individual who murdered Matthew Coleman.

During the course of the overall investigation it was determined on August 28, 2011—the day after the murder of Jere Melo and the attempted murder of Ian Chaney—that Laura Brickey, the biological mother of Aaron Bassler, had driven her son north on Highway 1 on August 10, 2011 and eventually dropped him off before noon at the driveway designated as 44000 North Highway 1. This is the same roadway leading out to the scene where Mr. Coleman was found murdered. A planned trip, Bassler had gone shopping at the Safeway and Purity markets in Fort Bragg for food and other provisions. Investigators know his mother took him to Safeway to shop on August 8, 2011. In addition to items purchased at the two stores, the mother also belatedly disclosed that her son was armed with a rifle when she transported him to the Point Vizcaino area.[8] She also said that this was not the first time that she had dropped Bassler off in this area.[9] Approximately one month prior, the mother had dropped Bassler off across the highway from this same location. Bassler had told his mother that he had two camps in the Westport area.[10]

When asked to provide background on her son, the mother explained to investigators that she believed something was wrong with her son because he had anger fits and he was paranoid around people. The mother placed blame for these personality manifestations on a claim that Bassler had used "acid" and had experienced a bad trip.[11] When asked about her son's Federal court-ordered counseling flowing from a 2009 incident where he lobbed notes about aliens and stars into the Chinese Consulate in San Francisco, the mother told law enforcement that no diagnosis of mental illness resulted from her son's nine-month long interaction with mental health professionals in that matter. The mother noted that her son had recently taken up chewing tobacco. When her son smoked marijuana, the mother said he would use the aluminum foil off of the top of plastic bottles, though she further added that she didn't think her son would ever smoke marijuana in the form of a joint. When asked about her son and opium poppies, the mother said he had tried to grow poppies wherever she had lived. She believed he was trying to get opium out of the plants.[12] Finally, when her son had access to a television, the mother reported that he only watched English language stations broadcasting the daily news of China or weather channels. Meanwhile, the father reported to law enforcement his opinion that his son was a "paranoid schizophrenic" who thinks that everybody is following him. A friend of Bassler reported that Bassler, starting in early 2011, was becoming more radical about being able to survive any type of armed encounter with the federal government. Bassler talked with this friend about making bunkers and how Bassler considered himself a survivalist.[13]

Further, after the death of Jere Melo, the mother also provided some information as to her son's whereabouts before and after Coleman's death. It was disclosed that the mother received a telephone call from her son on or about August 18, 2011 at about 2 o'clock in the morning. She told investigators that the son did not sound "screwed up" during the short call. The son told his mother not to call the Sheriff. He also wanted his father to be told that he had checked in so nobody would come looking for him.[14] This call was traced back to a cell phone of young woman who, when eventually located, confirmed that she had loaned her cell phone to a man she later was able to identify as Bassler from a photograph. The man approached the woman who was sitting in her vehicle at the Ettersberg Road junction of Briceland Road. He told the woman that he had walked to the junction from Usal and was looking for the nearest telephone. The woman offered the man the use of her cell phone. After he finished his call, the man asked the woman where she was heading and if he could have a ride. She replied she was heading towards Whitethorn. She agreed to give the man a ride and eventually dropped him off at the Shelter Cove/Whitethorn junction. When specifically asked, the woman could not remember the man carrying anything with him. After being dropped off by the woman, the man was last seen walking briskly into the night in the direction of Shelter Cove.

Murder of Jere Melo
Attempted Murder of Ian Chaney

As law enforcement's investigation into the death of Matthew Coleman continued without having been able to identify a viable suspect or suspects, a private citizen, Ian Philip Chaney,[15] age 31, made contact on August 23, 2011 with Jere Lynn Melo,[16] age 69, to report a bunker-type camp that Chaney had stumbled across on Hawthorne Timber property, private property timber lands that Melo helped manage and provide security.[17] Melo, in turn, contacted Deputy Jonathan Martin of the Mendocino County Sheriff's Office to pass on this information and to also make inquiry about an "Aaron," the person who Melo had been told was probably responsible for the bunker.[18] Deputy Martin responded by email to Melo that the Aaron in question was Aaron Bassler and that Bassler has been arrested for under the influence of controlled substances and that Bassler is "against law enforcement."[19] On August 25, 2011, Melo reported to Deputy Martin that he had attempted to locate the camp on August 24, 2011 but had been unsuccessful.[20] Deputy Martin responded by informing Melo that Bassler was not currently in custody. Unfortunately, neither Deputy Martin nor any other member of the Sheriff's Office was aware that Bassler had been in the Cape Vizcaino area when Coleman was murdered. Thus, no additional crime-specific warning of caution was provided to Melo.

On August 27, 2011, Melo and Chaney met so Chaney could lead Melo to the site of the bunker-type camp. As they got in the general area, the men found a water line that was now camouflaged [it had not been camouflaged when Chaney was last at the site] and the men followed that line to the open-topped bunker, a location that Chaney would later describe as a "great ambush spot." With Melo cutting the water line as they traveled to the bunker, neither man observed anybody at or around the bunker during their approach, nor did they hear or see anybody in the area. The land near the bunker had been terraced and there were plants growing on the terraces that Chaney believed to be opium poppies. At the bunker, Melo put down his wooden-handled axe he always carried, began taking photographs, and taking GPS readings near the bunker entrance. Chaney also took a picture of the bunker. As the men were looking south, Chaney heard crackling leaves behind and above the men. He whispered to Melo, "I think he's right behind us." The two men turned around to the north and saw Bassler hidden in brush about ten feet above and behind the men. Looking directly at Bassler, Melo announced, "Hey, what the f*ck are you doing over there?" Bassler immediately responded that he was an FBI agent and opened fire with what Chaney believed at the time to be a fully-automatic AK-47 assault rifle. Chaney heard three quick shots in rapid succession and, after the third shot, Chaney saw Melo "spin like a top," falling hard and sliding a short distance down the hill. Close enough to see the whites of his attacker's eyes, Chaney recognized the gunman as

Aaron. Dropping to the ground, Chaney took cover against the bunker.[21] Chaney returned fire with his 9mm semi-automatic handgun.[22] Bassler then stood up and began "unloading" his rifle on the spot where Chaney was seeking cover. Outgunned, Chaney decided to slide down the hill, reporting that he could hear bullets whizzing by his head, as the trees around him were being hit by bullets in rapid succession. As he slid down the hill, Chaney was also calling for Melo. At one point, Chaney, while looking back, observed Aaron standing on Melo's back and looking downhill towards Chaney as Bassler continued to fire on Chaney. Seeing Bassler trying to advance on him through the brush, Chaney got to his feet, used trees as cover, and ran hard from the area, continuing to return fire to keep the attacker back. As he was able to achieve separation, Chaney tried twice to connect to 911 with his cell phone.[23] Chaney eventually escaped to the Skunk railroad tracks, where he came upon an operator of a "speeder" cart at mile marker 6. Originally heading east, the speeder operator loaded Chaney, changed directions, and headed out to the west, with Chaney at the ready to fire should he see the attacker. When they got to Merritt's camp, Chaney was able to make contact with law enforcement and report what had happened.

After Melo's body was eventually recovered from the bunker location, evidence was located at that location that linked the Melo crime scene and the Coleman crime scene to a single perpetrator. Again, the tin foil marijuana pipe/blunt, scientifically tied to Bassler by DNA, was found at or near the location where it is likely Bassler was firing upon Coleman on August 11, 2011. Hershey's chocolate foils were also found at the Cape Vizcaino location, foils that were not associated with Coleman. Later, at least one marijuana blunt fashioned from tin foil was located at the bunker scene, along with more Hershey's chocolate foils. As one Sheriff's investigator noted in his report, finding the "marijuana pipe fashioned like a cigarette out of tin foil" at the bunker was only the second time in his law enforcement career that he had seen a smoking pipe fashioned from tin foil in this fashion. The first time, he noted, was at the Coleman murder scene. Hershey's chocolate foils were also a common denominator at the two crime scenes.

An autopsy performed on August 29, 2011 determined that Melo had sustained a lethal penetrating gunshot wound to his right central back, along with three additional grazing gunshots wounds to his right central back, left temporal head, and right foot. Toxicology tests revealed caffeine and theobromine[24] in Melo's blood. The cause of Melo's death was declared to be a gunshot wound causing massive internal trauma.

The District Attorney and sworn law enforcement members of the District Attorney's Office continuously monitored daily the progress of law enforcement's efforts to apprehend Bassler, including reviewing reports and evidence as they were prepared and reported, respectively. Based on the best information developed as of September 1, 2011 and in consultation with Sheriff Allman, District Attorney Eyster personally authorized and had filed on September 2, 2011 in the Ten Mile Division (Fort Bragg) of the Mendocino County Superior Court a felony complaint charging defendant Aaron James Bassler with the murders of both Coleman and Melo, and the attempted murder of Chaney. Special allegations and the special circumstance of lying in wait were also charged. Superior Court Judge Mayfield also signed a no bail warrant for the arrest of Aaron James Bassler that same day.

Attempted Murders of Alameda Sheriff's 3-Man Fugitive Apprehension Team

By September 29, 2011, Alameda County Sheriff Gregory J. Ahern had dispatched his eight-man "Special Response Unit" to provide mutual aid to Mendocino County Sheriff Thomas Allman to assist in the "fugitive apprehension" of a multiple homicide suspect in the woods east of Fort Bragg. In addition to a briefing held in Alameda County, this law enforcement team was briefed by Mendocino County law enforcement on the underlying evidence developed to date on the Coleman murder, the Melo murder, the suspect's tactics observed by Chaney during his narrow escape, that the suspect was armed with a high-powered rifle with significant quantities of ammunition, of the suspect's familiarity with the area and terrain, and on the descriptions and photographs of the suspect prior to their deployment. On the morning of September 29, 2011, a three-member partial team, consisting of Sergeant Wilhelm, Deputy Poole, and Deputy Shannon, of the eight-man Alameda County unit were deployed into the woods to relieve another apprehension team. Their assigned area was near the recent cabin break-ins around Northspur, fourteen miles east of Fort Bragg.

As the team was preparing to hunker down for surveillance and location security along a well-traveled dirt road, Sgt. Wilhelm caught a glimpse of something black moving in the woods. As Sgt. Wilhelm watched, a man Sgt. Wilhelm was able to positively identify as Bassler, wearing all black clothing, walking very fast, and carrying what appeared to be an assault-type rifle, came into view. Because of the task he was completing, Sgt. Wilhelm did not have his rifle at his side and was armed only with a sidearm. Fearing Bassler's superior firepower, Sgt.

Wilhelm remained still in the hope that he would not be seen, a tactic that initially worked. Bassler moved past Sgt. Wilhelm at a fast clip and extended the distance between the two men as a result of the suspect's very fast pace. As Sgt. Wilhelm stealthily tried to close the gap to get within pistol range, Bassler apparently sense something wrong, turned and looked directly at Sgt. Wilhelm. Sgt. Wilhelm repeatedly yelled, "Sheriff's Office, get on the ground." Bassler raised his rifle and fired at Sgt. Wilhelm. In response, Sgt. Wilhelm dropped to a crouch, fired 8 rounds, and quickly moved into the brush for cover. Likewise, Bassler moved into the woods for apparent cover. Upon hearing at a distance Sgt. Wilhelm's commands being directed at Bassler, Deputies Poole and Shannon moved in that direction, with Deputy Shannon eventually bringing Sgt. Wilhelm his rifle. Sgt. Wilhelm saw Bassler come back up to the road, where it appeared to Sgt. Wilhelm that Bassler was trying to assume a tactical fighting position. At that time, more rounds were fired in Bassler's direction. In the hope of creating a perimeter, the discovery and engagement of Bassler was also transmitted over the air to all available teams. Not knowing how fast reinforcements would arrive, the three-man team formed a strategic 360-degree cover for one another. While the law enforcement team was assuming its defensive formation, Bassler circled around through the woods and re-appeared back at the location where Sgt. Wilhelm had first observed him.[25] Bassler came out of the brush, using trees as cover. He raised his rifle and pointed it in the direction of the three men. The Alameda County team returned fired in Bassler's direction, as they heard two distinct shots fired by Bassler, including a "supersonic crack of a bullet" passing between Sgt. Wilhelm and Deputy Poole. It is noted that the members of the Alameda County team were each wearing soft body armor that would not have stopped the rifle rounds fired by Bassler. As Sgt. Wilhelm then tried to advance on Bassler's location while Deputies Poole and Shannon tried to keep

Bassler engaged, the fugitive again disappeared back into the brush and woods.

The Concluding Interaction

On September 29, 2011, Sacramento County Sheriff Scott R. Jones made the decision to dispatch members of his SWAT team to provide mutual aid to Mendocino County Sheriff Thomas Allman to assist in the apprehension of a homicide suspect in the woods east of Fort Bragg. The Sacramento County team members arrived early in the morning hours of September 30, 2011. In addition to a briefing held in Sacramento County on the 30th, this team was briefed by Mendocino County law enforcement, U.S. Marshals, and Alameda County personnel on Friday, September 29, 2011 on the underlying evidence developed to date on the Coleman murder, the Melo murder, the suspect's tactics observed by Chaney during Chaney's death-defying escape, that the suspect was armed with a high-powered rifle with significant quantities of ammunition, of the suspect's familiarity with the area and terrain, that the suspect had knowledge of military tactics, the descriptions and photographs of the suspect, and the suspect's tactics when contacted by the Alameda County apprehension team on the morning of September 29, 2011.

On the morning of Saturday, October 1, 2011, the Sacramento County Sheriff SWAT team members, along with other law enforcement personnel, were assigned to three-man teams and each team assigned to pre-selected observations posts along travel routes that the operations commander believed Bassler may still be using, based on the locations of recent burglaries and canine alerts.[26] Grouped as one team, Sacramento County Deputies Prehoda, Esty, and Owens were transported by

Mendocino County law enforcement personnel after a 7am briefing to their assigned area at Sherwood Road and Mud Springs Road, arriving between 8:30 and 9am. Having quickly developed a defensible observation post, the men commenced 360-degree observation coverage from that post. As the team members would be looking in different directions, non-verbal signals were agreed-upon should one of the team observed the suspect. Following Bassler's fire fight with and escape from the Alameda County team, the Sacramento County team was concerned that any audible signal might be heard by Bassler, allowing him to immediately fire on their position and/or escape again into the woods. Of special concern to the Sacramento County team, as well as the other teams, was the report from the Alameda County team who had been engaged by Bassler that he had opted to flank, re-engage and fire on the Alameda County team with the knowledge that they were law enforcement officers, instead of disengaging and using his honed survivalist skills to disappear into the woods.

Rotating positions throughout the morning, around 12:30 Deputy Owens saw a white male dressed in all black "walking with a purpose," as had been described by the Alameda County team. Deputy Owens characterized the man as moving so fast that he seemed to "explode out of the gulch." The man was armed with a rifle at the ready. The man was immediately recognized as Aaron James Bassler. Without giving a verbal warning,[27] Deputy Owens fired on Bassler. Despite believing that his shot had hit Bassler "center mass," Deputy Owens recounted that Bassler did not go down notwithstanding what Deputy Owens believed to be a hit. Bassler also did not release his grip on his rifle.[28] Believing there still to be a risk, Deputy Owens fired again, joined now by the other two team members. Having a magazine filled to its capacity of 30 rounds, Deputy Owens fired a total of six shots, stopping when he perceived no further risk to himself and others. Having a magazine

312

filled to its capacity of thirty rounds, Deputy Prehoda fired a total of three shots, stopping when he perceived no further risk to himself and others. Having a magazine filled to its capacity of thirty rounds, Deputy Esty fired a total of three rounds, stopping when he perceived no further risk to himself and others. A total of twelve shots were fired by the apprehension team as a whole. According to the results of the autopsy performed on October 4, 2011 in Ukiah, the pathologist was able to determine that seven of the 12 shots fired hit the deceased causing his death. The cause of death was determined to be multiple gunshots. The only substances of interest detected in Bassler's blood by toxicology tests were Delta-9 THC (16 ng/mL) and Delta-9 Carboxy THC (39 ng/mL).[29]

Officer-Involved Shooting Findings

In applying the totality of information developed by all investigators in the instant case to the previously mentioned criteria applicable for assessing whether the use of force is objectively reasonable, the District Attorney makes the following findings:

(1) The nature of the crimes at issue (two distinct and separate murders, as well as multiple attempted murders of a civilian and three law enforcement officers) are, not surprisingly, characterized in the Penal Code as violent offenses, the most violent conduct that society must address;

(2) It is and was objectively and subjectively reasonable for the Alameda County apprehension team members to defend themselves and fire on the suspect as the suspect posed an immediate and

extreme threat to the safety of the apprehension team, as well as other unengaged apprehension teams that were deployed in the general area. This is especially so because of the circumstances that, when Alameda County's team leader announced his presence and identified himself seeking the suspect's surrender, the suspect fired upon that team leader, then circled through the underbrush in an attempt to gain a tactical advantage, and re-emerged to re-engage and fire on the now assembled three-man team. Beyond self-defense, it is and was also subjectively and objectively reasonable for the Alameda County apprehension team to conclude that their use of lethal force was necessary to try and prevent a continuation of the ongoing threat to people living, working, and temporarily deployed in and around the forest;

(3) It is and was objectively and subjectively reasonable for the Sacramento County apprehension team members to conclude from observing the suspect's approach with an assumed loaded rifle at the ready that the defendant was an immediate and extreme threat to the safety of the apprehension team, as well as other unengaged apprehension teams that were deployed in the general area. This is especially so because of the information shared with the apprehension team that the suspect had recently fired on an Alameda County Sheriff's apprehension team, who had announced their presence and identified themselves seeking the suspect's surrender, and then circled that team through the underbrush in an attempt to gain a tactical advantage, firing again from a strategic location. It is also subjectively and objectively reasonable that the apprehension team concluded that there would be a continuation of the ongoing threat to people living, working, and temporarily deployed in and around the forest, a forest where the defendant had successful eluded apprehension by a numerically superior force for 36 of the 52 days of his crime spree;

314

(4) Given his earlier interaction with the Alameda County Sheriff's apprehension team, there is no question that the suspect was engaged in an ongoing attempt to evade arrest through utilization of both lethal resistance and flight;

(5) According to all accounts recorded close in time to the shooting, the degree to which the situation was tense, uncertain and evolving was extremely high, especially after the suspect's engagement with the Alameda County apprehension team. In reaching this conclusion, the previously mentioned legal guidance that officers regularly must act with little time to analyze and consider all circumstances is given great weight and consideration.

Notes

1: The phrase "serial killer" is being used herein to characterize a series of two or more murders, committed as separate events with an intervening "cooling off" period by one offender acting alone. Serial murder is a relatively rare event, estimated to comprise less than one percent of all murders in the United States committed in any given year. According to the Federal Bureau of Investigations, "The topic of serial murder occupies a unique niche within the criminal justice community. In addition to the significant investigative challenges they bring to law enforcement, serial murder cases attract an over-abundance of attention from the media, mental health experts, academia, and the general public. While there has been significant, independent work conducted by a variety of experts to identify and analyze the many issues related to serial murder, there have been few efforts to reach a consensus between law enforcement and other experts regarding these matters."

2: SWAT is a law enforcement acronym for Special Weapons and Tactics. The special weapons and tactics concept originated in the late 1960s as a result of several sniping incidents against civilians and police officers that had occurred around the country.

3: The California Mutual Aid System is an extension of the concept of "neighbor helping neighbor." The Law Enforcement Mutual Aid System was established in 1961, and has been used to restore order during emergencies, including civil unrest, and to provide assistance to local agencies during other unusual events. As a component of the Standardized Emergency Management System [SEMS], the Mutual Aid System is based on four organizational levels: cities, counties, regions and the state. (A county is an operational area along with its political subdivisions.) The state is divided into seven Law Enforcement Mutual Aid Regions. The County Sheriff is a key role player within the system. Each sheriff serves as the Regional Mutual Aid Coordinator. The basic concept provides that within the operational area, adjacent or neighboring law enforcement agencies will assist each other. Should the event require assistance from outside the county, the region will provide requested assistance to the impacted county. If the combined resources of the region are insufficient to cope with the incident, the Regional Coordinator contacts the State Law Enforcement Mutual Aid Coordinator at Cal EMA.

4: As will be noted elsewhere herein, a separate non-lethal shooting incident occurred between Bassler and members of the Alameda County Sheriff's Department on September 29, 2011. Bassler fired on the Alameda County apprehension team with the same rifle recovered from him on October 1, 2011. The deputies returned fire, and a short time later, having circled on them, Bassler again fired at the Alameda

County deputies from a different location. Bassler then escaped back into the cover of the woods.

5: No disrespect is intended to Mr. Coleman or his family by the use hereafter of just his surname.

6: A deputy who specialized in marijuana investigations flew the area on August 16, 2011 looking for possible marijuana gardens. None were located in or about the general area of the Coleman crime scene.

7: DNA testing by the California Department of Justice Laboratory in Redding concluded that the DNA extracted from the tin foil blunt or "joint" found at the Coleman murder scene came from Aaron James Bassler. Coleman was excluded as the source of the DNA. Additional DNA testing on the feces found left on the victim's body was not conducted due to the poor quality of the sample. However, it has been concluded that Bassler deposited his diarrheic feces on the deceased's remains post-mortem. It is believed by the prosecutor's office that this conduct by Bassler is indicative of some combination of an after-death demonstration of territorial or physical dominance, contempt of authority, and lack of remorse.

8: It has been documented in interviews that on Sunday, August 21, 2011 when Bassler's father, James Bassler, heard directly from his former wife at a family barbecue that she had dropped their son off with a rifle near the Point Vizcaino crime scene near in time to Coleman's death, he recommended that she call the Sheriff's Office and report what she knew. Brickey later confirmed that James Bassler had indeed asked her at the barbeque to report what she knew to the police. She explained that she did not contact law enforcement because she did not know at that time where to find her son and she didn't know for sure that her son had done anything wrong. In the final analysis, the mother did not believe her son was capable of murder so she did not want to be responsible for focusing law enforcement on him as a possible suspect, an unfortunate decision in hindsight.

9: Prior to August 28, 2011 there is no record that the mother had attempted to disclose important information to obviously interested law enforcement. The mother admitted, however, that she was aware of the timely media reports of the death of Coleman and the general location where it was reported Coleman had died.

10: In searching the entrance area at 44000 North Highway 1, investigators found a bucket hidden in the bushes near the unlocked gate that blocked that access road. While animals had apparently scattered the contents of the bucket, several Top Ramen noodle wrappers were found spread on the ground. A store receipt provided by the Safeway store in Fort Bragg documented that Bassler had purchased Top Ramen noodles on August 8th.

11: Acid generally refers to lysergic acid diethylamide, abbreviated LSD or LSD-25, also known as lysergide, and is a semi-synthetic psychedelic drug of the ergoline family. Well-known for its psychological effects and impacts, LSD effects can include altered thinking processes, closed and open eye visuals, synaesthesia, an altered sense of time, and altered spiritual experiences. When taken, LSD induces other physical effects in addition to hallucinations: tremors, dilated pupils, a rise in body temperature, an increase in heart rate, increased blood pressure and a loss of sleep due to sleeplessness. Users can also experience "bad trips," meaning terrifying thoughts or feelings, including fear of death, insanity or losing control of their lives or their bodies. Also reportedly common are flashbacks or hallucinations that occur long after taking the drug. These flashbacks can happen days, weeks, months or even years after one stops taking the drug, and they can include frightening thoughts, images, or colors. These flashbacks most often happen

318

to those who are using the drug on a regular basis, or who have a long history of LSD abuse.

12: Opium is a highly addictive narcotic drug acquired in the dried latex form from the opium poppy (Papaver somniferum) seed pod. Traditionally, the unripened pod is slit open and the sap seeps out and dries on the outer surface of the pod. The resulting yellow-brown latex, which is scraped off of the pod, is bitter in taste and contains varying amounts of alkaloids such as morphine, codeine, thebaine, and papaverine. The duration of chemical effects of opium is about four hours. The drug produces relaxation, relief of pain, anxiety, decreased alertness, impaired coordination, and serious problems with constipation. Repeated or chronic use produces tolerance to all the effects except constipation. Continued use may result in weight loss, mental deterioration, and death. Some degree of withdrawal sickness may occur if the drug is discontinued.

13: Some have attempted to use the crimes and tragedies described herein as a lightning rod for sparking a public debate on mental health policies in Mendocino County, in particular as those policies may relate to a local interest of some to implement Laura's Law. Having reviewed the Laura's Law criteria and compared same against the facts and background of the person in question, the District Attorney hereby finds that Aaron James Bassler would not have qualified for Laura's Law intervention pursuant to then-existing eligibility criteria. On the general topic of mental illness, it also should not go unmentioned that the Chinese-made rifle used by Bassler to commit his crimes was recently given to him by a family member. It is patently unreasonable for a family, even a broken one, if they truly believe that their son suffers from any form of a significant mental illness, to allow anybody, let alone another family member, to give that mentally-ill son a lethal assault rifle. If that were being contemplated, it seems reasonable that aggressive intervention to prevent such gifting should have taken place. It is also noted that even hidden mental frailties are often revealed and manifested in jail settings where staff is trained to look for such things. Having reviewed all jail records applicable to Bassler, there are no notations by trained and vigilant jail staff suggesting any suspicion of mental illness. (See, also, footnote 19.) It is strongly believed that Bassler's situational mental instability was primarily driven by alcohol and/or illicit drug abuse, both of which the local criminal justice system attempted to address at various times.

14: Bassler and his mother had an agreement that she would report him missing to the Sheriff's Office if he ever failed to check in with her within a week of his being gone from the immediate Fort Bragg area.

15: No disrespect is intended to Mr. Chaney or his family by the use hereafter of just his surname.

16: No disrespect is intended to Mr. Melo or his family by the use hereafter of just his surname.

17: Melo was a well-known Fort Bragg resident, having worked and served as a long-time forester and land manager. He was the former mayor of Fort Bragg, a community activist, and a sports enthusiast. At the time of his death, Melo was a current member of the Fort Bragg City Council.

18: Melo's August 23, 2011 email to the MCSO Deputy Martin reads as follows: "This morning I took a report from Ian Cheney [sic], a local who is married to a Balassi, and who is concerned about a bunker-type camp he observed on Hawthorne Timber Company property in the lower Noyo River area. I am asking for some guidance or information about the person who is the apparent grower. Mr. Cheney identified the person as a young man whose first name is Aaron, last name unknown. He is apparently an eccentric person. His mother lives on Sherwood Road, just about on top of the Skunk Railroad tunnel. Aaron apparently lives across Sherwood Road in a tile red (color only, no tiles) house, when he is around. Aaron is the person who ran his dark Toyota pickup into the tennis court fence at the Middle School a few months ago. Hopefully, that gives enough information for a positive identification. Mr. Cheney has seen Aaron on the Balassi property several times this year. He describes Aaron as a tall, young man who sports a skin head and dresses in dark clothing. Mr. Cheney has seen Aaron carrying potting soil and fertilizer bags across the Balassi property onto Hawthorne Timber Company property where he claims to have observed a "bunker" dug into the ground and surrounded by barbed wire. The Balassi family hears chain saws working at night. Mr. Cheney observed lots of cleared areas around the bunker. He told me that a fire had started in the area. He saw red poppies growing in the area. He did not stay around long enough to look for more, as Aaron is known to be a bit unstable. I reviewed the Hawthorne map this morning with Mr. Cheney, and my best estimate is that the site is near N 39 degrees 25.9 minutes and W 123 degrees 44.1 minutes. For a legal description, it is located in the E 1/2 of the SE 1/4 of Section 10 T18N R17W, above a mid-slope road. It is my plan to walk the area from South Fork on the Skunk Railroad tomorrow morning to get a better location. I will appreciate any information you might provide. Thank you. Jere."

19: As an aside, when Bassler was arrested by the Fort Bragg Police Department on September 13, 2010 for public intoxication and transported to jail, he requested during the jail screening process (while intoxicated) that he not be housed with other inmates. The reason he gave for this request was that he was a former police cadet. As with all his other bookings at the local jail, he was not perceived as an inmate needing to be referred to Jail Mental Health for evaluation. When Bassler was back in jail in March, 2011 following his DUI and resisting arrest, he again requested during the screening process (while intoxicated) that he be housed separate from other inmates. However, in the morning after he had sobered up, Bassler told jail staff that he had no problem being housed in a shared housing unit, which is where he was ultimately housed without incident. Again, during this last screening process and thereafter, Bassler was not determined to be an inmate who needed to be referred to Jail Mental Health for further evaluation.

20: Melo's August 25, 2011 email to the MCSO Deputy Martin reads as follows: "Jon: Thank you. Is he in custody now? I walked for six hours yesterday on the Hawthorne logging roads, overgrown for sure, and found nothing. I have an appointment at 8:00am, Saturday, to meet with Ian Cheney [sic] to get a better location. (It also occurs to me that this may be our guy in the Scout Camp incidents.) Jere." Melo's "Scout Camp incidents" comment refers to burglaries that had been reported as having happened at the Boy Scout camp on the Noyo River between June 23, 2011 and June 28, 2011. The camp is surrounded by Hawthorne Timber property. A person or persons unknown had broken into buildings and stolen bedding items, small hand tools, food, alcohol, [and] other items commonly used when camping. One of the breached padlocks had been shot off one building by a high-powered rifle. Deputy Martin told Melo about this incident and Melo, with the help of camp staff, later located the majority of the stolen items hidden under brush on a trail near the camp. A brown sleeping bag, folding chair, and other small items, however, were not recovered. The same day that Melo helped recover some of the stolen property from the brush, a man, identified only as a skinhead wearing camouflaged clothing and carrying an AK-47 rifle, was seen by railroad personnel walking on the railroad tracks within a quarter mile of the Boy Scout camp. In turn, Melo advised Deputy Martin that he believed there might be a survivalist camp in the area so Deputy Martin, acting on that tip, conducted an unsuccessful fixed-wing overflight looking for such a camp the following day.

21: Chaney described the man at the bunker ambush as a white male with a completely bald head. The man was wearing a thick black bulletproof vest and black pants. Known to Chaney for at least ten years as Aaron, the man had no shirt on underneath the vest. Chaney believed the vest was a bullet-proof vest because it had no pockets, there were Velcro straps holding the vest on the man's shoulders, and Chaney believed he struck Aaron with several of his 9mm rounds with the hits having no effect on the rifleman.

22: Chaney would later tell law enforcement that Melo did not like to carry a firearm while performing his security and land management duties. On the day in question, Chaney did not tell Melo that he was carrying a loaded firearm; though Chaney had previously told Melo he would not return to the location alone or without being armed.

23: While trying to escape Bassler's lethal onslaught, Chaney was also trying to also call for help. The first call got through but eventually dropped. However, while still connected, the following is a transcript of the harrowing conversation that took place: CHP Dispatch: 911 emergency reporting. Chaney: Hi, listen to me right now. My name is Ian Chaney. I'm here with Jere Melo out in the woods. We're being fired upon by some growers. I think Jere Melo might have been hit. CHP Dispatch: Where are you located? Chaney: I have no idea. We are right of the tracks, ummm… CHP Dispatch: What town are you in? Chaney: Fort Bragg, California. CHP Dispatch: Let me put you through to the

Sheriff's Office, just a moment... [Beeping sounds, then dialing tone; caller breathing heavily.] CHP Dispatch: You are being transferred. MCSO Dispatch: 911, what is your emergency? Chaney: Okay, listen to me right now. I'm being shot at... MCSO Dispatch: Where are you at? Chaney: I'm out in the woods and I think Jere Melo has been hit. I got... [several gunshots are heard in the background] Chaney: Sh*t. MCSO Dispatch: Where are you at? Chaney: God damn it. [tones as if buttons are being pushed on Chaney's cell phone keypad] Chaney: I'm out in the f*cking woods. [loud shuffling noise] MCSO Dispatch: Sir? Chaney: Are you still there? MCSO Dispatch: Yeah, where are... [recording ends].

24: Theobromine is a methylxanthine alkaloid found in tea and cocoa products.

25: The Alameda County team had arrived at their assigned area in a van. Inside the van were stored two sniper rifles, ammunition, and other law enforcement provisions. While the two deputies were setting up camp at a tactically-advantageous spot they had scouted out, Sgt. Wilhelm returned alone to camouflage the van, which he had finished just before he first saw Bassler. As expressed in each of their statements, all three team members were concerned that Bassler's final position of attack—after he had circled around—was very close to where the van had been hidden. Had Bassler discovered and been able to access the van, the officers were reasonably concerned that he might better arm himself and gain further tactical advantage.

26: Assigned by Sheriff Allman to head up the apprehension effort from the start, MCSO Captain Kurt O. Smallcomb served out of the Fort Bragg command post as the Operations Commander.

27: Just as any law enforcement officer lacks authority under the law to use deadly force against a suspect who has affirmatively indicated an intent to surrender and does not pose an immediate threat of serious harm to anybody, a law enforcement officer is nevertheless well within the breadth and scope of the law, proper police procedure, and tactical response to fire on a well-armed individual at first opportunity who presents as a high risk fugitive, who has answered an earlier opportunity to surrender to law enforcement with a double engagement and gunfire, and who continues to pose a life-threatening risk as an armed, escaping fugitive. As mentioned elsewhere herein, after being told face-to-face by at least one person that he was a wanted man, Bassler ignored literally weeks of self-surrender opportunities and, instead, escalated tensions in the woods by focusing lethal attacks on members of an apprehension team. Again, the more specific and applicable criteria in this case are the deadly force criteria announced by the Supreme Court in Tennessee v. Garner, supra. In Garner, the Supreme Court held that: "where the officer has probable cause to believe that the suspect poses a threat of serious physical harm, either to the officer or to others, it is not constitutionally unreasonable to prevent escape by using deadly force." (Tennessee v. Garner, 471 U.S. at 11; see also Chew v. Gates, 27 F.3d at 1441-1442 where the Chew Court interpreted Tennessee v. Garner as "holding that [the] fourth amendment permits use of deadly force to apprehend a fleeing felon where there is probable cause to believe the suspect poses a threat of serious physical harm.") The comments of one of the Sacramento County deputies, one who only secondarily engaged, are instructive. Had he been the deputy to first see the suspect fast approaching armed with a rifle with a high capacity magazine, Sacramento County Sheriff's Deputy Esty explained to DA investigators that he would have also fired on the suspect without announcing his presence because when Jere Melo tried to communicate with Bassler, Melo was immediately shot and killed. When Alameda County thereafter identified themselves as law enforcement, Bassler responded by firing on the sergeant, slipping into the brush to flank the team, and then coming out of hiding to again fire on all three team members. Had Bassler again escaped, there was concern on the part of at least Deputy Esty that Bassler would be a lethal threat to the other unengaged law enforcement officers in other observation posts spread throughout the area whom he may be able to take by surprise, especially given Bassler's recognized ability to move silently through the woods.

28: According to Mendocino County District Attorney Investigator Alvarado's on-scene investigation, the deceased was found at his final resting place on his right side with his right arm partially covering a pistol-gripped rifle that was almost completely wrapped in black electrical tape. That rifle was identified as a Chinese-made but modified Norinco SKS Sporter 7.62x39mm semi-automatic rifle. The rifle was loaded with a large capacity magazine and there was one live round taped just above the pistol grip on the left side of the receiver. The safety was off and there was a live round in the chamber, making the weapon fire ready. The large capacity magazine was loaded with 27 rounds of high velocity ammunition. The deceased also had with him a backpack that, among other things, contained 208 more rounds of 7.62x39 ammunition. Also found in the backpack was a .22 caliber rifle with a sawed-off barrel, accompanied by 26 rounds of .22 caliber ammunition. In viewing the chambered round removed from the Norinco SKS rifle, Investigator Alvarado determined that round was a dull silver Wolf 7.62mm. This round had the same color and was of the same make and caliber as casings recovered at the scene of the officer involved shootings on September 29, 2011, the incident involving the Alameda County apprehension team.

29: According to the certifying toxicologist's report of findings, "Marijuana is a DEA Schedule I hallucinogen. Pharmacologically, it has depressant and reality distorting effects. Collectively, the chemical compounds that comprise marijuana are known as Cannabinoids. Delta-9-THC is the principal psychoactive ingredient of marijuana/ hashish. It rapidly leaves the blood, even during smoking, falling to below detectable levels within several hours. THC concentrations in blood are usually about one-half that of serum/plasma concentrations. The active metabolite, 11-hydroxy-THC, may also fall below detectable levels shortly after inhalation. Delta-9-carboxy-THC (THCC) is the inactive metabolite of THC with peak concentrations attained 32 to 240 minutes after smoking and may be detected for up to one day or more in blood. Both delta-9-THC and THCC may be present substantially longer in chronic users. Reported usual peak concentrations in serum after smoking 1.75% or 3.55% THC marijuana cigarettes are 50 to 270 ng/mL after beginning of smoking, decreasing to less than 5 ng/mL by 2 hours. Corresponding delta-9-carboxy-THC concentrations range from 10-101 ng/mL about 32 to 240 minutes after the beginning of smoking and decline slowly.

ADDENDUM B
Laura's Law—an Overview

Wikipedia

Laura's Law is a California state law that allows for court-ordered assisted outpatient treatment or forced anti-psychotics in most cases. To qualify for the program, the person must have a serious mental illness plus a recent history of psychiatric hospitalizations, jailings or acts, threats or attempts of serious violent behavior towards self or others. A complete functional outline of the legal procedures and safeguards within Laura's Law has been prepared by NAMI (National Alliance on Mental Illness), San Mateo.

The law was named after Laura Wilcox, a mental health worker who was killed by an American citizen who had refused psychiatric treatment. Modeled on Kendra's Law, a similar statute enacted in New York, the bill was introduced as Assembly Bill 1421 by Assemblywoman Helen Thomson, a Democrat from Davis. The measure passed the California Legislature in 2002 and was signed into law by Governor Gray Davis. The statute can only be utilized in counties that choose to enact outpatient commitment programs based on the measure. As of 2010, Nevada County has fully implemented the law and Los Angeles County has a pilot project. In 2010, the California State Association of Counties chose Nevada County to receive its Challenge Award for implementing Laura's Law. Subsequently, in 2011, a National Association of Counties Achievement Award in Health was awarded to Nevada County for the Assisted Outpatient Treatment Program.

Background

Laura Wilcox, a 19-year-old sophomore from Haverford College, was working at Nevada County's public mental health clinic during her winter break from college. On January 10, 2001, she and two other people were shot to death by Scott Harlan Thorpe, a 41-year-old American citizen who resisted his family's attempt to force psychiatric treatment. Thorpe was found incompetent to stand trial and was sent to Atascadero State Hospital and was later transferred to California's Napa State Hospital. After the incident, Laura's parents chose to advocate for forced treatment of individuals considered to have mental illness. Scott Harlan Thorpe tried on several occasions to get help from Nevada County Mental Health by going in person and pleading with the staff to get psychiatric treatment. He was denied treatment on all occasions and told there was nothing the County could do, which was a severe contributing factor to the shooting.

Implementation at county discretion

The law is only operative in those counties in which the county board of supervisors, by resolution, authorizes its application and makes a finding that no voluntary mental health program serving adults, and no children's mental health program, was reduced in order to implement the law.

In 2004, Los Angeles County implemented Laura's Law on a limited basis. Since the passage of the MHSA [see Prop. 63 below], Nevada County fully implemented Laura's Law in May, 2008, and several other counties are discussing it, notably San Francisco County, San Mateo County, San Diego County, Marin County, and others.

In those counties that adopt outpatient commitment, an AB 1421 program will ensure individuals are provided the services and medical treatment (including medication) that will enable the person to have a good chance to recover. Nevada County Director Michael Heggarty best describes it as part of the recovery movement.

Proposition 63 impact

In November, 2004, California voters passed Proposition 63. When the California Department of Mental Health (DMH) released its draft plan requirements for county mental health administrators on February 15, 2005, they contained a provision that would allow MHSA funds to be used for "involuntary services" if certain criteria were met. Nevada County's Laura's law program and Los Angeles County's AOT pilot project are utilizing MHSA funding for services.

Assisted outpatient treatment eligibility criteria

As stated above, the patient must have a serious mental illness plus a recent history of psychiatric hospitalizations, jailings or acts, threats or attempts of serious violent behavior towards self or others. The recipient must also have been offered an opportunity to voluntarily participate in a treatment plan by the local mental health department, yet fails to the point that, without a Laura's Law program, he or she will likely relapse or deteriorate to the point of being dangerous to self or others. "Participation in the assisted outpatient program is the least restrictive placement necessary to ensure the person's recovery and stability." While a specified group of individuals may request an investigation to determine if a person qualifies for a Laura's Law program, only the county mental health director, or his or her designee, may file a petition with the superior court for a hearing to determine if the person should be court ordered to receive the services specified under the law.

A person may be placed in an assisted outpatient treatment if, after a hearing, a court finds that the following criteria have been met. The patient must:

—Be eighteen years of age or older

—Be suffering from a mental illness

—Be unlikely to survive safely in the community without supervision, based on a clinical determination

—Have a history of non-compliance with treatment that has either:
1. Been a significant factor in his or her being in a hospital, prison or jail at least twice within the last 36 months; or

2. Resulted in one or more acts, attempts or threats of serious violent behavior toward self or others within the last 48 months

—Have been offered an opportunity to voluntarily participate in a treatment plan by the local mental health department but continue to fail to engage in treatment

—Be substantially deteriorating

—Be, in view of his or her treatment history and current behavior, in need of assisted outpatient treatment in order to prevent a relapse or deterioration that would likely result in the person meeting California's inpatient commitment standard, which is being:

1. A serious risk of harm to himself or herself or others; or

2. Gravely disabled (in immediate physical danger due to being unable to meet basic needs for food, clothing, or shelter);

—Be likely to benefit from assisted outpatient treatment; and

—Participation in the assisted outpatient program is the least restrictive placement necessary to ensure the person's recovery and stability.

If the court finds that the individual meets the statutory criteria, the recipient will be provided intensive community treatment services and supervision by multidisciplinary teams of highly trained mental health professionals with staff-to-client ratios of not more than 1 to 10, and additional services, as specified, for persons with the most persistent and severe mental illness. The law specifies various rights of the person who is the subject of a Laura's Law petition as well as due process hearing rights. The bill also provides for voluntary settlement agreements as an alternative to the hearing process.

Debate over bill's efficacy and propriety

Supporters

Passage of the bill was supported by organizations such as the California Treatment Advocacy Coalition (an affiliate of the Treatment Advocacy Center), the California Psychiatric Association, the Police Chiefs Association, Mental Illness Policy Org., and the National Alliance on Mental Illness (NAMI). In an editorial endorsement of the law, the Los Angeles Times touted then-Governor Gray Davis's support, while limiting its comments on opponents to mentioning that the Citizens

Commission on Human Rights, which opposes virtually all psychiatric treatments, sponsored a rally at the Capitol against Laura's Law. The San Francisco Chronicle and The San Francisco Examiner have published positive articles on the topic. The Los Angeles Times won a Pulitzer Prize, in part for its coverage of Laura's Law.

Opposition

Mind Freedom International and the California Network of Mental Health Clients (CNMHC), along with allies in the psychiatric survivors movement, also fought the measure and its earlier versions, accusing such legislation as a regressive and reprehensible scheme to enforce coerced drug treatment regimens against the will of patients. The Church of Scientology and the Citizens Commission on Human Rights have also gained attention as opponents of the new law.

Outpatient commitment opponents make several varied arguments. Some dispute the positive effects of compulsory treatment, questioning the methodology of studies that show effectiveness. Others highlight negative effects of treatment. Still others point to disparities in the way these laws are applied. The psychiatric survivors movement opposes compulsory treatment on the basis that the ordered drugs often have serious or unpleasant side-effects such as anhedonia, tardive dyskinesia, neuroleptic malignant syndrome, excessive weight gain leading to diabetes, addiction, sexual side effects, and increased risk of suicide.

For those interested in further reading on this topic
Opponent views:

MindFreedom.org—"Bill for More Forced Psychiatry Passed by California Legislature, Goes to Governor," California Network of

Mental Health Clients (September 3, 2002)

Proponent views:

Mental Illness Policy Org. Laura's Law Home Page. Lauras-law.org

Psychlaws.org—"A Guide to Laura's Law: California's New Law for Assisted Outpatient Treatment," The California Treatment Advocacy Coalition and the Treatment Advocacy Center (January, 2003)

PsychLaws.org—"Landmark Legislation, Laura's Law, Brings Much-Needed Reform to California: AB 1421 will help those with severe mental illnesses who are too sick to help themselves" (opinion), Mary T. Zdanowicz, Treatment Advocacy Center (September 30, 2002)

PsychLaws.org—"Gov. Davis Signs Laura's Law: AB 1421 will help those with severe mental illnesses who are too sick to help themselves" (November 22, 2002)

The Treatment Advocacy Center—"Laura's Law"

☙

Jim Bassler, Father of Aaron Bassler
On Laura's Law
—Santa Rosa Press Democrat, July 17ᵗʰ, 2012

What Laura's Law is really about is whether the Mendocino County supervisors take the toughest cases of severe mental illness seriously ("Mendocino hopes to stop future Basslers," July 11 [2012]).

Laura's Law first provides a process to identify people with an illness who have proved, through hospitalizations or jailing, that they are not functioning well in the community. These are people who will continue to suffer, along with the community, unless we try to treat their illness.

334

This suffering can be deep and randomly distributed in the community, as recent history shows.

Laura's Law then requires high-level officials of the mental health and criminal justice systems to collaborate and oversee the delivery of proven services to the client. This collaboration and oversight is very important in gaining client cooperation and ensuring delivery of needed services to the client. The goal is wellness, and for these tough cases you need this team effort. For any kind of success, a team needs leadership, and this is where the board needs to set the goal and lay down the law by implementing Laura's Law.

Why Laura's Law and why not something else? Because the many parts of our county government have not worked very well together on this issue in the past. Asking them to come up with something else they all agree to would be asking too much.

The Board of Supervisors is too busy to micro-manage this issue. The fact is Laura's Law is available now, and it has proven to work very well to achieve the goal sought after. Unless you're looking for excuses, the only place you need look is to the Nevada County experience with the law.

Our two counties are similar in population and resources, yet look at the contrast. Read the Nevada County grand jury report and how it commended their mental health system, and then compare it to our grand jury report. The citizens I've talked to in both counties have generally the same opinion as their grand juries. I don't think they have better people in Nevada County government. The law was forced on them, and it worked. It's now considered a success by those in government.

There is a lot to learn by looking at Nevada County and how this law was implemented. Success is hard to ignore. If anything had gone wrong, it would have been news in every major paper in the state. Yet many like to look to other counties that have not implemented Laura's Law for excuses to do less.

With respect to severe mental illness, our county overall has a "can't do, can't change, can't fund and can't help" attitude. The supervisors need to provide the leadership to change that mindset.

I am aware of more than one case in the last several weeks that was very serious and possibly life-threatening, cases that were handled by low-level county employees who simply responded with, I can't help. We need the county to take these situations far more seriously. Laura's Law forces an effective serious response and provides some accountability to a system that lacks both.

To delay implementation or try to find an alternative is to waste money on jailing and hospitalizations while staff fumbles with ideas that may never happen. You will be feeding the "can't do" attitude. All the while a number of severely ill people, along with the community, suffer from lack of a needed response.

Please give us a mental health system for adults we can count on in this county. Give us a system that future grand juries can be proud of. Vote to implement Laura's Law as soon as possible.

గం

Jim Bassler, a Fort Bragg resident, is the father of Aaron Bassler, who killed two men before being slain following a month-long manhunt by law enforcement last year. Bassler had been concerned for years about his son's mental health.

Anderson Valley Advertiser, July 18, 2012
'Supes Spike Laura's Law'
by Mark Scaramella

"Laura's Law has always been a non-starter in Mendo. We can't afford it," said one County official involved in the preparation for last week's two-and-a-half-hour presentation on the "court assisted outpatient treatment" program.

Advocates think implementation of Laura's Law would help Mendo's diminished mental health services head off the volatile mentally ill before they hurt themselves or someone else. The murders of Matthew Coleman and Fort Bragg City Councilman Jere Melo last August by Aaron Bassler mobilized Laura's Law proponents who immediately regarded Bassler as a person who, if Laura's Law had been in effect, might have been helped before he became lethal.

Unlike the killer of Laura Wilcox after which Laura's Law is named, Bassler, so far as is known, never sought help. In fact, he did well when he was held for prior run-ins with law enforcement at the Mendocino County Jail, indicating that his psychotic state may have been induced by methamphetamine.

Bassler was shot and killed by a Sacramento SWAT team in the woods northeast of Fort Bragg after a 35-day intense manhunt. He was presumed to be mentally ill based on reports of family members and judged from episodes of bizarre behavior, but he was not undergoing therapy although he'd once been court-ordered to do so, attending the mandated sessions only sporadically.

The double murders prompted a number of Mendocino residents to assert that if Laura's Law was instituted in Mendocino County, seriously mentally ill people would get the help and treatment they need and Bassler-like tragedies might be averted.

But, as former Mental Health Department staffer Roanne Withers wrote for this newspaper last October, "In reality, the chances of anyone being murdered by someone with schizophrenia are about one in 14 million. You have a much better chance of being killed in a car accident or struck by lightning. And the murder rate is actually the same for someone with or without a psychotic disorder."

As passed by the California legislature, Laura's Law allows individual counties to opt into the Laura's Law program, but it also requires that a variety of mental health services be in place first, and that "patients" must first decline the in-place services before they can even begin to be considered for "court-assisted, voluntary" treatment.

The assumption here is that the dangerously mentally ill can rationally negotiate existing services much less even refuse them.

Since such comprehensive services are simply not in place in most California counties, only Nevada County has set up a Laura's Law program—under court order, not because their Board of Supervisors voted to implement it. And Nevada County was the site of the shocking murder of Laura and her two associates. And the killer had been refused existing mental health services.

No other counties have taken the plunge.

Supervisor Dan Hamburg introduced the subject last Tuesday with some history and a summary of the strict provisions of Laura's Law, noting that there is "no funding—that's a very important consideration here," he added.

According to Hamburg's background info, in the first two and a half years Laura's Law had been in effect in Nevada County after its launch in 2008, there have been 37 people considered for the program. Twenty-two of them agreed to enter the program "under court settlement" (i.e., court pressure with threats of jail or in-patient treatment) and 11 were court-ordered into the program involuntarily. Four declined treatment and went to court to argue against it being applied to them and won.

Laura's Law explicitly prohibits any corresponding reduction in other mental health services.

"Hundreds of people in Mendocino suffer from mental illness and lack of awareness of mental illness," said Hamburg, noting that "many times the mentally ill don't know they're mentally ill. But families do."

"It's better than jail," according to a San Mateo psychiatrist Hamburg cited. And it "ensures care before tragedies."

But, Hamburg said, it's expensive, it threatens civil rights of patients, and there is the possibility of a mental health court alternative.

"As a father of a mentally ill child who looked to County mental health services for assistance five years ago and came up empty, I think we do need to do better," Hamburg said, explaining why he favored giving Laura's Law full consideration. "If not Laura's Law, then something."

"Fortunately for me, my son is doing a lot better, but that's because my wife and I went outside and used very unconventional means to get help for our son. I know a lot of people in our County have to do the same thing. The Basslers unfortunately were not so fortunate. They apparently tried to get the attention of mental health workers and law enforcement officials but finally they resorted to some very dire situations, very difficult situations within their family and finally had to watch in horror as two men were killed and Aaron Bassler was shot dead. No parent or other loving relation of a severely mentally ill and violent person should have to go through what some of the families in this County have gone through. I'm not saying Laura's Law is a panacea, but I do think it's a potentially useful tool that we should have in our toolbox. Again, if not Laura's Law, something modeled after it just to assuage the pain and suffering that people are going through in this county."

Health and Human Services Director Stacey Cryer and recently appointed Mental Health Department Manager Tom Pinizzotto ran through a formal presentation on Laura's Law summarizing the pros and cons.

Predictably the cons substantially outweighed the pros.

"Some provisions are already in place and available," said Cryer, citing other laws that mandate mental health services—conservatorships, forced medication, etc. "But medications have side effects and the voluntary programs have not proven better than involuntary—although some disagree."

"Forced medication is not a provision of Laura's Law," noted Hamburg with agreement from Pinizzotto.

When people are nominated by family members for enrollment in the Laura's Law program they get a court hearing with a public defender and a mental health staffer who, with County Counsel, represent the County and its intent to push the patient into treatment.

In addition, counties have to prove that they have a variety of voluntary programs in place that have been turned down by the patient before they can pressure someone into court-pressured voluntary, much less involuntary, treatment.

Public Defender Linda Thompson described the burdensome legal process and strict criteria that must be met to even go to court for a given candidate.

"Very few of my clients would be within the criteria of Laura's Law," said Thompson, adding that the cost of Public Defender services would be high. "We'd be going to court every day," Thompson said with what sounded like exaggeration. Then there would be the usual time delays and follow-up hearings to continue the patient in the program.

On further consideration, Thompson estimated that there would probably be "three or four clients every couple of months. Many of them just don't understand what's going on. Competency questions arise."

Aaron Bassler's father, Jim Bassler, told the Board that mental health court is like Laura's Law and requires similar collaboration between various offices. "But it's not as comprehensive," he continued. "Nevada County proves that Laura's Law works. Yes, the services are not provided here now. But Laura's Law is what makes mental health providers really take mental health seriously. If you do, you will want Laura's Law."

Laura's Law advocate Sonya Nesch described how seven people on the Mendocino Coast now demand a variety of (mostly police) services which could be reduced if they were enrolled in a Laura's Law program.

"Laura's Law is not just for criminals. It gives you an opportunity to intervene before danger," she said.

District Attorney David Eyster was clearly opposed to the idea.

"The idea that Mental Health Court is just for criminals is not strictly true," said Eyster. "There are criminals and law-breakers. When mentally ill people violate the law they are not necessarily criminals. We are compassionate and give them a break when we can... I have completed my investigation on the officer involved shooting [of Aaron Bassler] and I'll have a written result coming out to the Fort Bragg City Council in early August. But I've found that if we had applied Laura's Law criteria, I don't believe Mr. [Aaron] Bassler would have been in the system. I don't think he'd have qualified. He would not have been in the Laura's Law structure. I say that not as an opinion or philosophy, but on the facts and looking at past jail records and Sheriff's reports and all sorts of things before me in reviewing the officer involved shooting. If we are doing things because we think it would have brought back Mr. Coleman or Mr. Melo or would have stopped that tragedy, that is no reason to do it because I don't think Laura's Law would have stopped that. We also have the distinction between those who are mentally ill and those who abuse drugs. We have to make sure we differentiate those. Some folks are self-imposed mentally ill [i.e., from substance abuse]; others are just that way. Some just need structure and help. If I had to take one of these options, I would say please invite one of the judges down here, perhaps Judge Henderson, presiding judge, because I will make sure that one of my attorneys goes to a mental health/homeless court as we did before and we would work with Ms. Cryer and Ms. Thompson and I think that's what we need to do because I don't see how Laura's Law will work effectively in Mendocino County. Nevada County put in a lot of mental health infrastructure for a relatively few people because of the strict criteria. But we have to decide what's good for the whole, not just a few."

Supervisor Hamburg pressed staff for advice on what a family would do now if they had a mentally ill family member. "What do people do when they need services? Who would Jim Bassler go to? I've been hearing lately that the letters that they sent never arrived at the offices they were sent to, which is kind of amazing."

Unfortunately, Hamburg didn't explain this provocative remark which suggests, well, it suggests the letters might not exist.

"But who would they go to now?" Hamburg continued. "Where would I start? What I like about Laura's Law is that it has that efficient process to get you in the door. I couldn't find a way to get in the door."

First to attempt a reply was Supervisor John McCowen.

"One of the problematic issues is that Laura's Law, even for people who, apparently, even for people with serious problems, may also not be the way to get in the door."

"It's not a panacea, I know," replied Hamburg.

Mr. Pinizzotto then launched into a buzzword-laced non-answer soliloquy that shed zero light:

"What's different now is we're more focused on outreach and engagement. Our culture within the mental health department is changing as we have gone through the last couple of years of reorganization and restructuring. Aggressive outreach engagement. We're enhancing these programs as we speak. Just on the coast, most recently, we have awarded several service contracts. Hospitality House won a federal grant which gives additional dollars on the coast for outreach and engagement of homeless folks and people in need. Also we've enhanced services as we speak. What's different now is we have increased psychiatric medication support services on the coast from 16 hours a week to 36 hours a week... This is a timeline as well. In the past six months we've met with our stakeholders and have increased and expanded mental health services act programs throughout the coast. Working closely with our community partners we have funded additional children's services. We are finding economies of scale and efficiencies and integrating and talking more. In terms of access we are now in the process of moving forward with monitoring the amount of time from when someone is first seen and our goal is to have that in five days or less."

Next time, Mr. P., please provide subtitles for us English speakers.

Hamburg diplomatically replied, "You're talking about people who are looking to get some help. But I'm talking about people who are not looking to get some help because they think they're fine. But they're scaring the *bejesus* out of everybody who comes in contact with them. Those are the people who I'm concerned about, frightened about, frightened for their families."

It fell to Health and Human Services Director Stacey Cryer to state the obvious:

"It's not a popular option, but one thing you can do today is you can always call law enforcement. They will make a determination on whether or not they should go to the emergency room, and if they need to be evaluated further."

Cops as therapists and mental health evaluators, given the Blue Meanie mindset of Mendolib, is not what Mendolib ever wants to hear, but most cops are not only experienced in dealing with 5150s, they're better at it than many "helping professionals."

Hamburg laughed at Cryer's bluntness. "That's what I was always told. If I wanted to get help for my son I should put him out on the street and let him get arrested. Then he'd go to jail!"

Cryer tried to soften the point: "You don't have to let them get arrested, you just call law enforcement."

[Sheriff Allman estimates that at any one time at least 20% of his jail inmates are mentally ill.]

Hamburg (sarcastically): "And he'd get his treatment."

Cryer repeated, "They don't have to necessarily get arrested."

Hamburg: "They have to do something wrong to get stopped."

The cop treatment option having been set-aside, Supervisor McCowen said he was "happy to see the mental health/homeless court option up there. Two sergeants with the Ukiah Police Department, Eric Baarts and Sean Kaeser, approached me probably six to eight months ago with the idea of a homeless court. They do exist in other jurisdictions. They're effective. We currently don't have a good system of dealing with what I would call the low level social offenses that homeless people are prone to commit. A lot of times it's kind of a crossover. Is it mental illness? Is it homelessness? Is it substance abuse? All of the above? But the information that I read says that homeless court was an effective means of causing the people who are committing the offense to have to address their behavior and the intent was to get them to address their behavior, not to inflict punishment. But if they were not willing to change their behavior or take the steps that would be consistent with making the effort to change their behavior then there would be some consequences that would ensure that. Instead of just going to court, get a fine, go to jail, it would be get a citation, change your behavior, go to court, don't go to jail, don't get a fine, maybe start developing the skills that would get you out of the situation you were in. That did show a lot of promise. I had a very brief preliminary discussion with Public Defender Thompson and District Attorney Eyster. They were both favorable to the concept. I was getting pulled in other directions so I didn't pursue it, so I'm happy to see that on the list."

Hamburg: "If the judges are willing to participate in this we have to pull a cast of characters together and we need to do something like this because I do believe that when people go to court it's kind of a wakeup call, particularly when that judge has some power over people's lives. I really welcome getting the judges involved."

Public Defender Thompson then launched into a windy recitation about how hard it would be to get the judges—much less those unruly crazy people—to show up, much less participate, concluding, however, that she'd talk to the judges about it and if she had to she'd put in her own time to do whatever they end up doing.

Along the way Thompson declared that the courts are about to take a 35% budget cut themselves, a number we've not heard and are unable to verify.

The Board finally voted to ask staff to come back with "a plan" in late September incorporating some of the options that were discussed— not including Laura's Law.

If history is any guide, "the plan" will be that Mendocino County will continue to muddle along with what few mental health options the County offers.

ADDENDUM C
The Mendocino County Marijuana Culture

By Jack Rikess
Toke of the Town
Northern California Correspondent

Conventional wisdom for anyone living north of Santa Rosa is that marijuana is an integral component of California's economy. In the beginning, growers were tolerated by the locals as misfits of society who had migrated north to avoid the world of straight jobs and/or had fled to 'Mendo' with the 'back to the county' movement to grow their organic beans and fruit.

Venerable local institutions such as the timber and fishing industries were leery of the young freaks with their torn jeans and rusting VW vans. Their fears were soon justified when that first generation found that there were endless acres of hidden land stashed in "them there hills."

If a guy could find a secluded patch in the hills that was close to water and had sun, he had the makings of his first clandestine start-up "garden." The Timber giants viewed the encroaching growers as threats to their land, their water, and to the political dominance that they held in NorCal [Northern California] since the mid-19th century.

By the 1980s, the marijuana industry was entrenched and blooming, much to the chagrin of local law enforcement and community leaders. These former lazy rejects were driving new trucks, sending their kids to school, and buying their veggies at Safeway just like everyone else.

Thirty years later it is estimated that cannabis industry generates around 13 billion dollars in annual sales. And that's what is available to count. The timber industry is now a hollow trunk of its former self. The salmon and other fish populations have been so drastically depleted in the last few decades that fishermen can't rely on their yield from season to season. Many fishing boats on the coast have gone belly up.

While these formerly thriving industries in Mendocino and Humboldt scale back, local residents are having difficulty finding jobs that will support their families. Imagine the impact on Detroit if the auto industry hadn't received its bailout. That could have possibly been Northern California without marijuana.

In the last five years the growers in the three counties that make up the Emerald Triangle, Mendocino, Humboldt and Trinity, have been able to make a legitimate living because the counties chose to regulate marijuana instead of creating a war. The influx of cash that came from providing product to the medical marijuana dispensaries not only provided a light at the end of the forest for the growers, but, as with the auto industry, the tertiary markets began to thrive.

Dusty buildings and tiny strip malls in Willits, Hopland and Ukiah that had lay vacant after the economic downturn of 2007-2008 were being replaced with successful garden centers and irrigation equipment suppliers.

Under George W. Bush, medical marijuana in California found its roots and was beginning to take hold. The Emerald Triangle was experiencing an unspoken moratorium on busting growers. In turn, the three counties had more legitimate cash flow at their disposal than any time in recent history.

The growers became part of a three-pronged arrangement in what is called 'a loop system.' The medical marijuana dispensaries could contract a grower for his or her crop, sign papers, the grower then worked under the umbrella of the dispensary. The patient came to a dispensary for their medicine; the dispensary provided the medicine that the grower delivered.

Unlike the previous generation of isolated, tight-lipped cultivators, today's grower was part of a network that was totally legal and above board in the eyes of the State of California. For a moment it looked like there was détente between growers and cops while a more thorough resolution could be found until the fall of 2011.

In 2011 the Federal Government launched an attack on Northern California called Operation Full Court Press (OFCP). The stated goal behind OFCP was to find and eradicate illegal or possible Mexican gangs or cartels that were powering major industrial grows in the national forests of Northern California.

While the Feds say that their efforts were successful, the locals point out a different perspective. OFCP was a large scale undertaking with many federal officers branching out in all directions in Mendocino County.

What they saw was a budding, extremely transparent cannabis community. They were able to see, first-hand for themselves, what was going on in NorCal, and declared unequivocally that medical marijuana was "a sham." Apparently two-story billboards along the freeways and highways glorifying the benefits of the cannabis additives, "Bloom Grow" and "Kush King Formula One," are not as prevalent back east as they are along the dusty brown grassy knolls of our 101 North.

At the tail end of 2011, after OFCP, the Feds returned with a vengeance to Northern Cali with a to-do list of persons whom they felt were flaunting their liberties a little too openly. The Feds pulled the rug out from under the locals who, up to that point, felt free to provide product directly and indirectly to Medical Marijuana patients.

The DEA and other federal agencies harassed law-abiding medical marijuana dispensaries and collectives indiscriminately, as if on a whim. Suddenly, what was considered business as usual for many over the prior three years, came to a halt.

Today growers and farmers are once again suspicious of law enforcement. The tentative bridges that were built with the local cops have been torn down and confusion about who to trust prevails. In the middle of all this is Mendocino County's Sheriff Tom Allman. Interestingly, my first introduction to the sheriff of Mendocino County came through these aforementioned, so-called outlaws of the region.

When I initially began reporting about California's number one cash crop, it was in Tom Allman's backyard where I did most of my research. This eventually led to stories, anecdotes, and flashes from the front dealing with the struggles or achievements of the local marijuana farmer. Invariably the name of Tom Allman came up during my interviews and reports on stories of local interest.

To my surprise, many of the players who I came in contact with would say the same thing to me. If they ever had to turn themselves in to a cop, the only cop who they would trust is Tom Allman. On several occasions, the Sheriff has been called during off-hours to meet up with a deputy because a cornered suspect will only turn themselves in to Allman.

It was Tom Allman's involvement in lengthy debates between the Mendocino growers and the District Attorney's office that led to the legendary 9.31 program which provided a manageable and scalable solution to the cannabis issue.

Allman's resume is stellar. He was the temporary top cop in New Orleans in the aftermath of Katrina, organizing a network of out-of-state police. At the end of the '90s the Sheriff was part of a global team that led and trained an international police force in Kosovo until order could be restored by local constables.

[Allman is] smart, funny, and may have one of the hardest jobs in the cop world. He's stuck between societies' growing acceptance of marijuana and the civic leaders who are content to let him take the fall for the marijuana problem. When he does something good, they take credit.

From the Feds he gets that he's too soft on pot. From the voters who put him into office, he's not doing enough. And to the ganjateers, the growers, those who are in favor of legalization, and the believers that Mendocino could do for weed like its neighbor, Napa Valley, did for wine; he's holding back a potential gazillion dollar enterprise that could turn the Golden State around financially.

Beyond that, he encounters the same rising challenges with crime and budget cuts as his fellow law enforcers. This includes dealing with a heavy meth problem, weekly spousal shootings, and DUIs to go, all taking place over a blindingly forested countryside almost the size of Rhode Island.

In my opinion… having to answer to the Feds, the voters, marijuana growers, and the general Kmart-going citizenry of his jurisdiction on any given day, might send your average cop into a tizzy. Not Tom Allman. He's generally humorous, thoughtful, and not afraid to be painfully direct if needed, while still maintaining his composure.

Tom Allman brings a thoughtful understanding to an ever-changing job that has earned him respect in both worlds.

☙

Interview:
Mendocino County Sheriff Tom Allman

Operation Full Court Press—The Aftermath

By Jack Rikess

Rikess: Let's pick up where we last left off, Operation Full Court Press.

Sheriff: Let's go! It was a huge success!

Rikess: Let me ask the questions please. (pause) Was it a huge success?

Sheriff: It was a success on several planes. It was, if you are just looking for numbers, it was a success. 57,000 pounds of garbage was brought out. 152 arrests were made. 17% of those were illegal immigrants from Mexico. Thousands and thousands of marijuana plants taken out.

However... that's certainly not how you judge a success. How I judge success is the fact that six rural sheriff's offices came together with one goal in mind and that is, "We are either going to sink or swim, seeing if we can coordinate our efforts and see if we can make a difference."

There are a lot of things that have come out of Full Court Press which are both good and very disturbing. I will start with the good.

I have the three sheriffs to the east all telling me that they have had zero activity of people transporting irrigation and hydroponic stuff up to the Mendocino National Forest. Normally, you would say, "Hooray! Let's have a toast to that."

On the other hand, I have people in Covelo saying that this year they've seen more traffic than any other year.

I shake my head and say, "Wait a minute, this is Mendocino National Forest. Don't growers know that Mendocino County came up with Operation Full Court Press? Don't they know that we were the ones pushing for the arrests, that we were the ones pushing for the success?"

Now we are seeing an influx of people who are growing full-bore on the western face of the Mendo National Forest?

So now, where I thought this year we were going to be able to focus on trespass grows on timber tracks, we are going to have to take away some of that energy and focus on the Mendocino National Forest again. When you and I first met three years ago, I told you that we had five enforcement objectives. Do you remember those?

Rikess: No.

Sheriff: We have had five enforcement objectives... for two years. This year we have a sixth. When I tell you the sixth you will understand.

When I say enforcement objectives... I am looking at marijuana eradication—the eradication of illegal marijuana as a business plan. Not a business plan to create income for the Sheriff's office, that's not it at all. But how am I going to gauge success? Donald Trump gauges success for every million dollars that he puts in the bank. Good for him. That is not how I am going to gauge my success in my life.

If someone said to me, "Tom, we have fewer marijuana growers in the Mendocino National Forest than ever before on the Mendocino side, that is success for me. Let me talk about our five enforcement objectives.

The first four are very obvious. (Well, the last four.) This is the only one we will really disagree on. [First] I say, go after large commercial marijuana operation, but that begs for someone to ask me to define what a large commercial marijuana operation is. Some might say its 100 plants; some might say its 1000 plants.

Rikess: I am sorry, not to push you but what would you define it as?

Sheriff: I am saying that we look at each year on an individual basis. And we certainly know what this year is looking at. This year a large operation is going to be between 300 and 500 plants. I hope I am correct when I say this... but we've seen the last of 15,000-plant grows.

Since I have been the sheriff we have had 15,000-plant grows. We haven't had one for a while. I have told the deputies that instead of you saying, "You know what, that guy has always been growing marijuana, and I am going to go after him. I am going to get a search warrant and take 30 plants."

I said, "He's been getting away with it for a long time but so is the guy who is smarter than him. He's been getting away with 400 plants. So I want you to go after the guy with 400 plants."

It doesn't take any longer to write a search warrant for 400 plants as it does for 30 plants. So the business plan to the deputies is, "I want you to go after the greedy people. Those are the ones who are truly abusing our county." So THOSE are the ones that are the large, commercial growers.

Now, when I talk about the other four [kinds of illegal grows or gardens we're pursuing], it's very possible that they are going to be tied into large commercial growers.

Next are public lands. We have to remind the citizens that even though Proposition 215 is alive and well in California, there's no public land where you can grow. None.

You cannot say, "I have a doctor's recommendation and I am going to the national forest to grow marijuana." The public lands do not allow for the growth of marijuana.

The next is large, timber tracks—large parcels where we have trespass grows. Trespass grows, this is what history has shows us… what happens in a trespass grow… First of all for those who don't know—timber, for the most part is not being harvested out of Mendocino County. It is part of our economy. It's an important part of our economy. The price of fir right now is the same price it was in 1970.

Two more [types of illegal grows we're going after are]: environmental degradation. If we can see it from the air, we are going to land there.

Rikess: That has to be hard to see from the air.

Sheriff: No it is NOT! I am not kidding when I tell you this. It makes me sick to my stomach when I see this. This was several years ago… this guy with a dozer had taken the tops off of two mountains and fill in the valley. You know what! May you rot in hell! There is a special place in hell for them.

This is number five: illegal water diversion or water theft. This is the sex appeal that juries love.

If you go tell a jury of 12 people, "This guy grew 100 plants," the jury is going to fall asleep. (Acting like a bored jurist:) "Okay, he grew 100 plants" (ho hum). If you say, "This guy grew 100 plants and he was illegally sucking water out of the Eel River using a three-inch water pipe," they say, "What?! You can't do that!" We say, "Hooray!" We've got their attention.

The last is obvious. I don't use the C-word—cartel—I use the term organized crime. If we have an indication that organized crime has set up a grow, they have brought in a low-level grunt to do it… that is important to me. Because if we allow that one garden to be successful this year, then that one garden is going to be two gardens next year and four gardens the year after. That's where I'm focused on. That's my business plan. Well, let me tell you what those six things say. Those six things are so important because if you talk to any legitimate medical marijuana grower, he's going to agree with you. If you talk to any legislator in Sacramento, he or she is going to agree with you. We have found commonality, worked it into a business plan.

We are out here increasing our numbers, decreasing the complaints. We don't have near the complaints from citizens that we used to [like], "How come you took my weed?" Because we are not taking Ma and Pa Kettle's weed [anymore]. We are truly focused on the people who want to make their million bucks in one year.

Rikess: Operation Full Court Press happened. It's my understanding that the Feds came in here and said, "Marijuana is a sham in Northern California. It's a joke. What these guys are doing is pulling the wool over our eyes and we are going to come back here. We are going to show them who [is] the boss. And they came back here and they did exactly that...

Sheriff: They went after one garden and we have...

Rikess: No. They went through the state. They [were] in Long Beach yesterday. They're constantly, every day—they swoop in dispensaries. Legal, law-abiding dispensaries.

Sheriff: And I am going to go right back to what I said. The law is so ambiguous that 215 should have been corrected by the voters to talk about dispensaries, to talk about consistent laws that people could possess, and that's one of our...

Rikess: So, the Feds came in, "it's a sham, it's a joke... We're going to stop this." My point is that it pushed us back.

Sheriff: I agreed when I said we took a step backward. That's Matt Cohen...

356

Rikess: Not just Matt Cohen, I mean up and down...

Sheriff: In my county I had Matt Cohen. What dispensaries were closed in Mendocino County? I didn't see that list? Oh wait! There were none...

Rikess: Where is Potter Valley?

Sheriff: In my county, Mendocino. It might have been a cooperative, it wasn't a dispensary.

Rikess: I'll get back to you on that one. But be that as it may, the Feds are pushing the growers back to a Black Market economy. Do you think we should just bide our time and see where it's going? Where is the solution?

Sheriff: Well, let's start with what you call the Black Market, and I call illegal diversion.

Rikess: It is my understanding after the Feds came through with Operation Full Court Press, that there were vast amounts of garbage left behind from either deserted or busted grows. When they came to eradicate...

Sheriff: That we left garbage? We didn't remove all of the garbage that the growers had. But we didn't leave anything.

Rikess: I'm not saying that you brought in anything...

Sheriff: Yes, absolutely. It's not like a crime scene where we have to get in there and clean up.

Rikess: Why not? Seriously? We both want to reclaim the forest. Now someone is walking through the forest and they have come upon desolation row.

Sheriff: That is a really fair question.

Rikess: When are the Feds going to come in and do something like that...?

Sheriff: Like what?

Rikess: Clean up our forest... Shouldn't it be a turnkey operation?

Sheriff: In a perfect world. Snow White would have them do that. However let's be very basic about this. The 57,000 pounds of garbage that was removed represents approximately sixty percent of the gardens we went into. We made sure that all fertilizer or poisons were removed from all grows. We made sure that the infrastructure of long term grows, and when I say infrastructure, I mean buried water lines that would run to latrines or kitchens or places where they clean their laundry... Yes, they had underground two-inch pipes going into these things that they used year after year. Those were removed. The garbage from... the living garbage... from... the empty cans of food, the wet clothes, the sleeping bags, the tents, the human feces, that garbage... While we would have loved to have cleaned it up, the volunteer effort from the Sierra Trail Club is somewhat limited—they were in there hustling.

What we have this year going is a 501(c)3 foundation here in the county called "The Mendocino Public Safety Foundation." They have raised a lot of money to pay the sheriff's office; we are now sending law enforcement deputies with these volunteers. Last week we did 60 hours of garbage cleaning in Covelo. We sent deputies to provide security for them while they do the cleanup. So yes, I agree, I wish we would have cleaned it up more.

However, of the money that we spent last year, 40 percent of it was spent towards clean-up and trying to reclaim the land. Only 60 percent was spent toward eradication.

Rikess: Let's be clear. I know you differentiate between growers. You obviously do. Operation Full Court Press in its real nature was supposed to go after what was going on in the [National] forest, which in a sense meant organized crime, Mexican disorganized crime, cartels, and things like that. I know for a fact that your local growers here would have assisted you, Tom Allman, and pointed out in our forests [where the Mexican gangs are growing]. They would work with you. Is that correct?

Sheriff: They have worked [with us], and some of them have been some of our largest contributors.

Rikess: Yes, so we want to differentiate Operation Full Court Press and the Feds coming down on marijuana...

Sheriff: It's night and day, Jack.

Rikess: But it doesn't feel like night and day to the grower of Mendocino County. They feel lumped in with what's happening...

Sheriff: Well, it would... Let me tell you this. We had a 99-plant grow literally a mile from the landing pad in Covelo. Every helicopter that carried law enforcement officers had to fly over this 99-plant grow daily. These helicopters were maybe only 200 feet off the ground at that point because they were approaching the heliport and I think that the fact...

Rikess: For the people at home—this is a legal grow.

Sheriff: This is a legal grow. So for growers to say, "Oh, my gosh! They brought in all this attention. They have gone after all these people who are growing." I am here to say, really? Because I could take you to the place in Covelo where 200 cops flew over [a grow] every day and no one touched it.

Rikess: Didn't touch it. But there is a great consensus of opinion, and I will just use that as a point, there were other examples, but by them flying over the 99-plant grow every day, it just ate at them. It killed them.

Sheriff: Why was my money this year from the Feds cut and reduced?

Rikess: Tough times.

Sheriff: Why were the dollars... Okay, I guess they are looking at their priorities the correct way.

Rikess: But they found money for CAMP [Campaign Against Marijuana Planting].

Sheriff: No, they didn't.

Rikess: Yes, they did.

Sheriff: Well, instead of six helicopters, the state has three.

Rikess: But.

Sheriff: HOLD ON! Let me finish, and instead of three weeks, I'll have less than two, a week and a half, so we certainly don't see that the Feds were that concern[ed]. If we can continue to supply money to South Korea and Japan, I would hope that we could because, Jack, as many people who say marijuana is innocent, [that] marijuana is not the scourge on society, I may agree with some of them but I will tell you, there are bad people involved in some marijuana grows.

The kind of people who would just as soon throw nuclear waste down into one of our valleys... Bad, bad people who don't care about Mendocino County or the people who live here...